CHAOS AND ORDER IN
THE CAPITAL MARKETS

WILEY FINANCE EDITIONS

CHAOS AND ORDER IN
THE CAPITAL MARKETS
A New View of Cycles, Prices, and Market Volatility
Second Edition

Edgar E. Peters

John Wiley & Sons, Inc.
New York • Chichester • Brisbane • Toronto • Singapore

To my children, Ian and Lucia; my mother, Michiko; and the memory of my father, Edgar. And finally: To Sheryl, who always believed in me.

Copyright © 1996 by Edgar E. Peters

Published by John Wiley & Sons, Inc.

Library of Congress Cataloging-in-Publication Data:
Peters, Edgar E., 1952–
    Chaos and order in the capital markets : a new view of cycles,
  prices, and market volatility / Edgar E. Peters. — 2nd ed.
      p.   cm. — (Wiley finance editions)
  Includes bibliographical references and index.
  ISBN 0-471-13938-6 (cloth : alk. paper)
    1. Capital market—Mathematical models. 2. Futures market-
-Mathematical models. 3. Fractals. 4. Chaotic behavior in systems.
  I. Title. II. Series.
  HG4523.P47   1996
  332'.0414—dc20   96-18533

Preface to the Second Edition

When I wrote the first edition of this book I hoped that it would be read by enough people to stimulate further study. The reaction has been far wider than I thought possible. That is not to say that my work has become overwhelmingly widespread, but readership has been broad enough so that the effort has been worthwhile. When I set out, my goal was to write a conceptual introduction to chaos theory and fractal statistics for practitioners, particularly as it could be applied to economics and finance. Others had written and researched on this topic before, but they had been mostly economists. While it was (and continues to be) almost a joke to say that we had to prove that the market was "chaotic," very little had been published on the topic by financial economists. What had been published was mostly in academic journals. I also wished to reintroduce *rescaled range (R/S) analysis* back into the researcher's toolbox.

When the time came to write *Chaos and Order in the Capital Markets* I had two basic objectives. The first was to write an introduction to nonlinear studies that was comprehensive enough to be useful, but not so detailed that I would lose most readers. My second purpose was to expand nonlinear concepts to market and economic analysis, *and* contrast that with prevailing theory. Mainstream theory was, and continues to be, about efficient markets and rational investors. Because of the dual objectives, the book came out as a polemic. It both explains the basics of what is generically known as chaos theory and makes a case for applying that methodology to market and economic analysis. I am gratified that so many have found this approach thought provoking. Many readers of the first edition have taken my work and expanded it further, either in graduate study at universities or in practice. I am also gratified that some have taken the time to criticize my approach. I have learned much from them.

The first edition was written in 1990, and much has changed since then. Many new concepts have been learned, and many new nonlinear technologies have become widespread. Since the introductory nature of the book continues to be useful, and the empirical studies convincing, an update of the book to incorporate recent advances seemed like a good idea. I was faced with a challenge, however. I had already written a second book, *Fractal Market Analysis*, that was more technical than *Chaos and Order in the Capital Markets*. In *FMA*, I discussed more comprehensive tests than were available in 1990. If I included those tests in the second edition of *Chaos and Order* it would become a clone of the second book. Also, while I wished to discuss new technology, such as genetic algorithms and fuzzy logic, comprehensive discussions of those talks would make the book overly long and cumbersome.

I decided that much of the original book would remain unchanged. The discussions of chaos and fractals that were aimed at an intuitive rather than an overwhelming mathematical level remain informative. As such, they should remain "as is." Instead, in much of the text I have corrected errors pointed out by many readers. I also decided to leave the empirical studies as they were. *Chaos and Order* continues to be a conceptual introduction. However, I have augmented the text in many places with discussions and references to complexity theory. *Complexity theory* is a more general nonlinear field of study. Chaos and fractals turn out to be subsets of the larger field.

The major additions to the book are found in the latter part. In 1990 there were very few investment professionals who used nonlinear methods. In addition, there was the aforementioned growth in nonlinear technologies. Thus, a new Part IV has been added that deals with applications of nonlinear technologies and some of the practitioners who use them. In keeping with the nature of this book, the material is mostly conceptual. References are listed for technically inclined readers, and enough mathematics to get started.

Finally, the BASIC programs have been upgraded to Visual BASIC from the old BASICA code of the first edition. A diskette with these programs is included. A BASIC program for R/S analysis has been added, as well.

The book continues to be aimed at investment professionals and interested academics. An individual with undergraduate-level exposure to basic statistics should have little trouble following the text. The preface to the first edition continues to state the purpose behind the writing of this book. Progress has been made in the last five years, but there is still much work to be done. It is often said that the most interesting times for a field are when it is in transition. Investment finance is currently in such a state. As I point out in the text, the nonlinear view of markets is merely a *generalization* of the prevailing linear view. By relaxing the restrictive assumption of linearity, nonlinearity naturally arises. If more people become involved in the transition to the nonlinear view because of this book, then it will have continued to serve its purpose.

EDGAR E. PETERS

Concord, Massachusetts
May 1996

Acknowledgments

In addition to all those mentioned in the first edition, I would like to thank the following people at PanAgora Asset Management: Peter Rathjens, Jarrod Wilcox, and Paul Samuelson for their insights; Georgeanne Nicozisine and Bob Casey for listening to me go on about this stuff while on the road; and Rick Wilk and David Liddell for covering for me on my many days out of the office.

Special thanks go to Michael Corning for not only rewriting the BASIC programs, but also establishing and maintaining the FMA Home Page on the World Wide Web. His enthusiasm for spreading the word on nonlinearity has helped keep my interest in the subject from flagging. I would also like to thank Christopher May for our interesting discussions, as well as for the information he keeps sending me.

Finally, I would like to again thank my family for their continued support and encouragement.

Preface

This book is a conceptual introduction to fractals and chaos theory as applied to investments and, to a lesser degree, economics. In recent years, research in the capital markets has been producing more questions than it has been answering; the need for a new paradigm, or a new way of looking at things, has become more and more apparent. The existing view, based on efficient market assumptions, has a distinguished history going back some 40 years, but it has not, for some time, significantly increased understanding of how markets work. This book attempts a shift away from the concept of efficient markets and toward a more general view of the forces underlying the capital market system. In this new paradigm, the existing paradigm still exists as a special case. Therefore, this shift is an evolution in capital market research and, I believe, a logical next step.

The book is not meant as a textbook. It is intended to communicate the concepts behind fractals and chaos theory, as they apply to the capital markets and economics. I have supplied no proofs of the theorems. Those interested in such full mathematical treatments are referred to the bibliography, where an abundance of mathematical and scientific texts and papers is offered. The book is addressed to investment professionals and interested academics, and assumes a firm grounding in capital market theory, elementary statistics, and elementary calculus. Anyone with a MBA should have little trouble understanding the text, and those with undergraduate degrees in business or economics should also benefit. The informal style is meant to provoke thought and present new ideas. Formal proofs are available elsewhere.

I would like to acknowledge the help of the following people who, through the years, provided advice and information: Richard Crowell, Eugene Hawkins, Mark Zurak, Robert Wood, Jr., Eric Korngold, David Lawrence, Berry Cox,

Warren Sproul, Maurice Larrain, Tonis Vaga, Bruce West, Hassan Ahmed, James Vertin, Charles D'Ambrosio, Frank Fabozzi, Bruce Clarke, Fred Meltzer, Ken Johnson, and Mike Jones. In addition, I would like to thank James Rullo, Kris Lino, Desiree Babbitt, Mimmy Cooper, and Kathleen Williams at PanAgora Asset Management, for their indulgence and help while this manuscript was being completed. Finally, I would like to thank my wife and children for their continued support during the time it took to complete this project.

EDGAR E. PETERS

Concord, Massachusetts
September 1991

Contents

PART TWO   FRACTAL STRUCTURE IN THE CAPITAL MARKETS

PART ONE
THE NEW PARADIGM

A paradigm is a mental model, a way of looking at things in a global sense. Financial economics has been dominated in the last 40 years by a linear paradigm. That is, a view that for every action there is a proportionate reaction. However, the markets are rarely so orderly. Often, when you least expect it, there is an exponential over-reaction to an action. This is the essence of non-linearity, and most practitioners recognize its connection with reality. Many academics and quants also admit that the markets react in a non-linear fashion. However, they assume that linear restrictions do not affect the usefulness of their models even if the systems have non-linearities. Linear models are much easier to work with than messy non-linear ones. The benefits of the simple linear model outweigh the potential dangers of its limitations. Chaos theory and the sciences of complexity teach us otherwise.

In this section we will review conventional capital market theory, and explore both its good points and its problems. This will lead into the benefits of a new paradigm: one of non-linearity and complexity.

1
Introduction: Life Can Be So Complicated

Throughout recorded time (and probably before), people have been trying to make life structured and organized. How else can we explain our legal system, bureaucracy, and organization charts? To order time, calendars and clocks were created, and they govern the proper organization and coordination of daily activities. We publish encyclopedias, dictionaries, books, and newspapers, to organize knowledge. Yet, no matter how finely detailed the laws or organization charts, we still have trouble understanding the process underlying a structure, whether it is a natural system, like the weather, or one of our own social creations. That is why we need a court system to interpret laws, we need consultants to help us understand the group dynamics of our corporations, and we need science to understand nature.

No matter how we try to make it so, the world is not orderly; nature is not orderly, nor are the human creations called institutions. Economies and the capital markets are particularly lacking in orderliness. The capital markets are our own creation; yet we do not understand how they work. Some of our best thinkers spend their lifetime trying to understand how capital flows from one investor to another, and why. To make the capital markets neater, models have been created in an effort to explain them. These models are, of necessity, simplifications of reality. By making a few simplifying assumptions about the way investors behave, an entire analytic framework has been created to help us understand the markets, which we have also created. The models have not worked well. They explain some of the structure, but they leave much unanswered and often raise more questions than they answer. Economists find that their forecasts, contrary to theory, have limited empirical validity.

As an example, a *Forbes* article entitled "Dreary Days in the Dismal Science," written by W. L. Linden, quoted studies of economic forecasts by McNees (1983, 1985, 1987, 1988), who found that economists have made serious forecasting errors at every major turning point since the early 1970s, when the studies began. Included in the group studied was Townsend-Greenspan, run by Fed Chairman Alan Greenspan. McNees found that forecasters tend to be off *as a group* at these turning points. Forecasts, when correct, were relevant in only a short time frame. A small change in one variable seemed to have a much bigger impact than theory would suggest.

In addition, evidence continues to mount that the capital markets do not behave as the random walk theory, which is largely taught as fact, has predicted. For instance, the stock market has more large changes (or "outliers") than can be attributable to noise alone. Other anomalies to the existing paradigm of the capital markets will be discussed later, but they are too numerous to be dismissed.

Forty years ago, econometrics was supposed to give us the ability to forecast our economic future and prepare accordingly. Today, economic forecasts are often the subject of derision. Wall Street and corporate America have begun dismantling their economics departments because, as Linden said, their forecasts "proved entertaining and interesting—but not very useful." What went wrong?

First, there is the concept of equilibrium. Econometric analysis assumes that, if there are no outside, or exogenous, influences, then a system is at rest. This is an economist's definition of equilibrium. Everything balances out. Supply equals demand. By perturbing the system, exogenous factors take it away from equilibrium. The system reacts to the perturbation by reverting to equilibrium in a linear fashion. The system reacts immediately because it wishes to be at equilibrium and abhors being out of balance. The system wants tidiness, everything in its proper place.

However, if we look at the ecology of a living world—that of the Earth, for example—we see that nature abhors equilibrium. If a species or a system is to survive, it must evolve; it must be, as Prigogine states, "far from equilibrium." The Moon is in equilibrium. The Moon is a dead planet.

A free-market economy is also an evolving structure. Attempts to control an economy and make it more stable (or keep it at equilibrium) have failed.

The recent collapse of Leninist Communism is but one example. Other "utopian" societies have also tried to create an equilibrium economy, but all of them have failed.

Equilibrium implies a lack of emotional forces, such as greed and fear, which cause the economy to evolve and to adapt to new conditions. Regulation of these human tendencies can be desirable, to keep their effects somewhat dampened, but to do away with them would take the life out of the system, including the far-from-equilibrium conditions that are necessary for development. Equilibrium in a system means the system's death.

An "efficient market" is one in which assets are fairly priced according to the information available, and neither buyers nor sellers have an advantage. However, other considerations besides fair price are important to the functioning of markets. For instance, any trader will confirm that a low-volatility market is an unhealthy market. New financial instruments that have low interest eventually die, even if they are fairly priced. A recent example is the Index Participation contracts, designed to give program trading capability to individuals or institutions without using futures. This was a fine idea, and the contracts were usually fairly priced, but the concept died because of lack of interest. Trading volume was too low to sustain the market. A healthy market is one with volatility, but not necessarily fair price.

Should we then endorse the notion that a healthy economy and a healthy market *do not* tend to equilibrium but are, instead, far from equilibrium? Economists who are using equilibrium theories to model far-from-equilibrium systems are likely to produce dubious results.

A second problem with the econometric view of the world is its treatment of time. It ignores time or, at best, treats time as a variable like any other. The markets and the economy have no memory, or only limited memory, of the past. If, ten years from now, all of the variables that affect interest rates were to be identical to their current values, then interest rates would also have their current values. The combination of events that might lead to those two separate points in time is irrelevant. At best, econometrics deals with a short-term memory; the memory effects quickly dissipate. The idea that one event can change the future is foreign to econometrics—a fact that may explain why economists missed the turning points in the McNees studies mentioned earlier.

As an example, let us say that interest rates (r) are dependent solely on the current rate of inflation (i) and the money supply(s). A simple model would be:

$$r = a*i + b*s$$

In this oversimplistic case, if the coefficients a and b are fixed, then r depends on current *levels* of i and s. It does not matter whether i and s are both rising or falling, or one is rising and the other is falling. History is irrelevant.

What is missing, of course, is the qualitative aspect that comes from human decision making. We are influenced by what has happened. Our expectations of the future are shaped by our recent experiences. This feedback effect, the past influencing the present and the present influencing the future, is largely ignored, particularly in capital market theory. In the next chapter, we shall examine a rational person built to justify econometric techniques. This rational person is unaffected by past events except, perhaps, those of the near past. Real feedback systems involve long-term correlations and trends, because memories of long-past events can still affect the decisions made in the present.

All of these considerations make capital markets messy. The neat, optimal solutions do not apply. Instead, we have multiple possible solutions. These characteristics—far-from-equilibrium conditions and time-dependent feedback mechanisms—are symptomatic of nonlinear dynamic systems.

When I was an undergraduate studying mathematics, the differential equations we studied were linear. We studied linear differential equations because they could be solved for one, unique solution. They had practical applications to engineering and physics. They were tidy.

Nonlinear differential equations were viewed as not useful, because they had multiple, seemingly unrelated solutions. They were complex, messy, and to be avoided.

We have found that most complex, natural systems can be modeled by nonlinear differential, or difference, equations. These equations are useful for the very reasons that had made them something to be avoided. Life is messy. There are many possibilities. We need models with multiple solutions.

To illustrate, let's take a simple nonlinear system. Suppose we have a stock with a price (P_t) and further define it as a penny stock selling for less than \$1. Because enough buyers come into the market, their demand causes the price to rise at a particular rate (a). The future value of P_t at time t + 1 would then increase in the following manner:

$$P_{(t+1)} = a*P_t \tag{1.1}$$

The equation assumes that there are only buyers. To make the model more realistic, we should add an effect from sellers. Suppose that while prices increase at $a*P_t$, sellers reduce the price at $a*P_t^2$. Equation (1.1) becomes:

$$P_{t+1} = a*P_t - a*P_t^2$$

or

$$P_{t+1} = a*P_t*(1 - P_t) \tag{1.2}$$

This model is not realistic, but it explains that, as buying pressure raises prices by a rate of a, selling pressure decreases prices at a rate of $a*P_t$. At low levels of buying pressure, the price goes to zero and the system dies. At a higher level of buying pressure (but not too high), the price will converge to a steady state, or "fair value."

Suppose the buying pressure results in a growth rate of a = 2, and P_0 = 0.3. By iterating equation (1.2), a fair price of 0.50 is eventually reached. (I suggest that the reader try this on a personal computer, using a spreadsheet. Simply copy equation (1.2) down for 100 cells or so. A calculator can also be used if the CALC button is repeatedly pressed.) Thus, at moderate volume, prices converge to a single value. However, if the growth rate is increased to a = 2.5, there are suddenly two possible fair prices and the system oscillates between them. Why is this happening? At that *critical level,* buyers and sellers are not entering the market equally. There is a lag as $a*P_t^2$ becomes a bigger drag than the growth rate, (a). However, once the price hits the lower possibility, the growth rate dominates, pulling the price back up to the higher price. There are two fair values: at one, the sellers sell; at the other, the buyers buy. It does not stop here, however.

As the growth rate continues to rise, 4, 16, and 32 possible fair values appear. Finally, at a = 3.75, an infinite number of fair values is possible. Because the system cannot agree on what the fair price is, it fluctuates in a seemingly random, chaotic fashion. Figure 1.1 is a bifurcation diagram showing the critical values of the growth rate, (a), where the number of fair values increases.

The model is unrealistic; it assumes, for instance, that selling pressure is directly related to the growth rate due to buying (a). However, it illustrates how complex results can originate in even a simple nonlinear system. We can begin to imagine the complexities in a large nonlinear system such as the weather and the actively trading stock market. Equation (1.2) is the celebrated *Logistic Equation,* which has been extensively analyzed in the literature. Chapter 10 examines its behavior in more detail.

From this simple example, we can see a number of important characteristics of nonlinear dynamic systems. First, they are *feedback* systems. What

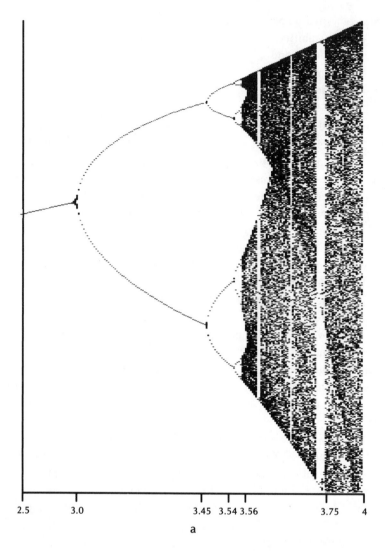

2.5   3.0   3.45 3.54 3.56   3.75   4

a

FIGURE 1.1   Bifurcation diagram: The Logistic Equation.

happened yesterday influences what happens today; P_{t+1} is a product of P_t. Second, there are *critical levels,* where more than a single equilibrium exists. In the Logistic Equation, the first critical level is when a = 2.5. Third, the system is a *fractal.* This term will be elaborated on in Part II, but fractal characteristics are evident in Figure 1.1. At a = 3.75, there is a "band of stability." However, inside each figure is a smaller figure, identical to the larger figure. If the smaller figure were to be enlarged, that figure would contain another band of stability, where another even smaller version of the main figure resides. At smaller and smaller scales, the same repetition would be found. This *self-similar* property is a characteristic of nonlinear dynamic systems and is symptomatic of the nonlinear feedback process. This complexity occurs only when the system is far from equilibrium.

Finally, there is *sensitive dependence on initial conditions*. If equation (1.2) now becomes a forecasting model, then a slight change in P_t will result in a very different price at time $(t + n)$, even though they may have been close in the beginning.

These characteristics indicate that, if the capital markets are nonlinear dynamic systems, then we should expect:

1. Long-term correlations and trends (feedback effects);
2. Erratic (critical levels) markets under certain conditions, and at certain times;
3. A time series of returns that, at smaller increments of time, will still look the same and will have similar statistical characteristics (fractal structure);
4. Less reliable forecasts, the further out in time we look (sensitive dependence on initial conditions).

In general, these types of characteristics arise only when a system is far from equilibrium. The characteristics seem to describe the market that we know from experience, but they do not fit the Efficient Market Hypothesis (EMH), which has dominated quantitative investment finance, or financial economics, for the past 30 years. The failure of the EMH as a paradigm is the subject of the next two chapters.

The EMH assumes that investors are rational, orderly, and tidy. It is a model of investment behavior that reduces the mathematics to simple linear differential equations, with one solution. However, the markets are not orderly or simple. They are messy and complex.

COMPLEXITY

Over the last few years, it has become clear that chaos theory and fractals are a subset of a much larger universe of discourse: *complexity theory*. Complexity theory deals with processes where a large number of seemingly independent agents act coherently. Complexity can be a dynamical process, or an object. We recognize the qualitative aspects of complex objects without being able to precisely measure them. Trees, handwriting, and river beds are all objects that are individual yet have global characteristics. Complexity assures that they are different in detail while similar in concept. That is, they are locally random, but globally deterministic. They are fractal.

We also see this in many dynamical systems, such as the world ecosystem. Kauffman (1993) has postulated that spontaneous coherent structures are a more likely mechanism for evolution than the slowly changing theory of Darwin. This work has been inspired by fossil evidence that new species appear simultaneously in bursts of natural creativity. Likewise, in the social sciences there have been many instances where scattered individuals working independently become schools of thought, like the Transcendentalists, or schools of art, like the Impressionists. Likewise, a disorganized rabble can become a coherent mob. The mob can act as if of one mind. The group can perform actions that none of the individuals would contemplate if working alone.

Traditional modeling techniques cannot handle the complexity of true life situations like these. Only in the last decade with the power of the computer have we been able to explore nature's, and the capital market's, secrets.

STRUCTURE OF THIS BOOK

This book is designed as both an introduction to new analytical techniques and a plea to reexamine the methods that have been in use for the past 40 years. In particular, we need to examine the assumptions under which our existing models operate. Part One, a brief review and critique, covers both the foundations and the history of current capital market theory. Most readers will be familiar with much of this material, but it is an important reminder of both how we came to this point in the evolution of our field, and why we developed along the line we did. It is time to question some of the assumptions under which we have created the efficient markets concept. We do this in Chapter 2. In Chapter 3, we review some of the empirical evidence that contradicts existing theory. Chapter 4 forms a bridge to the need for new concepts to explain the deficiencies in the current paradigm.

Part Two covers fractal analysis. Like the rest of the book, it is mostly a conceptual discussion. Fractals offer a new, broader statistical analysis that is a logical extension of current capital market theory. In Chapters 5 and 6, we cover crucial characteristics of fractals, and, in Chapter 7, the analysis of fractal time series through rescaled range analysis (R/S). Chapter 8 examines analysis of the capital markets using fractal techniques, and Chapter 9 covers the specifics of fractal statistics.

Part Three goes on to nonlinear dynamic analysis, or chaos theory. Chapters 11 and 12 define and analyze chaotic systems. Chapter 13 examines the capital markets for evidence of chaotic tendencies.

Part Four deals with applications designed to cope with the complexity underlying the real world. Throughout, the text attempts to present new ways of looking at old problems. Some of these ways are radically different from those previously used—at least, at first glance, they appear to be different. However, when these approaches are examined more closely, I believe that the new paradigm will be seen as a more general form of the existing paradigm. The new paradigm allows for investors who are not rational and for statistics that do not conform to the normal distribution. The existing paradigm remains a special case of the new nonlinear paradigm, but, as a special case, it does not appear often. This generalization makes the problem of understanding markets and economies much more complicated, but much more realistic. The implications are both exciting and frightening. They are exciting, in that we will have a deeper insight and understanding of the nature of markets, but they are frightening because they reveal how much work still remains to be done.

2
Random Walks and Efficient Markets

No concept in investment finance has been as widely tested and little believed as "efficient markets." Yet, the concept is the bedrock of quantitative capital market theory, and the past 30-plus years of research have depended on it. The Efficient Market Hypothesis (EMH) actually has roots dating back to the turn of the century. The EMH has one primary function: to justify the use of probability calculus in analyzing capital markets. If the markets are nonlinear dynamic systems, then the use of standard statistical analysis can give misleading results, particularly if a random walk model is used. Therefore, it is important to reevaluate the premises that underlie current capital market theory.

Efficient markets are priced so that all public information, both fundamental and price history, is already discounted. Prices, therefore, move only when new information is received. An efficient market cannot be gamed because not only do the prices reflect known information, but the large number of investors will ensure that the prices are fair. In this regard, investors are considered rational: they know, in a collective sense, what information is important and what is not. Then, after digesting the information and assessing the risks involved, the collective consciousness of the market finds an equilibrium price. Essentially, the EMH says that the market is made up of too many people to be wrong.

If the safety-in-numbers assumption is true, then today's change in price is caused only by today's unexpected news. Yesterday's news is no longer important, and today's return is unrelated to yesterday's return; the returns are independent. If returns are independent, then they are random variables and follow a random walk. If enough independent price changes are collected, in the limit (as the number of observations approaches infinity), the probability distribution becomes the normal distribution. This assumption regarding the normality of returns opens up a large battery of statistical tests and modeling techniques, which can create optimal solutions for decision making.

This is the random walk version of the EMH; in many ways, it is the most restrictive version. Market efficiency does not necessarily imply a random walk, but a random walk does imply market efficiency. Therefore, the assumption that returns are normally distributed is not necessarily implied by efficient markets. However, there is a very deeply rooted assumption of independence. Most tests of the EMH also test the random walk version. In addition, the EMH in any version says that past information does not affect market activity, once the information is generally known. This independence assumption between market moves lends itself first to a random walk theory, and then to more general martingale and submartingale models. Although not all versions of the EMH assume independence, the techniques used for statistical testing have independence assumptions, as well as built-in finite variance. Because of these characteristics, the random walk version of the EMH is the one generally referred to as the Efficient Market Hypothesis, although technically this is not true.

Actually, assuming that returns follow, a random walk came first, through both observation and the statistical analysis of returns. The rationalization for the use of statistical analysis, with its independence assumptions, came much later. The EMH was the culmination of this rationalization process.

Any scientist will complain that developing a theory to justify methods is putting the cart before the horse—it is bad science. If market returns had been shown to be normally distributed, then a hypothesis and its implications could have been developed. In capital market theory, the assumptions of normality and finite variance, as well as models based on those assumptions, were developed even as empirical evidence continued to contradict theory.

In this chapter, we will review capital market theory and its development. Of necessity, the discussion is brief. The purpose here is to show that, if the random walk assumption of capital market prices is flawed, much of the current theory, empirical research, and research methodology utilized is seriously weakened. New methods must replace the old, and they must not depend on independence, normality, or finite variance. The new methods must include fractals and nonlinear dynamics whose characteristics appear to conform more closely to observed behavior. In addition, the nonlinear paradigm must allow for the concept of a "long memory" in the markets: an event can influence the markets for a long, perhaps indefinite time into the future. The current paradigm allows for a short memory at best, in the submartingale form.

DEVELOPMENT OF THE EMH

The original work using statistical methods to analyze returns was published in 1900 by Louis Bachelier, who applied to stocks, bonds, futures, and options the methods created for analyzing gambling. Bachelier's paper is the work of pioneering foresight, many years ahead of its time. Among its accomplishments was the recognition that the random walk process (later formalized by Weiner) is brownian motion. Einstein rediscovered this relationship a decade later.

Bachelier offered the first display of option payoffs, the now familiar kinked line graphs, as well as graphs for straddles and other option-related strategies. However, little empirical evidence is given to support his contention that market returns are independent, identically distributed (IID) random variables, the assumption that was crucial to his analysis.

Bachelier's thesis was revolutionary, but largely ignored and forgotten. Application of statistical analysis to the markets languished (with the exception of work by Holbrook Working and Alfred Cowles in the 1930s) until the late 1940s. Progress then became rapid. A body of work that became the basis of the EMH was collected by Cootner in his classic volume (1964b) *The Random Character of Stock Market Prices,* first published in 1964. Cootner's anthology, the standard bearer of the first "golden age" of quantitative analysis, deals strictly with market characteristics, not portfolio theory. The work of Markowitz, Tobin, and Sharpe, which also appeared during this period, is therefore not included. The book does present the rationale for what was to be formalized as the EMH in the 1960s by Fama.

During the decades of the 1920s through the 1940s, market analysis was dominated by Fundamentalists (followers of Graham and Dodd) and Technicians (or technical analysts, followers of Magee). The 1950s added a third group, the Quants (or quantitative analysts, followers of Bachelier).

By nature, the Quants had more sympathy for Fundamentalists than the Technicians did, because the Fundamentalists assumed investors to be rational, in order for value to reassert itself. The Technicians assumed that the market was driven by emotion, or "animal spirits," as Lord Keynes said.

Bias against technical analysis is represented in Roberts's paper (1964) in Cootner's anthology. Roberts makes an appeal for widespread use of statistical analysis based on work by Kendall (1964), who had said:

... changes in securities prices behaved nearly as if they had been generated by a suitably designed roulette wheel for which each outcome was statistically independent of past history and for which relative frequencies were reasonably stable through time.

Roberts further states that the "change model insists on independence," and the probabilities "must be stable over time." The rationale for accepting the chance model is that, if the market were an imperfect roulette wheel, "people would notice the imperfections and by acting on them, remove them." Roberts offers this as a rationale without accepting it, however. His paper makes a plea for further research.

The claim that stock prices follow a random walk is formalized by Osborne (1964) in his very formally developed paper on brownian motion. Osborne offers a process in which changes in stock market prices can be equivalent to the movement of a particle in a fluid, commonly called brownian motion. He does so by stating a number of assumptions and drawing conclusions from these results.

The first two assumptions deal with minimum price moves (one-eighth of a dollar) and with the fact that the number of transactions per day is finite and not important. However, Osborne goes from there to a number of assumptions regarding investor perception of value. His Assumption 3 states that "price and value are related" and that relationship is the prime determinant of market returns. Assumption 4 says that, given two securities with different expected returns, the logical decision is to pick the stock with the highest expected return. "Expected return" is the sum of the probabilities of a return times the associated return. The probabilities add to 1, so the expected return is the probability weighted return, or the expected value of the random variable.

Assumption 5 states that buyers and sellers "are unlikely to trade unless there is equality of opportunity to profit." In other words, the buyer cannot have an advantage over the seller or vice versa, if a transaction is to be accomplished. Osborne says that Assumption 5 is "a consequence" of Assumptions 3 and 4.

Thus, a general equilibrium price (Assumption 5) occurs because investors are most concerned with paying the right price for value (Assumption 3), and, given two variables with expected values, investors will pick the one with the highest expected return (Assumption 4); as a result, a buyer and seller find the price mutually advantageous. In other words, because investors are able to rationally equate price and value, they will trade at the equilibrium price based on the information available at that time. The sequence of price changes is independent, because price is already equated to available information.

Osborne's Assumption 7 is the culmination of Assumptions 3 through 6. Assumption 7 (which is really a conclusion) states that, because price changes are independent (i.e., they are a random walk), we would expect the distribution of changes to be normal, with a stable mean and finite variance. This is a result of the Central Limit Theorem of probability calculus, or the Law of Large Numbers. The Central Limit Theorem states that a sample of IID random variables will be normally distributed as the sample gets larger.

Despite the fact that we are about to question Osborne's logic, his accomplishment is in no way diminished. Osborne collected various concepts underlying random walk theory, which, in the end justifies the use of probability calculus. Essentially, this group of academics knew that statistical analysis offered a vast array of modeling and research tools. The tools, however, had limits regarding their underlying assumptions. Paramount among these was: the subject under study must be an IID random variable. It was thus postulated that, because the stock market and other capital markets are large systems that have a large number of degrees of freedom (or investors), current prices must reflect the information everyone already has. *Changes* in price would come only from unexpected new information.

The founding fathers of capital market theory were well aware of these simplifying assumptions and their implications. They were not trying to minimize the impact of these assumptions on the theory. They did, however, feel that the assumptions did not materially affect the usefulness of the model, especially if certain assumptions about investor behavior were accepted. The concept of the *rational investor* was crucial to what became the EMH.

Osborne had already touched on this concept, as we have seen. Osborne said that investors value stocks based on their expected value (or expected return), which was the probability weighted average of possible returns. It was assumed that investors set their subjective probabilities in a rational and unbiased manner.

As a simple example, we will say that an investor sees three possible economic scenarios: positive growth, no growth, and negative growth. If the economy experiences positive growth, the investor feels that the market will be up 12 percent. With no growth, the market will be down 1 percent. If the economy slips into recession, the market will go down 8 percent. The investor also has done an economic analysis and has decided that the growth scenario has a 60 percent probability of occurring, the no-growth, 30 percent, and the recession, 10 percent. The expected return would be:

$$0.6*12\% + 0.3*(-1\%) + 0.1*(-8\%) = 6.1\%$$

Many investors do make decisions this way. Investors judge the probabilities and possible payoffs of different scenarios, but they do not necessarily base their final decision on probabilities. Later, we will discuss some research into human decision making; for now, state lotteries can be used as an example. The expected return of state lotteries is typically negative. It has to be, or the state would not make any money. Yet, millions of people play the lottery, even though it's not something a "rational investor" would do. Lottery players evidently feel that the possibility of a large return offsets the risk of a small loss, even if the probabilities are against them. This is not "rational," yet it is human nature.

Fama (1965a) finally formalized these observations into the Efficient Market Hypothesis (EMH), which states that the market is a martingale, or "fair game"; that is, information cannot be used to profit in the marketplace. The EMH is similar to Osborne's Assumption 5. In its pure form, the EMH does not require independence through time or accept only IID observations. However, the random walk model does require those assumptions. If returns are random, then markets are efficient. The converse may not be true, however.

The concept of efficient markets finally branched out to attack fundamental analysis as well as technical analysis. Up to this point, the focus had been that past *price* information was not related to future prices. By 1973, Lorie and Hamilton (1973), in their excellent survey, said:

> The assertion that a market is efficient is vastly stronger than the assertion that successive changes in stock prices are independent of each other. The latter assertion—the weak form of the efficient market hypothesis—merely says that current prices of stocks fully reflect all that is implied by the historical sequence of prices so that a knowledge of that sequence is of no value in forming expectations about future prices. The assertion that the market is efficient implies that current prices reflect and impound not only all of the implications of the historical sequence of prices, but also *all that is knowable* about the companies whose stocks are being traded . . . it suggests the fruitlessness of efforts to earn superior rates of return by the analysis of all public information.

This attack on fundamental analysis has generally been unacceptable to the investment community, and it divided the EMH into "weak" and "strong" forms. The strong form suggested that fundamental analysis was a useless activity, because prices already reflected "all that is knowable," or all public and private (insider) information. As a compromise, the "semistrong" form was articulated.

In the semistrong version of the EMH, prices reflect all "public" information. Security analysts, using Graham-and-Dodd techniques, formulate value based on information that is available to all investors. A large number of *independent* estimates results in a "fair" value by the aggregate market. Analysts, thus, become the *reason* markets are efficient. Fundamental analysts form a fair price by consensus.

The semistrong form of the EMH was much more acceptable to the investment community because it said that markets were efficient *because of* security analysis, not in spite of it. In addition, the semistrong form implied that changes in stock prices were random because of influences outside the price series itself. That is, price changes were random, not because the market itself was a "crap shoot," but because of the evaluation of the changing fundamentals of a company, caused by both micro- and macro-economics. By the mid-1970s, the semistrong version of the EMH was the generally accepted theory. When one referred to the Efficient Market Hypothesis, the semistrong version was understood. For the remainder of this book we will generally refer to the semistrong version of the EMH, which states that *markets are efficient because prices reflect all public information. A weak-form efficient market is one in which the price changes are independent and may be a random walk.*

The academic community had undergone a 30-year paradigm shift, from the "animal spirits" of Keynes to the "rational investor" of the EMH. By 1970, the academic community had generally accepted the EMH (the investment community took a few years longer), and what Kuhn (1962) called "normal science" had taken over financial economics. The major studies undertaken to prove the EMH to be true will be discussed in Chapter 3.

MODERN PORTFOLIO THEORY

Meanwhile, Modern Portfolio Theory (MPT) was also being developed. Markowitz (1952) made the distribution of possible returns, as measured by its variance, the measure of riskiness of the portfolio. Formally, the population variance is defined by the following formula:

$$\sigma^2 = \sum_{i=1}^{\infty} (r_i - r_\mu)^2 \tag{2.1}$$

where σ^2 = variance
         r_μ = mean return
         r_i = return observation

At the limit, the variance would measure the dispersion of possible returns around the average return. The square root of the variance, or standard deviation, measures the probability that the return deviates from the mean. If we use Osborne's concept of expected return, we can estimate the probability that actual return will deviate from average return. The wider the dispersion, the higher the standard deviation will be, and the riskier the stock would be. Using the variance requires that the returns be normally distributed. However, if stock returns follow a random walk and are IID random variables, then the Central Limit Theorem of calculus (or the Law of Large Numbers) states that the distribution would be normal, and variance would be finite. Investors would thus desire the portfolio with the highest expected return for a level of risk. Investors were expected to be risk-averse. This approach became known as "mean/variance efficiency." The curve shown in Figure 2.1 was called the "efficient frontier" because the dark curve contained the portfolios with the highest level of expected return for a given level of risk, or standard deviation. Investors would prefer these optimal portfolios, based on the rational investor model.

These concepts were extended by Sharpe (1964), Litner (1965), and Mossin (1966) in what came to be known as the Capital Asset Pricing Model (CAPM),

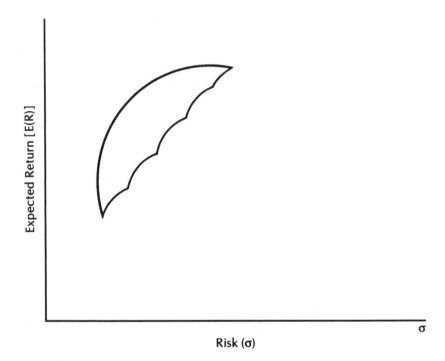

FIGURE 2.1   The efficient frontier.

the name coined by Sharpe. The CAPM combined the EMH and Markowitz's mathematical model of portfolio theory into a model of investor behavior based on rational expectations in a general equilibrium framework. In particular, it assumed that investors had homogeneous return expectations—that is, they interpreted information in the same manner. The CAPM was a remarkable advance, arrived at independently by the three developers.

Because the CAPM has been extensively discussed in the literature, the discussion here is limited mostly to aspects that are relevant to the premise that a new paradigm is needed. The CAPM begins by assuming that we live in a world free of transaction costs, commissions, and taxes. These simplifying assumptions were necessary to separate investor behavior from constraints imposed by society. Physicists often do the same thing when they assume friction's nonexistence. Next, CAPM assumes that everyone can borrow and lend at a risk-free rate of interest, which is usually interpreted as the 90-day T-Bill rate. Finally, it assumes that all investors desire Markowitz mean/variance efficiency—that they want the portfolio with the highest level of expected return for a given level of risk, and are risk-averse. Risk is again defined as the standard deviation of returns. Investors are, therefore, rational in the sense of Osborne and Markowitz.

Based on these assumptions, the CAPM goes on to draw a number of conclusions about investor behavior. First, the optimal portfolio for all investors would be combinations of the market portfolio (all risky assets capitalization weighted) and the riskless asset. This type of portfolio is shown in Figure 2.2: a line is tangent to the efficient frontier at the market portfolio (M) and the Y-intercept, which is the risk-free rate (r). Levels of risk can be adjusted by adding to the riskless asset, to reduce the standard deviation of the portfolio, or by borrowing at that rate to lever the market portfolio. The portfolios that lie along this line, called the Capital Market Line (CML), dominate the portfolios on the efficient frontier; investors would prefer these portfolios to all others. In addition, investors are not compensated for assuming nonmarket risk, because the optimal portfolios are along the CML. The model also states that assets with higher risk should be compensated for by higher returns. Because risk is now relative to the market portfolio, a linear measure of the sensitivity of the security risk to the market risk is used. The linear measure is called beta. If all risky assets were plotted on a graph of their betas versus their expected returns, the result would be a straight line that intercepts the Y-axis at the risk-free rate of interest and passes through the market portfolio. This result, called the Security Market Line (SML), is shown in Figure 2.3.

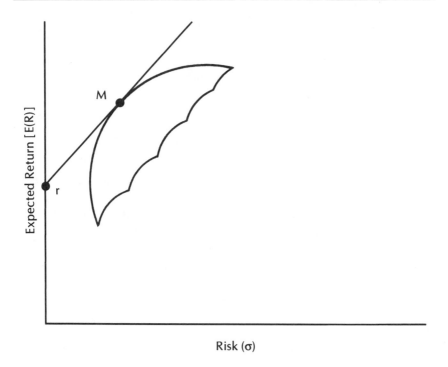

FIGURE 2.2   The capital market line.

This short and necessarily incomplete discussion of the CAPM is intended to show the substantial dependence on standard deviation as the measure of risk. By implication, the CAPM needs efficient markets and normally or log-normally distributed returns, because variances are assumed to be finite.

The CAPM, which made quantitative methods practical, remains the standard for any new model of investor behavior. Markowitz portfolio theory explained why diversification reduced risk. The CAPM explained how investors would behave, if they were rational. Practitioners needed to be convinced that the CAPM's underlying assumptions, which were simplifying assumptions, did not detract from the usefulness of the model. The EMH became extensively used as a rationale for the Gaussian assumption of log-normally distributed returns. This struggle for acceptance probably made the early champions of quantitative methods insist that the EMH was true. Their merger of the EMH with the CAPM and its modifications came to be known generally as Modern Portfolio Theory, or MPT. This same struggle for acceptance may have caused discussion of possible mis-specification to be pushed to the background.

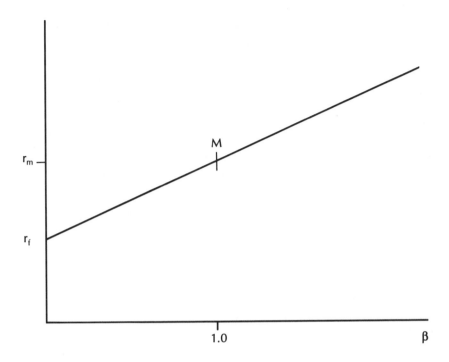

FIGURE 2.3   The security market line.

The EMH reinforced MPT, and the investment community accepted variance and standard deviation as *the* measures of risk. Again, the early founders
of capital market theory were well aware of these assumptions and their limitations. Samuelson, Sharpe, and Fama (among others) all published work modify-
ing MPT for nonnormal distributions. Empirical evidence continued, through
the 1960s, to favor the Stable Paretian Hypothesis of Mandelbrot (1964), which
said that, because returns are nonnormal, there was a need for possible revision
of the EMH and MPT. (We will discuss the Stable Paretian Hypothesis in detail
in Part Two, when we deal with fractals.) The evidence that returns were non-
normally distributed was strong when Sharpe (1970), and Fama and Miller
(1972) published their texts; both books included sections on needed modifications to standard portfolio theory, to account for Stable Paretian distributions.

By the 1970s, such discussion had ceased, except for a few isolated academic
papers, notably by Roll (1977). Advances in financial economics continued,
based on the weak-form EMH and its assumption that price changes were independent. In addition, the normal distribution, with its Gaussian assumptions to

model independence, was convenient to use. Applications of econometrics to capital markets became more complex as the EMH gained wider acceptance and was questioned less and less. Major advances included the option pricing model of Black and Scholes (1973) and the Arbitrage Pricing Theory (APT) of Ross (1976). The APT, a more general pricing model than the CAPM, said that price changes came from unexpected changes in factors; the APT could therefore handle nonlinear relationships. However, in practice, standard econometrics (including finite variance assumptions) have been used, in attempts to implement the APT. The APT did present an alternative theoretical pricing model that did not depend on quadratic utility functions.

In recent years, theoretical models have become less frequent. Research in the 1980s generally focused on empirical research and applications of existing models.

The only theoretical advance to gain a wide following in recent years postulates that market volatility is time varying. That is, volatility is conditional upon its recent levels. These models had their genesis in the autoregression conditional heteroskedastic (ARCH) models of Engle (1982). Since Engle's original work, many variations have developed on the basic ARCH model. However, all keep the basic assumption of short-memory processes and some form of market efficiency.

SUMMARY

In its current form, capital market theory is based on a few key concepts:

1. *Rational investors.* Investors require mean/variance efficiency. They assess potential returns by a probabilistic weighting method that generates expected returns. Risk is measured as the standard deviation of returns. Investors want assets that give the highest expected return for a level of risk. They are risk-averse.

2. *Efficient markets.* Prices reflect all public information. Changes in prices are not related, except possibly for some very short-term dependence, which dissipates quickly. Value is determined by the consensus of a large number of fundamental analysts.

3. *Random walks.* Because of the two concepts above, returns follow a random walk. Therefore, the probability distribution is approximately normal or log-normal. Approximately normal means that, at a minimum, the distribution of returns has a finite mean and variance.

This listing indicates that capital market theory is, in general, dependent on normally distributed returns. Empirical studies have attempted to prove this Gaussian assumption, but have often delivered contrary results. We will discuss some of these studies in the next chapter.

Through the 1950s and 1960s, the impact of the normality assumption was understood. A nonnormal return distribution was always considered a possibility, even if it was not desirable. However, during the 1970s, and particularly during the 1980s, the EMH was generally taught as fact. Because of the large number of MBAs earned during the 1980s, a perception that the EMH is a proven truth has resulted. This general acceptance of the EMH may have come from the efforts of academics in the 1960s and the early 1970s to get their theories accepted. A healthy skepticism was not maintained, as it should be at all times.

Two possibilities have been ignored: particularly that markets and securities are interdependent and that the rational investor model is not realistic. As we will see, people do not behave in the manner described by rational expectations theory. The view that investors may not know how to interpret all known information and may react to trends, thus incorporating past information into their current actions, was considered an unnecessary complication that should be assumed away, like transaction costs and taxes. However, understanding how people interpret information may be more crucial than previously acknowledged, even if the mathematics get messy. In particular, current capital market theory is based on a linear view of society. In this view, people see information and adjust to it immediately, and securities do so through their betas, which are the slope of a linear regression between a stock and the market portfolios' excess returns. The linear paradigm is built into the normality assumption. However, we will see that people, and nature in general, are *nonlinear*. Unlike assuming away taxes, assuming that investors are rational changes the nature of the system. That is why the linear paradigm, despite its simplicity and conceptual elegance, is seriously flawed. In the next chapter, we will deal with tests of the linear paradigm, and what they have found.

3
The Failure of the Linear Paradigm

Before the Efficient Market Hypothesis (EMH) was fully formed, exceptions to the normality assumption were being found. One anomaly was apparent when Osborne (1964) plotted the density function of stock market returns, and labeled the returns "approximately normal": there were extra observations in the tails of the distribution, a condition that statisticians call "kurtosis." Osborne noted that the tails were fatter than they should be, but did not see their significance. By the time Cootner's classic was published (1964b), it was generally accepted that the distribution of price changes had fat tails, but the implications of this departure from normality were widely debated. Mandelbrot's (1964) chapter in the Cootner volume suggested that returns may belong to a family of "Stable Paretian" distributions, which are characterized by undefined, or infinite, variance. Cootner contested the suggestion, which would have seriously weakened the Gaussian hypothesis, and offered an alternative in which sums of normal distributions may result in a distribution that looks fat-tailed but is still Gaussian. This debate continued for almost ten years.

The linear paradigm says, basically, that investors react to information in a linear fashion. That is, they react as information is received; they do not react in a cumulative fashion to a series of events. The linear view is built into the rational investor concept, because past information has already been discounted in security prices. Thus, the linear paradigm implies that returns should have approximately normal distributions and should be independent.

The new paradigm generalizes investor reaction to accept the possibility of nonlinear reaction to information, and is therefore a natural extension of the current view.

TESTS OF NORMALITY

The first complete study on daily returns was done by Fama (1965a), who found that returns were negatively skewed: more observations were in the left-hand (negative) tail than in the right-hand tail. In addition, the tails were fatter, and the peak around the mean was higher than predicted by the normal distribution, a condition called "leptokurtosis." Sharpe also noted this in his 1970 textbook, *Portfolio Theory and Capital Markets*. When Sharpe compared annual returns to the normal distribution, he noted that "normal distributions assign little likelihood to the occurrence of really extreme values. But such values occur quite often."

More recently, Turner and Weigel (1990) performed an extensive study of volatility, using daily S&P index returns from 1928 through 1990, with similar results. Table 3.1 summarizes their findings. They found that "daily return distributions for the Dow Jones and S&P 500 are negatively skewed and contain a larger frequency of returns around the mean interspersed with infrequent very large or very small returns as compared to a normal distribution."

Figure 3.1(a) is a frequency distribution of returns, which I compiled to illustrate this point. The graph shows a frequency distribution of the 5-day

Table 3.1   Volatility Study: Daily S&P 500 Returns, 1/28–12/89

Decade	Mean	Standard Deviation	Skewness	Kurtosis
1920s	0.0322	1.6460	−1.4117	18.9700
1930s	−0.0232	1.9150	0.1783	3.7710
1940s	0.0100	0.8898	−0.9354	10.8001
1950s	0.0490	0.7050	−0.8398	7.8594
1960s	0.0172	0.6251	−0.4751	9.8719
1970s	0.0062	0.8652	0.2565	2.2935
1980s	0.0468	1.0989	−3.7752	79.6573
Overall	0.0170	1.1516	−0.6338	21.3122

Adapted from Turner and Weigel (1990).

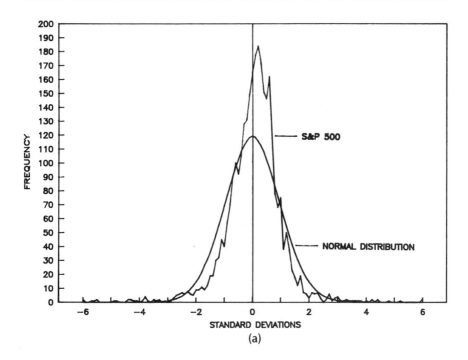

FIGURE 3.1a Frequency distribution of S&P 500 5-day returns, January 1928–December 1989: Normal vs. actual returns.

logarithmic first difference in prices for the S&P 500 from January 1928 to December 1989. The changes have been normalized so that they have a zero mean and a standard deviation of one. A frequency distribution for an equal number of Gaussian random numbers is also shown. The high peak and fat tails noted quantitatively in Table 3.1 can be clearly seen. In addition, the return data have a number of four- and five-sigma events in both tails. Figure 3.1(b) illustrates the differences between the two curves in Figure 3.1(a). The negative skewness can be seen at the count three standard deviations below the mean. The stock market's probability of a three-sigma event is roughly twice that of the Gaussian random numbers.

Any frequency distribution that includes October 1987 will be negatively skewed and will have a fat negative tail. However, earlier studies showed the same phenomenon. In another recent study of quarterly S&P 500 returns, from 1946 through 1988, Friedman and Laibson (1989) point out that "the

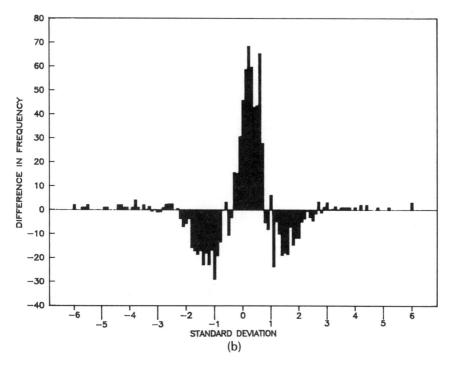

FIGURE 3.1b   Difference in frequency, S&P 500 5-day returns: Normal.

22.6 percent *one-day* decline in stock prices on October 19, 1987, was unique, but from the perspective of a quarterly time frame the 1987:4 episode was one of several unusually large rallies or crashes." These authors note that, in addition to being leptokurtotic, "large movements have more often been crashes than rallies" and significant leptokurtosis "appears regardless of the period chosen."

These studies offer ample evidence that U.S. stock market returns are not normally distributed. If stock returns are not normally distributed, then much statistical analysis, particularly diagnostics such as correlation coefficients and t-statistics, is seriously weakened and may give misleading answers. The case for a random walk in stock prices is also seriously weakened.

Sterge (1989), in an additional study of financial futures prices of Treasury Bond, Treasury Note, and Eurodollar contracts, finds the same leptokurtotic distributions. Sterge notes that "very large (three or more standard deviations from the norm) price changes can be expected to occur two to three times as often as predicted by normality."

The failure of the linear paradigm and of the weak-form EMH to describe the probabilities of returns is therefore not confined to the U.S. stock market, but can be extended to other markets as well. In particular, there is little basis to the assertion that the distribution of market returns is "approximately normal."

THE CURIOUS BEHAVIOR OF VOLATILITY

Given that market returns are not normally distributed, it is not surprising that studies of "volatility" have found it to be disturbingly unstable. This stands to reason, because variance is stable and finite for the normal distribution alone, if the capital markets fall into the "Stable Paretian" family of distributions, as postulated by Mandelbrot.

Studies of volatility have tended to focus on stability over time. For instance, in the normal distribution, the variance of 5-day returns should be five times the variance of daily returns. Another method, using standard deviation rather than variance, is to multiply the daily standard deviation by the square root of 5. This scaling feature of the normal distribution is referred to as the $T^{1/2}$ Rule, where T is the increment of time.

The investment community often "annualizes" risk, using the $T^{1/2}$ Rule. Annual returns are usually reported, but volatility is calculated based on monthly returns. The monthly standard deviation is therefore converted to an annual number by multiplying it by the square root of 12—a perfectly acceptable method, if the distribution is normally distributed. However, we have seen that returns are not normally distributed. What are the implications?

Studies show that standard deviation does not scale according to the $T^{1/2}$ Rule. Turner and Weigel found that monthly and quarterly volatility were higher than they should be, compared to annual volatility, but daily volatility was lower than it should be. Chapter 9 presents further evidence of this, using numbers compiled by the author.

Finally, there is the work of Shiller, collected in his book *Stock Market Volatility* (1989). Shiller's approach to volatility is not based on looking at the distribution of returns. Instead, Shiller is concerned with the amount of volatility that should be expected in a rational market's framework. Shiller notes that rational investors' valuation of stocks would be based on expected dividends from owning the stock. Prices, however, are much too volatile to be due to changes in expected dividends, even when adjusted for inflation. He goes on to assert that there are two types of investors: "noise traders," who follow fashions and fads, and "smart money traders," who invest according to value. Shiller feels that "smart money" does not necessarily describe investment professionals. Noise traders tend to overreact to news that may affect future dividends, to the profit of smart money.

The excessive market volatility observed by Shiller challenged (1) the idea of rational investors, and (2) the concept that, by having large numbers of investors, the achievement of market efficiency would be ensured.

Finally, there is the autoregressive conditional heteroskedastic (ARCH) model of Engle (1982). This model sees volatility as conditional upon its previous level. Thus high volatility levels are followed by more high volatility, while low volatility is followed by more low volatility. This is consistent with Mandelbrot's (1964) observation that the size of price changes (ignoring the sign) seems to be correlated. Statistical evidence compiled by Engle (1982) and LeBaron (1990) among others supports the ARCH model family. In recent years this has led to increasing recognition that standard deviation is not a standard measure, at least over the short term. ARCH also results in fat-tailed probability distributions. Therefore, ARCH has had the most impact upon option pricing and technical trading rules. The impact of ARCH upon portfolio management has been negligible.

THE RISK/RETURN TRADEOFF

We have been focusing on empirical evidence of the distribution of market returns, and have seen that the evidence does not support the random walk assumption or a Gaussian normal distribution. In this section, we will look at investigations of investor behavior and will challenge the rational investor constructed to validate the concept of the EMH.

The studies of the CAPM are too numerous to describe here. Best known is the test by Black, Jensen, and Scholes (1972), which set a standard for tests of capital market theory. These authors constructed portfolios with different beta levels, to see whether the risk/return tradeoff specified by the CAPM could be supported empirically. In particular, they compared the shape of the realized Security Market Line (SML) to that predicted by theory. The SML (Figure 2.3) is the beta of a security plotted versus its expected return. Because, in the CAPM, investors are not compensated for bearing nonmarket risk, all securities should fall on the SML. The SML is a line that intercepts the risk-free rate of interest and is drawn through the market portfolio. Each security falls on the line because of its beta, or sensitivity to market returns (see Figure 2.3). In

their study, Black, Jensen, and Scholes used actual returns rather than expected returns, to see whether the realized SML conformed to theory.

They found that the realized SML for the 35-year period from 1931 to 1965
sloped upward for the full period, as predicted by the CAPM. Risky stocks
with higher betas *did* have higher returns than lower beta stocks; the relationship was approximately linear. However, the slope was flatter than predicted
by theory. The intercept was higher than the risk-free rate of interest. Higher
beta stocks gave less return than predicted by theory, and low-risk stocks gave
more return.

In addition, four subperiods of 105 months were tested. The betas remained fairly stationary over time, but the risk/return tradeoff was decidedly
unstable. The intercept was negative for the first subperiod, and positive for
the last three. The slope of the SML was steep for the first sub-period, positive but flatter for the second, flat for the third, and negative for the fourth.
The last two subperiods were contrary to the direction predicted by theory. In
the third subperiod (July 1948–March 1957), return was virtually the same,
regardless of risk. In the fourth period (April 1957–December 1965), higher
risk meant less return, even over an interval of almost nine years.

Black, Jensen, and Scholes then recapped an earlier article by Black
(1972), in which the traditional CAPM is adjusted, if riskless borrowing is not
available. This adjustment patches up the theory by using a zero beta stock return as the intercept, instead of the traditional risk-free rate, because such a
rate is unavailable to borrowers. The theory then becomes more realistic, because we must always borrow at a higher rate than the government. However,
the instability of the slope was not explained.

The only real critique of the CAPM came from Roll (1977), and it caused a
good deal of publicity. Roll showed that the empirical tests of the CAPM depended on the proxy used for the market portfolio. In the formal statement of
the CAPM, the market portfolio was the portfolio of *all* risky assets, not just
stocks. Yet, the tests of the CAPM centered on stocks, and a stock market
index was used as a proxy for the market portfolio. Roll proved that the return
on an asset is always a linear function of beta, if the proxy chosen is any efficient portfolio. Any "proof" of the CAPM will always support the CAPM, if
the proxy chosen is efficient. Roll went on to state that we can never truly test
the CAPM unless we use the true market portfolio. All we are testing is
whether the proxy for the market portfolio is efficient.

Roll's work does not contradict the CAPM, or the assumptions underlying
the EMH. He suggested that the CAPM can never truly be tested. I cover his
work to show that the only substantial criticism of the CAPM still does not

address the crucial issue of market efficiency. Roll criticized the techniques used to test the theory, not the theory itself. Even in this controversial work, the question of market efficiency does not arise.

ARE MARKETS EFFICIENT?

This brief review indicates that serious questions have been raised about the EMH. In Chapter 2, we saw that the EMH was necessary to justify the assumption that price changes follow a random walk; that is, a random walk model is not justified without the EMH, though the relationship is not necessarily reversible. A random walk was necessary for application of statistical analysis to a time series of price changes. Statistical analysis was necessary, if portfolio theory was to be applicable to the real world. Without normality, a large body of theory and empirical work becomes questionable. We also saw that the traditional risk/return tradeoff did not necessarily apply.

In addition, there have been numerous market anomalies in which excess nonmarket returns could be achieved, contrary to the "fair game" of the semistrong EMH. In the stock market, these include the small firm effect, the low P/E effect, and the January effect. Rudd and Clasing (1982) document excess returns realized from nonmarket-factor returns generated by the BARRA E1 six-factor risk model. This CAPM-based model found that four sources of nonmarket risk (market variability, low valuation and unsuccess, immaturity and smallness, and financial risk) all offered the opportunity for significant nonmarket returns. Rudd and Clasing say that these factor returns are "far from random," suggesting that the semistrong EMH is flawed. These anomalies have long suggested that the current paradigm requires an adjustment that takes these anomalies into account.

Perhaps the real question is related to how people make decisions. The EMH is heavily dependent on rational investors. Rationality is defined as the ability to value securities on the basis of all available information, and to price them accordingly. In particular, investors are risk-averse. However, are people rational (by this definition) even in aggregate? When faced with the potential for gains and losses, how do people react?

Conventional theory says that investors are risk-averse. If they are to accept more risk, investors must be compensated with more return. Recent research presented by Tversky (1990) suggests that, when losses are involved, people tend to be risk-seeking: they are more likely to gamble if gambling can minimize their losses.

Tversky gives the following example. Suppose an investor has a choice between (1) a sure gain of $85,000, or (2) an 85 percent chance of receiving $100,000 and a 15 percent chance of receiving nothing. Most people will prefer the sure thing, even though the expected return, as defined by Osborne in Chapter 2, is identical in both cases. People are risk-averse, as suggested by theory.

Tversky then switches the situation around. Suppose the investor now has a choice between (1) a sure loss of $85,000, or (2) an 85 percent chance of losing $100,000 and a 15 percent chance of losing nothing. Again, the expected return is identical for both choices, but, in this situation, people will gamble. Evidently, the chance to minimize losses is preferable to a sure loss, even if there is a significant chance of further loss. People become risk-seeking, because the nature of the gamble is different.

Capital market theory also assumes that all investors have the same single-holding-period investment horizon. This is necessary for the expected returns to be comparable, but it is well known that this is not the case. When offered the opportunity of receiving $5,000 today, or $5,150 a month from now, most people will take $5,000 today. However, if offered $5,000 one year from now, or $5,150 thirteen months from now, most will opt for the longer holding period. This, again, is inconsistent with the rational investor model.

Tversky also addresses how people act under conditions of uncertainty. The rational expectations hypothesis says that the beliefs and subjective probabilities of rational investors are accurate and unbiased. However, people have a common tendency to make overconfident predictions. The brain is probably designed to make decisions with as much certainty as possible, after receiving little information. For survival purposes, confidence in the face of uncertainty is a desirable characteristic. However, overconfidence can cause people to ignore information that is available to others. Therefore, in assigning subjective probabilities, the forecaster is more likely to assign to a particular economic scenario a higher probability than is warranted by the facts. In part, the forecaster may be trying not to appear indecisive. In an example in Chapter 2, an investor was 60 percent sure of economic growth, 30 percent sure of no growth, and 10 percent sure of a recession. In reality, an investor who was fairly certain of the growth scenario would increase the probability to 90 percent, with a 10 percent probability of flat growth, so as not to appear overconfident. Recession will probably "not be a possibility at this time." This wording is notable for its similarity to pronouncements by the White House Council of Economic Advisors, when asked whether recession is a possibility.

Tversky and Kahenmann's work has since spawned a subcategory called *behavioral finance*. This field began, in essence, with the publication of a paper by DeBondt and Thaler (1986) entitled "Does the Stock Market Over-react?" Their work is discussed in more detail in Chapter 14.

Alongside Tversky's view of how people make decisions is my own view, which needs empirical confirmation. I believe that people do not recognize, or react to, trends until they are well established. For instance, they will not begin to extrapolate a phenomenon like rising inflation, until inflation has been rising for some time. They will then make a decision that incorporates information they have ignored until that time. This behavior is quite different from that of the rational investor, who would immediately adjust to new information. However, the statement that people do not recognize relevant information if it does not fit in with the current forecast of the future more closely describes human nature, and this description is consistent with Tversky's view that people tend to be overconfident about their forecasts. They are, therefore, less likely to change their forecasts, unless they receive enough confirming information that the environment has changed. They are more likely to react to trends than to forecast changes in them. If investors do react to information in this way, the market cannot be efficient, because all information is not yet reflected in prices. Much is ignored, and reaction comes later.

When individual investors are unlikely to react in the defined rational way, there is no reason to believe that the aggregate is any better. Anyone who has read Mackay's (1841) *Extraordinary Popular Delusions and the Madness of Crowds* will acknowledge historical precedent for believing otherwise. More recent examples could include the gold bubble of 1980 and the U.S. stock market of 1987.

WHY THE FAT TAILS?

The exact nature of the leptokurtosis (fat tails and high peak) of the distribution of returns has been widely debated. It is now generally accepted that the distribution is leptokurtotic, but debate centers on whether the random walk theory is therefore in serious danger. The most common explanation of the fat tails is that information shows up in infrequent clumps, rather than in a smooth and continuous fashion. The market reaction to clumps of information results in the fat tails. Because the distribution of information is leptokurtotic, the distribution of price changes is also leptokurtotic.

As noted earlier, Mandelbrot (1964) suggested that capital market returns follow a family of distributions he called Stable Peretian. Stable Paretian distributions have high peaks at the mean, and fat tails, much like the observed frequency distribution of stock market returns (see Table 3.1 and Figure 3.1). Stable Paretian distributions are characterized by a tendency to have trends and cycles as well as abrupt and discontinuous changes, and they can be adjusted for skewness. However, variance is infinite, or undefined, in these distributions. Cootner (1964b) and Shiller (1989) found the concept of infinite variances unacceptable, preferring instead to reformulate existing theory in terms of normal distributions rather than face the possibility that the past 40 years of economic and capital market research may be seriously flawed. Cootner (1964a), in his critique of Mandelbrot's paper, stated that we could not be sure that measuring the tails proved that the distribution was not merely a leptokurtotic Gaussian distribution. Cootner mentioned that, if Mandelbrot were right, "almost all of our statistical tools are obsolete. . . ." He felt that we needed more proof before consigning centuries of work to the trash heap. Stable Paretian distributions can now be called fractal distributions and will be discussed in detail in Chapter 9. Using fractal analysis, we can now distinguish between a fat-tailed Gaussian distribution and a fractal distribution.

Finally, we must once again examine how people react to information. We have discussed how the common explanation for fat tails comes from the infrequent *arrival* of information. Once the information arrives, it is still digested and immediately reflected in prices. But what if it is the *reaction* to information that occurs in clumps? If investors ignore information until trends are well in place, and then react, in a cumulative fashion, to all the information previously ignored, we could well have fat tails. It would mean that people react to information in a nonlinear way. Once the level of information passes a critical level, people will react to all the information that they have ignored up to that point. This sequence implies that the present is influenced by the past, a clear violation of the EMH. In the EMH, information is reacted to in a cause-and-effect manner. Like Newtonian physics, information is received and reacted to by changing the price to reflect new information.

THE DANGER OF SIMPLIFYING ASSUMPTIONS

From this discussion, we can see that the simplifying assumption of a rational investor has led to an entire analytic framework that may be a castle built on sand. The rational investor concept and the Efficient Market Hypothesis were constructed to justify the use of probability calculus by giving an economic framework to the crucial assumption of independence of observations or returns. Capital market theory attempted to make the investment environment neater, or more orderly, than it really is. Among the factors that make it messy, by EMH standards, are the following:

1. People are not necessarily risk-averse at all times. They can often be risk-seeking, particularly if they are faced with what are perceived to be sure losses for not gambling.
2. People are not unbiased when they set subjective probabilities. They are likely to be more confident in their forecasts than is warranted by the information they have.
3. People may not react to information as it is received. Instead, they may react to it after it is received, if it confirms a change in a recent trend. This is a nonlinear reaction, as opposed to the linear reaction predicted by the rational investor concept.
4. There is no evidence to support the belief that people in aggregate are more rational than individuals. For proof, one only has to look at the social upheavals, fads, and fashions that have occurred throughout human history.

Once again, the attempt to simplify nature by making it tidy and solvable has led to misleading conclusions.

Econometric analysis was desirable because it could be solved for optimal solutions. However, if markets are nonlinear, there are many possible solutions. Trying to find a single optimal solution can be a misguided quest.

We must judge how seriously the current paradigms are affected if we release the simplifying assumptions. The founding fathers of capital market theory were well aware of the impact of these simplifying assumptions, but they felt that they did not seriously reduce the usefulness of the model.

Prior to Galileo, it was commonly assumed that heavy objects fell faster than lighter objects. Making this assumption changes the nature of the interaction of bodies.

The assumption that investors react to information in a linear way, as the information arrives, can profoundly change the nature of the markets if, instead, investors react in a nonlinear, or delayed, fashion. I contend that the assumption that investors are rational (and, therefore, price changes are independent) cannot be endorsed without substantial empirical evidence. The case for investor rationality has not been convincingly made.

4

Markets and Chaos: Chance and Necessity

Chapters 2 and 3 have indicated that the EMH has often failed to explain market behavior. Models based on the EMH, like the CAPM, have likewise exhibited serious shortcomings. Nevertheless, much market behavior does conform to the EMH. For instance, studies have shown that active managers have failed to consistently beat the "market" over time. Proponents of the EMH have pointed to this fact as proof that markets are efficient. Critics of the EMH say that the results merely prove the incompetence of investment managers, particularly nonquantitative active managers. Despite all the empirical studies, only a handful of which have been discussed here, debate continues over the efficiency of the market.

Fueling the debate is the fact that, although there is little conclusive evidence that markets are efficient, there is also little evidence that they are not; practitioners have shown mixed results regarding their investment performance. Fundamental analysis often works, but it often fails. Technical analysis often works, and then it does not work. Economists speak of economic cycles, but none can be found analytically. Traders speak of market cycles; they too cannot be proven. To top it off, the critics of the EMH have been unable to offer an alternative that takes all the discrepancies into account. In few other areas are theory and practical experience in such little agreement.

Animosity between the two camps is high. Quants say that reason proves the nonexistence of market cycles. Practitioners say that the Quants are living in a dream world and have proven nothing. This split between practice and theory has been common throughout history in the physical sciences. Quants often refer to technical analysis as a form of market astrology, perhaps overlooking the fact that the astrologers were also the first astronomers, and alchemists were the first chemists. Quants should also remember that current scientific knowledge is not always correct.

In the 16th century, it was widely believed by scientists that projectiles, like cannonballs fired toward an enemy, fell straight down after they reached their apex, because gravity pulled them down in a linear fashion, as specified by Aristotle. Practitioners (in this case, soldiers) said that this theory was nonsense: cannonballs followed a curved path. They knew, because they were busy knocking down castles. Not until Descartes' work in the 17th century would mathematicians admit that they (and Aristotle) had been wrong.

Quants must be careful to keep their assumptions from biasing their conclusions, if the assumptions themselves have not been proven. Regarding the cannonballs' path, it was assumed that Aristotle was always right. He was right about many things, but he was wrong about projectiles. Practitioners must be careful not to "mystify" what they do, because it is not fully understood. An example of mystification is the technical analysts' assertion: "The market speaks in its own language." What does that mean? That external information is useless? If so, why? No answer has been given.

There must be a melding of these two viewpoints. Only a combination of theory and practice can produce profitable technology.

In a time series of market returns, we have a clear split between what reason tells us and what intuition advises. Reason says that there is no order in the markets, because findings, using analytical methods, have been inconclusive. Intuition tells us that something is there, but it cannot be isolated. Perhaps the problem goes back to our definition of order. What do we mean by order?

CAN CHANCE AND NECESSITY COEXIST?

In general, we assume that randomness and order are mutually exclusive. Noise can interfere with a system, but if order is there, it will dominate. If a television transmission is interfered with by random static, or "snow," the transmission itself will still be apparent. The noise remains independent of the transmission. With this view in mind, market studies typically look for some variation on a periodic order underlying the market mechanism, with random noise superimposed. This approach is much like Shiller's concept of noise traders and smart money. Technical analysts often make this same assumption when they say that 200-day moving averages have some predictive power—that a moving average smooths out the noise superimposed on the underlying trend. Typical studies, usually using spectral analysis, have looked for a periodic order beneath a random noise that is superimposed over the order. No studies have convincingly either supported or rejected the EMH.

Many systems have now been found where randomness and determinism, or chance and necessity, integrate and coexist. In particular, they have been found in thermodynamics where "far from equilibrium" conditions prevail. Our answer may lie here.

In economics and capital market theory, we have long used the Newtonian assumption that a system left alone tends to equilibrium. In the physics of motion, equilibrium has been tied to a body at rest. Motion is achieved by perturbing the system with an exterior force. In applying Newtonian dynamics to economics and capital markets, we have also modeled the system as being naturally at equilibrium unless perturbed by an exogenous shock. Thus, there is a natural balance between supply and demand, unless an exogenous shock changes the supply or demand, which will cause the system to seek a new equilibrium. This is an extension of equilibrium theory in nature.

Nature maintains a natural balance in which organisms compete and coexist in an ecological system whose workings are stable over time—at least, that has long been the view. However, even in ecology, the "natural balance" theory is being replaced by acknowledgment that nature is actually in a continually fluctuating state.

As we said in Chapter 1, static equilibrium is not a natural state, and it's time that economics and investment finance faced that possibility. In nonlinear dynamic systems, chance and necessity coexist. Randomness is combined with determinism to create a statistical order. Therefore, order may be a dynamic process in which randomness and order are merged, not a periodic phenomenon with noise imposed.

Complexity theory recognizes that this combination of local randomness and global order results in processes which are more robust with respect to their environment. That is, they are adaptable to changing conditions because they react in seemingly unpredictable ways. They cannot be second-guessed by other species or systems, and so compete more effectively. A static system would react in predictable linear ways, and be doomed to extinction. Its resources would be cornered by its more adaptable cousins.

The current paradigm, based upon efficient markets and linear relationships between cause and effect, postulates a market that would eventually be arbitraged away. The new paradigm treats the markets as complex, interactive, and *adaptable* systems. Their complexity offers rich possibilities and interpretations, but no easy answers.

In Part Two, we will review the fundamentals of nonlinear dynamic systems by examining nonlinear systems statistically, using fractals, and then analytically, using nonlinear dynamic systems, or chaos theory. The two are closely related, as we will see. It is hoped that the methods and evidence presented here will spur the investment community to look beyond random walks and related theories, toward models of complexity.

PART TWO
FRACTAL STRUCTURE IN THE CAPITAL MARKETS

Since the first edition of this book, fractal images have become fairly commonplace. Many coffee table books with interesting alien looking landscapes have been sold. Fractals are used as tools in computer generated graphics, including movies. Fractals even decorate tee-shirts and ties. However, fractals are more than pretty pictures. Fractals have changed the way we view the world. Fractal geometry allows us to generate complex shapes through simple iterated rules. We can perceive, though not yet precisely, that the complexity that surrounds us in nature is closely tied to this new geometry. Because of this, many market technical analysts have incorrectly assumed that fractal geometry will help them to recognize new patterns in stock market charts. The real usefulness of fractals is far deeper than that.

Fractals have had an impact on statistical analysis that is not widely appreciated. Nature is not a series of repeating patterns, but instead characterized by a local randomness and global order. Each real-life fractal is different in detail while similar in overall concept. All oak trees, for instance, are different while easily recognizable as oak trees. Fractals in the real world are governed by a global statistical structure, while maintaining a local randomness. For market and economic analysis this can have a profound effect.

In this section we will discuss fractals. They will change not only the way you view market and economic analysis, but nature itself.

5
Introduction to Fractals

The development of fractal geometry has been one of this century's most useful and fascinating discoveries in mathematics. With fractals, mathematicians have created a system that describes natural shapes in terms of a few simple rules. Complexity emerges from this simplicity. Fractals give structure to complexity, and beauty to chaos. The realization that nonlinear dynamic systems create fractals interests us. Most natural shapes, and time series, are best described by fractals. Nature is, therefore, nonlinear, and fractals are the geometry of chaos.

Fractal geometry's view of the world is very different from that of Euclidean geometry. Euclidean geometry, which we learned in high school, reflects the philosophy of the ancient Greeks who developed it.

The ancient Greeks were responsible for bringing reason to Western culture. While observing that life was full of seemingly chaotic random events, they searched for pure forms and order, hidden beneath the noise of daily life. They wished to reduce nature to these pure forms. Mathematics was their tool. Much has been written of the ancient Greeks' mystical relationship with mathematics. In many ways, our need to find structure in nature is a legacy from those ancient times. There are strong parallels between the view that pure forms underlie the noise of daily life, and economists' search for cyclical order beneath the noise of daily transactions, which we discussed in Chapter 3. The ancient Greeks believed in the order of numbers and its relationship with the order of the universe. They worked to integrate numbers with nature through a system of natural laws.

Euclid was responsible for taking separate laws, developed by Pythagoras, Aristotle, and others, and making a system of them. His basic structure (axioms, theorems, and proofs), which was used to develop plane geometry, is still very much in use today. Engineering and land surveying rely heavily on these ancient laws.

Euclid reduced nature to pure and symmetric objects: the point, the one-dimensional line, the two-dimensional plane, and the three-dimensional solid. Solids have a number of pure symmetrical shapes, such as spheres, cones, cylinders, and blocks. None of these objects has holes in it, and none is rough. Each is a pure, smooth form. To the Greeks, symmetry and wholeness were signs of perfection. Only perfection would be created by nature.

In reality, nature abhors symmetry as much as it abhors equilibrium; the two are probably equivalent. Natural objects are not roughed-up versions of the pure euclidean structures. Consequently, creating a computer image of a mountain, using euclidean geometry, is a daunting task that requires many lines of code and substantial amounts of random access memory (RAM). With fractal geometry, a mountain can be created by using a few rules continuously repeated.

Benoit Mandelbrot can be considered the Euclid of fractal geometry. He has collected the observations of mathematicians concerned with "monsters," or objects not definable by euclidean geometry. By combining the work of these mathematicians with his own insight, he has created a geometry of nature that thrives on asymmetry and roughness. Mandelbrot has said that "mountains are not cones, and clouds are not spheres."

Perhaps the failure of euclidean geometry to describe natural objects is best exemplified by the following property. In euclidean geometry, the closer one looks at an object, the simpler it becomes. A three-dimensional block becomes a two-dimensional plane becomes a one-dimensional line until one finally arrives at the point. A natural object, on the other hand, shows more detail the closer one looks at it, all the way down to the subatomic level. Fractals have this property. The closer they are examined, the more detail can be seen.

So, what is a fractal? No all-encompassing, final definition of fractals exists. Mandelbrot (1982) originally defined fractals based on topological dimension. He has since rejected that definition. We will use the following as a working definition:

A fractal is an object in which the parts are in some way related to the whole.

Fractals are self-referential, or self-similar. One of the most easily perceived natural fractals is a tree. Trees branch according to a fractal scale. Each branch, with its smaller branches, is similar to the whole tree in a qualitative sense.

Fractal shapes show self-similarity with respect to space. Fractal time series have statistical self-similarity with respect to time. Fractal time series are random fractals, which have more in common with natural objects than the pure mathematical fractals we will cover initially. We will be concerned primarily with fractal time series, but fractal shapes give a good intuitive base for what "self-similarity" actually means. Along the way, we will ease into fractal time series. However, to whet your appetite, think of a time series of stock returns. Figure 5.1 shows daily, weekly, and monthly S&P 500 returns for 40 consecutive observations. With no scale on the X and Y axes, can you determine which graph is which? Figure 5.1 illustrates self-similarity in a time series.

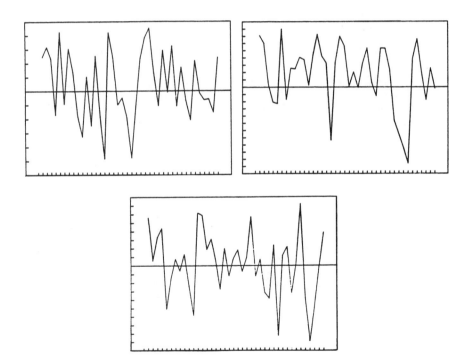

FIGURE 5.1 Self-similarity in S&P 500 returns: Daily, weekly, and monthly returns. (Can you guess which is which?)

FRACTAL SHAPES

Fractal shapes can be generated in many ways. The simplest way is to take a generating rule and iterate it over and over again. Figure 5.2 shows an example. We start with a solid equilateral triangle (Figure 5.2(a)). We then remove a equilateral triangle from within that triangle. We are left with three smaller triangles and an empty triangular shape in the middle, as shown in Figure 5.2(b). We now remove a triangle from within each of the three triangles (Figure 5.2(c)). If we keep repeating this process we end up with the structure shown in Figure 5.2(d), a triangle that has an infinite number of smaller triangles within it. If we were to magnify a portion of this triangle, we would see even more, smaller triangles within the larger ones. An infinite number of triangles is trapped in the finite space of the original triangle. We have infinite

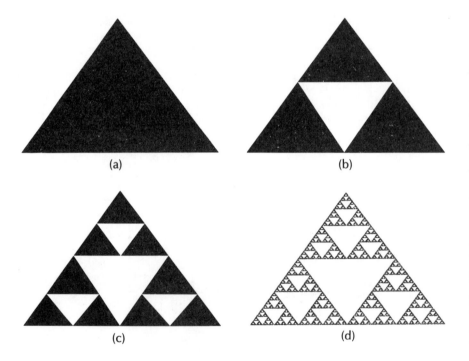

(a)

(b)

(c)

(d)

FIGURE 5.2 Generating the Sierpinski Triangle. (a) Start with a solid equilateral triangle. (b) Remove an equilateral triangle from the center. (c) Remove a triangle from the remaining triangles. (d) Repeat for 10,000 iterations, triangles within triangles.

complexity generated in a finite space by a simple rule. This particular fractal, called the Sierpinski triangle, is relevant to time series analysis, as we shall see later.

Now try applying euclidean geometry to the Sierpinski triangle. It is not one-dimensional, because it is not a line. It is not two-dimensional, like a solid triangle, because it has holes in it. Its dimension is between one and two. It is 1.58, a fractional or fractal dimension. Fractional dimensions are the chief identifying characteristics of fractals. Mandelbrot's insight, that fractional dimensions are natural and do exist, can be compared to the invention of the number zero by medieval Islamic mathematicians, or the invention of negative numbers by early Hindu mathematicians. Fractional dimensions are an obvious reality. Previously overlooked, they profoundly expand the descriptive power of mathematics.

We tend to think that any object that is "flat" is two-dimensional. Mathematically speaking, this is not true. A euclidean plane is a flat surface with no gaps. Likewise, we tend to think that any object that has "depth" is three-dimensional. Again, in euclidean geometry, this is not true. A three-dimensional object is a pure solid form. In mathematical terms, it is differentiable across its entire surface. It has no holes or gaps in it. Therefore, an object with depth is not necessarily three-dimensional. As an example, a wiffle ball is a hollow ball with holes in it. In euclidean terms, a wiffle ball is not three-dimensional because it is not differentiable over its entire surface. It is not continuous.

Again, consider a time series of stock prices, which appears as a jagged line. The jagged line is not one-dimensional, because it is not straight. It is also not two-dimensional, because it does not fill a plane. Dimensionally speaking, it is more than a line and less than a plane. Its dimension is between one and two. (In Chapter 9, we will find that the S&P 500 has a dimensionality of 1.24.)

Another example of a fractal shape is the Koch snowflake. Unlike the Sierpinski triangle, the Koch snowflake is created by an additive rule. Figure 5.3 shows its creation. Start with an equilateral triangle (Figure 5.3). On the middle third of each side, place another equilateral triangle, to create the shape shown in Figure 5.3(b). Keep repeating step (b) and the result will be the snowflake in Figure 5.3(c). The snowflake, conceptually, has an infinite length, because triangles can be added indefinitely. Here, the circle that encloses the original triangle limits this space. We have an infinite length within a finite space. Also, the closer one looks at the snowflake, the more detail is seen. Smaller versions of the larger snowflake are visible. Once again, we have

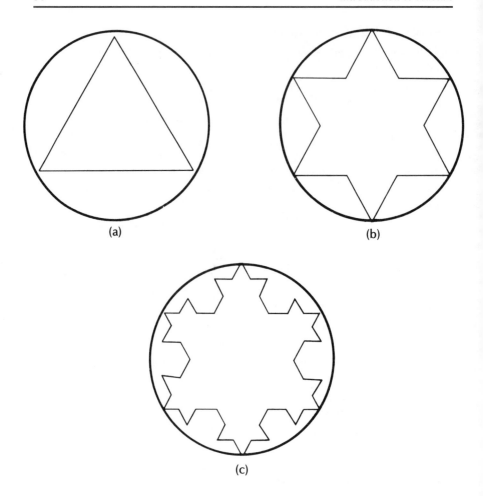

FIGURE 5.3 Generating a Koch Snowflake. (a) Start with an equilateral triangle. (b) Add an equilateral triangle to the middle third of each side. (c) Continue to add an equilateral triangle to the middle third of each side.

created an object of infinite complexity, contained within a finite space, using a simple iterative rule.

These two examples, the Sierpinski triangle and the Koch snowflake, are symmetrical fractals. They are often called deterministic fractals because they are generated by deterministic rules. As we have stated, natural objects are never truly symmetric. These two fractal shapes, therefore, are not truly representative of nature or of the capital markets, but they do illustrate some of the important characteristics of fractals. They are objects created by iterating a simple rule to create a self-similar object with a fractal dimension. Random fractals are more realistic.

RANDOM FRACTALS

Coastlines are a good example of random fractals. From an airplane, at a high altitude, a coastline looks like a smooth, irregular line. The lower the airplane flies, the more jagged the coastline appears, until, at a close distance, each rock is visible. Stock prices are comparable to coastlines. The jagged line of stock prices, or returns, initially looks like a coastline. The closer we look at the time series (e.g., the smaller the time increment in Figure 5.1), the more detail we see.

Random fractals are combinations of generating rules chosen at random at different scales. We can use the structure of the mammalian lung as an example. Our lung has a main stem, the trachea, which has two primary branches. The two branches have more branches. The diameter of the branches decreases according to an exponential power law, on average. This scaling is fractal. However, the lung is not a symmetrical fractal like the Koch snowflake. Each generation has a decreasing diameter, on average, but individual branches can vary in size as well. The scaling of each generation does not occur by a characteristic scale. The natural "rule" that causes this multiple scaling appears to be tied to the adaptability of the system. If one diameter fails at a particular branch generation, there are other sizes to compensate. Natural selection appears to favor random fractal scaling, even though it is random. This combination of randomness coupled with a deterministic generating rule, or "causality," can also make fractals useful in capital market analysis.

THE CHAOS GAME

Michael Barnsley, of Iterated Systems, Inc., has developed a useful system called Iterated Function Systems (IFS) for generating fractal shapes. In one subset of IFS are fractals that are created by a deterministic rule implemented in a random fashion. The results are not what you might think. Barnsley calls this algorithm the Chaos Game.

One form of the Chaos Game is shown in Figure 5.4. Start with three points equidistant from each other, as in Figure 5.4(a). Label point A as (1, 2), point

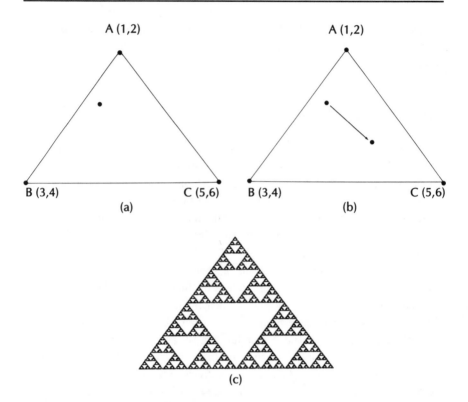

FIGURE 5.4 The Chaos Game. (a) Start with three points, an equal distance apart, and randomly draw a point within the boundaries defined by the points. (b) Assuming you roll a fair die that comes up number 6, you go halfway to the point marked C(5,6). (c) Repeat step (b) 10,000 times and you have the Sierpinski triangle.

B as (3, 4), and point C as (5, 6). This is the playing board. Choose any point within the triangle defined by points A, B, and C.

To play the game, roll a die (make sure it is a fair one). Move halfway to the point that has the rolled number, and plot a new point. For instance, if you roll a 5, move halfway from the initial point to point C (5,6) and plot a new point, as shown in Figure 5.4(b). Continue this about 10,000 times. (Hint: It's easier using a computer.) After about 10,000 iterations, you end up with the result shown in Figure 5.4(c), which should look familiar because it is the Sierpinski triangle. The actual starting point does not change the result, which is always the Sierpinski triangle, even though the points are plotted in a different order each time. The order depends on all the points plotted before it. Even so, the Sierpinski triangle is the end result. How can this be?

Barnsley says that the triangle is the limit of this IFS. All the points are attracted to this shape.

Let's examine what is going on in the Chaos Game. Information from the roll of the die is random. The system has no idea where it is going, until the die is rolled. Forecasting the direction of the system is impossible. Yet, once the system receives information, it is processed according to internal, deterministic rules. The result is a limited *range* of possibilities, but the *number* of possibilities is infinite. The structure—infinite possibilities within a finite range—is the attractor, or limiting set, of the IFS.

Note that the attractor is not random, although it has an infinite number of possible solutions. Each point within the triangle is not equally likely to occur. The spaces within the triangles have a zero probability of occurring, even though there is an infinite number of spaces.

Each point is dependent on the point that was plotted before it. Actually, each point is dependent on all of the points that were plotted before it, even though the information used to plot the IFS was randomly generated.

This combination of random events and dependence characterizes fractal time series, as we shall see in Chapter 7.

What, then, is a fractal? A fractal is the attractor (limiting set) of a generating rule (information processor), when the information is generated randomly. It is self-similar in that smaller pieces of it are related to the whole. Finally, it has a fractal dimension. This is a more complete definition than the working version stated earlier. Still, it is not a precise definition. Perhaps, someday, a precise definition will be developed, but it is possible that a precise definition will never be developed, because fractal geometry is the geometry of nature. Defining nature in one line is a daunting task.

We have seen that there are two types of fractals: deterministic and random. Deterministic fractals are generally symmetric. Random fractals do not necessarily have pieces that *look* like pieces of the whole. Instead, they may be qualitatively related. In the case of time series, we will find that fractal time series are qualitatively self-similar in that, at different scales, the series have similar statistical characteristics. If this sounds like the normal distribution, it is. However, fractal time series can have fractional dimensions; the normal distribution has an integer dimension of 2, which changes many of the characteristics of the time series.

We have, so far, skimmed over the concept of the fractal dimension. This concept is important enough to warrant a chapter of its own.

6
The Fractal Dimension

The page you are reading is a three-dimensional piece of paper. Suppose the page had no thickness, but was, instead, a true two-dimensional piece of paper, or a euclidean plane. If you were to detach the two-dimensional sheet from the book and crumble it into a ball, the ball of paper would no longer be two-dimensional, but it would not exactly be three-dimensional either. It would have creases; its dimension would be less than three. The tighter the ball got crumpled, the closer it would get to becoming three-dimensional, or solid. Only if the original page were made of a sticky substance, like clay, could the crumpled ball become truly three-dimensional. Paper will always have creases.

The crumpled ball has a fractional, or "fractal" dimension. It is noniteger. Euclidean geometry, with its pure, smooth forms, cannot describe the dimensionality of the crumpled paper ball. The paper ball cannot be reproduced using euclidean geometry, except through a large number of linear interpolations. Using calculus, its surface is not differentiable.

We tend to think of any object that has depth as "three-dimensional." Mathematically, this is not true. A line plotted in a three-dimensional space has depth, but the line is still one-dimensional. A true three-dimensional object is a solid; that is, the object has no holes or gaps in its surface. This explains why reproducing natural-looking objects using euclidean geometry is so difficult. Most real objects are not solid in the classical, euclidean sense; they have gaps and spaces. They merely reside in three-dimensional space.

The failure of euclidean geometry to describe most natural objects severely limits its ability to help us understand how the object is formed. For time series, classical geometry offers little help in understanding the underlying causality of the structure, unless it is a random walk—a system so complex that prediction becomes impossible. In statistical terms, the number of degrees of freedom or factors influencing the system is very large.

The fractal dimension, which describes how an object (or time series) fills its space, is the product of all the factors influencing the system that produces the object (or time series).

If a rock is randomly bombarded equally on all sides by rushing water, it will, after a millennium or two, become perfectly round. Each part of the rock will have experienced equal erosion. The number of streams of water (or the number of degrees of freedom) would have to be infinite.

If a small number of streams of water were eroding it, the rock would not be a smooth ball. Only the parts of the rock hit by the streams would erode, so the rock could not be round. If there were three streams, then there would be three depressions in the rock. If one of the three streams is likely to have a more forceful flow than the others, then one depression would be deeper than the others.

As a result, a rock eroded by a large number of equally likely streams will be smooth, symmetrical, and euclidean. The rock with few unequal biases will be rough and nonsymmetric.

A time series is only random when it is influenced by a large number of events that are equally likely to occur. In statistical terms, it has a high number of degrees of freedom. A nonrandom time series will reflect the nonrandom nature of its influences. The data will clump together, to reflect the correlations inherent in its influences. In other words, the time series will be fractal.

Typically, we embed an object in a space that is larger than its fractal dimension. We tend to think of the crumpled ball of paper as three-dimensional, even though it does not fill the three-dimensional space. The space we place the object in is called the embedding dimension, or topological dimension. When objects have dimensions between two and three, we tend to think of them as three-dimensional. Examples are mountains and clouds.

We tend to think of coastlines as two-dimensional, when they are actually less than that. Time series fit into the same category. Only a random time series would fill a plane and be truly two-dimensional.

One of the characteristics of fractal objects is that they retain their dimensionality when they are placed in an embedding dimension that is greater than their fractal dimension. Random distributions (white noise) do not have this characteristic. White noise fills its space much the same way a gas fills a volume. If a fixed amount of gas is put into a larger volume container, the gas will simply spread out in the larger space, because there is nothing to bind the molecules of the gas together. A solid, on the other hand, has molecules that are bound together. In a parallel way, correlation holds points together in a fractal time series, but there are no correlations to hold the points together in a random series. In a fractal, like the Sierpinski triangle, each point is correlated with the point plotted before it. If we increase the dimension used to plot the triangle in, the correlations will still exist, and will pull the points together into clumps. These clumps retain the dimensionality of the original series.

A random series would have no correlation with previous points. Nothing would keep the points in the same vicinity, to preserve their dimensionality. Instead, they will fill up whatever space they are placed in.

The fractal dimension is determined by how the object, or time series, fills its space. A fractal object will fill its space unevenly because its parts are related, or correlated. To determine the fractal dimension, we must measure how the object clumps together in its space.

There are many ways of calculating dimension, but all of them involve figuring out the volume or area of the fractal shape, and how it scales as the volume or area is increased.

Coastlines are a good example, especially considering the geometric similarity between coastlines and time series. Mandelbrot (1982) has postulated that we can never actually measure the length of a coastline, because the length we calculate depends on the length of the ruler we use to measure it.

Suppose, for example, we wish to measure the coast of Maine. We begin at the northernmost point and measure by placing a six-foot-long ruler on the ground. We measure in six-foot increments, end-to-end down the coast, and arrive at a number. Next, we repeat the exercise using a three-foot ruler, again measuring from end to end. This time, because we have measured with a smaller ruler, we are able to capture more detail. Because we can account for more of the crevices and inlets, we end up with a longer length for the coast of Maine. If we decrease the ruler length to one foot, we get even more detail and a longer length. The smaller the ruler, the longer the coastline. The length of the coastline is dependent on the size of the ruler!

Because this is true for all coastlines, length is not a valid way to compare coastlines. Instead, Mandelbrot proposes using the fractal dimension to compare them. Coastlines are jagged lines, so their fractal dimension is greater

than one (which is their euclidean dimension); how much greater than one
would depend on how jagged the coastlines are. The more jagged they are, the
closer their fractal dimension would approach two, the dimension of a plane.

The fractal dimension is calculated by measuring this jagged property. We
count the number of circles, with a certain diameter, that are needed to cover
the coastline. We increase the diameter, and again count the number of circles.
If we continue to do this, we will find that the number of circles has an exponential relationship to the radius of the circle. The number of circles scales according to the following relationship:

$$N*(2*r)^D = 1 \qquad\qquad\qquad (6.1)$$

where   N = number of circles
            r   = radius
           D = fractal dimension

Equation (6.1) can be transformed using logarithms:

$$D = \frac{\log N}{\log(1/2*r)} \qquad\qquad\qquad (6.2)$$

We can use a piece of the Koch snowflake as a simple coastline; the middle
third of a line is replaced by an equilateral triangle. If the end-to-end length of
this curve is one unit, then we need four circles of diameter 0.3 to cover the
curve. (See Figure 6.1.) The Koch curve has a fractal dimension of:

$$D = \frac{\log(4)}{\log(1/0.3)} = 1.26.$$

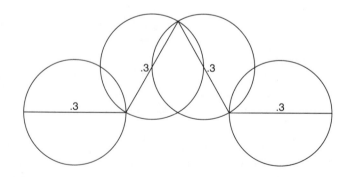

FIGURE 6.1 Calculating the fractal dimension.

For real coastlines, we find a similar property. The coastline of Norway, for instance, has a fractal dimension of 1.52, while the coastline of Britain is 1.30. This means that the coastline of Norway is more jagged than the coastline of Britain, because its fractal dimension is closer to 2.00. In a similar way, we could compare different stocks by noting their fractal dimensions. Typically, we compare the riskiness of different securities by looking at their volatilities. The concept, which had its first wide exposure in Markowitz (1952), is that the more volatile a stock is, the riskier it is perceived to be. Volatility, or risk, is stated as the statistical measure of standard deviation of returns—or its square, variance. Volatility is supposed to measure the dispersion of returns. Does it?

Standard deviation measures the probability that an observation will be a certain distance from the average observation. The larger this number is, the wider the dispersion. Wide dispersion would mean that there is a high probability of large swings in returns. The security is risky. However, it is often overlooked that standard deviation as a measure of dispersion is only valid if the underlying system is random. If the observations are correlated (or exhibit serial correlation), then the usefulness of standard deviation as a measure of dispersion is considerably weakened. Because numerous studies (see Chapter 3) have consistently shown that the distribution of stock returns is not normally distributed, standard deviation as a measure of comparative risk is of questionable usefulness.

As an example, let's take two possible return series, labeled S1 and S2 in Table 6.1. S2 is not normally distributed. S1 is a trendless series, and S2 shows a clear trend. S1 has a cumulative return of 1.93 percent, compared to S2's 22.83 percent. However, S1 has a standard deviation of 1.70, while S2

Table 6.1 Standard Deviation versus Fractal Dimension

Observation	S1	S2
1	+2	+1
2	−1	+2
3	−2	+3
4	+2	+4
5	−1	+5
6	+2	+6
Cumulative return	+1.93	+22.83
Standard deviation	1.70	1.71
Fractal dimension	1.42	1.13

has a virtually identical standard deviation of 1.71. In this hypothetical example, two stocks with virtually identical volatilities have quite different return characteristics. Purists will say that *both* series are not normally distributed, which makes this comparison invalid. That is exactly the point. Because stock returns are clearly not normally distributed, using standard deviation as a measure of comparative risk is as invalid as length is in comparing coastlines. The fractal dimension of S1 is 1.42, versus 1.13 for S2. S1 is clearly a more jagged series than S2, and fractal dimension is one way of differentiating the two in a qualitative way.

Two stocks with similar volatilities, therefore, can have very different patterns of returns. One can have "choppy" (near random) behavior; the other can have a persistent trend. Volatility is not a proper measure of risk in comparing two securities. Their fractal dimensions can tell another story, as we shall see in the next chapters.

SUMMARY

The fractal dimension shows us how the shape or time series fills its space. The way an object fills its space is determined by the forces involved in its formation. For a coastline, the relevant forces are the geological phenomena involved in its formation, such as water pressure and volcanic activity. For a time series of stock returns, the micro- and macroeconomic data influence investors' perceptions of what is good value. Different stocks can react differently to the same macroeconomic news because of differences in a company's industry, balance sheet, and prospects. However, the circle-counting method of determining fractal dimension is not practical.

We have not yet explored the impact of the fractal dimension on probability distributions. We have seen that fractal shapes and time series are characterized by long-term correlations. They do not necessarily follow a random walk. Their probability distribution is not a normal distribution (the well-known bell-shaped curve), but a different shape.

In the next chapters, we will examine the impact, on time series, of the long-term correlations that produce fractals. We will see that our statistical notion of risk—the standard deviation of returns—is in serious need of correction.

7
Fractal Time Series—
Biased Random Walks

In Chapter 2, we discussed the Efficient Market Hypothesis (EMH), which basically states that, because current prices reflect all available or public information, future price changes can be determined only by new information. With all prior information already reflected in prices, the markets follow a random walk. Each day's price movement is unrelated to the previous day's activity. EMH implicitly assumes that all investors immediately react to new information, so that the future is unrelated to the past or the present. This assumption was necessary for the Central Limit Theorem to apply to capital market analysis. The Central Limit Theorem was necessary to justify the use of probability calculus and linear models.

Do people really make decisions in this manner? Typically, some people do react to information as it is received. However, most people wait for confirming information and do not react until a trend is clearly established. The amount of confirming information necessary to validate a trend varies, but the uneven assimilation of information may cause a biased random walk. Biased random walks were extensively studied by Hurst in the 1940s and again by Mandelbrot in the 1960s and 1970s. Mandelbrot called them fractional brownian motions. We can now call them fractal time series.

THE HURST EXPONENT

Hurst was a hydrologist who began working on the Nile River Dam project in about 1907 and remained in the Nile region for the next 40 or so years. While there, he struggled with the problem of reservoir control. An ideal reservoir would never overflow; a policy would be put in place to discharge a certain amount of water each year. However, if the influx from the river were too low, then the reservoir level would become dangerously low. The problem was: What policy of discharges could be set, such that the reservoir never overflowed or emptied?

In constructing a model, it was common to assume that the uncontrollable part of the system—in this case, the influx of water from rainfall—followed a random walk. This is a common assumption, when dealing with a large system that has many degrees of freedom. The ecology of the Nile River area was involved. Surely, there were many degrees of freedom in this system!

When Hurst decided to test the assumption, he gave us a new statistic: the Hurst exponent (H). H, we will find, has broad applicability to all time series analysis, because it is remarkably robust. It has few underlying assumptions about the system being studied, and it can classify time series. It can distinguish a random series from a nonrandom series, even if the random series is non-Gaussian (i.e., not normally distributed). Hurst found that most natural systems do not follow a random walk, Gaussian or otherwise.

Hurst measured how the reservoir level fluctuated around its average level over time. As could be expected, the range of this fluctuation would change, depending on the length of time used for measurement. If the series were random, the range would increase with the square root of time. This is the $T^{1/2}$ Rule, mentioned earlier. To standardize the measure over time, Hurst decided to create a dimensionless ratio by dividing the range by the standard deviation of the observations. Hence, the analysis is called rescaled range analysis (R/S analysis). Hurst found that most natural phenomena, including river discharges, temperatures, rainfall, and sunspots, follow a "biased random walk"—a trend with noise. The strength of the trend and the level of noise could be measured by how the rescaled range scales with time, that is, by how high H is above 0.50.

Our intention is to extend Hurst's study of time series of natural phenomena into economic and capital market time series, to see whether these series are also biased random walks. To reformulate Hurst's work for a general time series, we must first define a range that would be comparable to the fluctuations of the reservoir height levels. We begin with an existing time series, t, with u observations:

$$X_{t,N} = \sum_{u=1}^{t} (e_u - M_N) \tag{7.1}$$

where $X_{t,N}$ = cumulative deviation over N periods
           e_u = influx in year u
          M_N = average e_u over N periods

The range then becomes the difference between the maximum and minimum levels attained in (7.1):

$$R = \text{Max} (X_{t,N}) - \text{Min} (X_{t,N}) \tag{7.2}$$

where   R = range of X
     Max (X) = maximum value of X
     Min (X) = minimum value of X

In order to compare different types of time series, Hurst divided this range by the standard deviation of the original observations. This "rescaled range" should increase with time. Hurst formulated the following relationship:

$$R/S = (a*N)^H \tag{7.3}$$

where   R/S = rescaled range
         N = number of observations
         a = a constant
        H = Hurst exponent

According to statistical mechanics, H should equal 0.5 if the series is a random walk. In other words, the range of cumulative deviations should increase with the square root of time, N. When Hurst applied his statistic to the Nile River discharge record, he found H = 0.90! He tried other rivers. H was usually greater than 0.50. He tried different natural phenomena. In all cases, he found H greater than 0.50. What did it mean?

When H differed from 0.50, the observations were not independent. Each observation carried a "memory" of all the events that preceded it. This was not a short-term memory, which is often called "Markovian." This memory is different: it is long-term; theoretically, it lasts forever. More recent events had a greater impact that distant events, but there was still residual influence. On a broader scale, a system that exhibits Hurst statistics is the result of a long stream of interconnected events. What happens today influences the future. Where we are now is a result of where we have been in the past. Time is important. Like a pebble dropped in water, today's events ripple forward in time. The size of the ripple diminishes until, for all intents and purposes, the ripple vanishes.

Inclusion of a "time arrow" is not possible in standard econometrics, which assumes series are invariant with respect to time. Instead, we find that time is an iterative process, like the Chaos Game in Chapter 5. The impact of the present on the future can be expressed as a correlation:

$$C = 2^{(2H - 1)} - 1 \qquad\qquad\qquad (7.4)$$

where   C = correlation measure
         H = Hurst exponent

There are three distinct classifications for the Hurst exponent (H): (1) H = 0.50, (2) $0 \leq H < 0.50$, and (3) $0.50 < H < 1.00$. H equal to 0.5 denotes a random series. Events are random and uncorrelated. Equation (7.4) equals zero. The present does not influence the future. Its probability density function can be the normal curve, but it does not have to be. R/S analysis can classify an independent series, no matter what the shape of the underlying distribution. In statistics courses, we are taught that nature follows the normal distribution. Hurst's findings refute that teaching. H is typically greater than 0.5. Its probability distribution is not normal.

Before we examine that class, a brief discussion of $0 \leq H < 0.5$ is in order. This type of system is an antipersistent, or ergodic, series. It is often referred to as "mean reverting." If the system has been up in the previous period, it is more likely to be down in the next period. Conversely, if it was down before, it is more likely to be up in the next period. The strength of this antipersistent behavior depends on how close H is to zero. The closer it is to zero, the closer C in equation (7.4) moves toward −0.50, or negative correlation. This kind of series would be choppier, or more volatile, than a random series, because it would consist of frequent reversals. Despite the prevalence of the mean reversal concept in economic and financial literature, few antipersistent series have yet been found.

When $0.5 < H < 1.0$, we have a persistent, or trend-reinforcing, series. If the series has been up (down) in the last period, then the chances are that it will continue to be positive (negative) in the next period. Trends are apparent. The strength of the trend-reinforcing behavior, or persistence, increases as H approaches 1.0, or 100 percent correlation in equation (7.4). The closer H is to 0.5, the noisier it will be, and the less defined its trends will be. Persistent series are fractional brownian motion, or biased random walks. The strength of the bias depends on how far H is above 0.50.

Persistent time series are the more interesting class because, as Hurst found, they are plentiful in nature, as are the capital markets. However, what causes persistence? Why does it involve a memory effect?

HURST'S SIMULATION TECHNIQUE

Perhaps the best way to understand how Hurst's statistics can arise, and what they mean, is to examine Hurst's own method for simulating a random walk.

Hurst was working in the 1940s, when computers were only a theoretical possibility and were certainly not available in Egypt. Hurst tried to simulate random walks by flipping coins, but found the process slow and tedious. Instead, he constructed a "probability pack of cards." The cards in this pack were numbered -1, $+1$, -3, $+3$, -5, $+5$, -7, and $+7$. The pack had 52 cards, and the numbers were distributed so that they approximated the normal curve. By shuffling and cutting the deck, and then noting the cut cards, Hurst could simulate a random series much faster than by flipping coins.

To simulate a biased random walk, Hurst would first shuffle the deck, then cut it, and note the number. Assume the number was $+3$. Hurst would then replace the card, reshuffle the deck, and deal two hands of 26 cards, which we will call hands A and B. Because he had previously cut a $+3$, he would take the three highest cards from hand B and place them in hand A. Then he would remove the three lowest cards out of hand A. Finally, a joker would be placed in hand A, and hand A would be reshuffled. Hand A now had a bias to the order of $+3$. Hurst would use hand A as his random number generator by cutting hand A and noting the number. When the joker was cut, the entire 52-card deck would be reshuffled (minus the joker), and a new biased hand would be created.

Hurst did six experiments, each consisting of 1,000 cuts of the deck. He found H = .714 ± .091, much as he had observed in nature. Again, what did it mean?

Hurst's bias was randomly generated by cutting the deck. In the above example, the cut produced a $+3$. The change in the bias also occurred by a random cut of the deck, which yielded the joker. Yet, no matter how many times the experiment is repeated, H = .714 continues to appear. (This result is very similar to the Chaos Game of Chapter 5, where a generating rule randomly applied produces the same fractal. Once again, randomness creates order.)

In the Hurst simulator, a random event (the initial cut of the deck) determines the degree of the bias. Another random event (the arrival of the joker) determines the length of the biased run. However, these two random events have limits. The degree of the bias is limited to the extremes of $+7$ or -7. The bias in this system changes, on the average, after 27 cuts of the deck, because there are 27 cards in the biased deck. Again, a combination of random events with generating order creates a structure. Unlike the Chaos Game, however, this is a statistical structure, and it requires close scrutiny: if the capital markets exhibit Hurst statistics (and they do), then their probability distribution is not normal. If the random walk does not apply, much of quantitative analysis collapses, especially the Capital Asset Pricing Model and the concept of risk as standard deviation or volatility.

It is easy to conjecture how Hurst statistics could arise in a capital market framework. The bias is generated by investors who react to current economic conditions. This bias continues until the random arrival of new information (an economic equivalent of the joker) changes the bias in magnitude, direction, or both.

THE FRACTAL NATURE OF H

Persistent time series, defined as $0.5 < H \leq 1.0$, are fractal because they can also be described as fractional brownian motion. In fractional brownian motion, there is correlation between events across time scales. Because of this relationship, the probability of two events following one another is not 50/50. The Hurst exponent (H) describes the likelihood that two consecutive events are likely to occur. If $H = 0.6$, there is, in essence, a higher probability that, if the last move was positive, the next move will also be positive. This is not a true probability; it is merely a measure of "bias."

Because each point is not equally likely (as it is in a random walk), the fractal dimension of the probability distribution is not 2; it is a number between 1 and 2. Mandelbrot (1972) has shown that the inverse of H is the fractal dimension. A random walk, with $H = 0.5$, would have a fractal dimension of 2. If $H = 0.7$, the fractal dimension is $1/0.7$ or 1.43. Note that a random walk is truly two-dimensional and would fill up a plane.

Figure 7.1 shows simulated series for $H = 0.50, 0.72$, and 0.90. As H draws closer to 1, the series becomes less noisy and has more consecutive observations with the same signs. In Figure 7.2, the data in Figure 7.1 are plotted as cumulative time series. Again, as H increases, the cumulative line becomes smoother and less jagged. There is less noise in the system and the "trends," or deviations from the average, become more pronounced. The Hurst exponent (H) measures how jagged the time series is. A perfectly deterministic system would produce a smooth curve. A fractal time series separates a pure random series from a deterministic system perturbed by random events.

Appendix 3 reproduces a BASIC program for simulating a fractional brownian motion series from a Gaussian series. The methodology offers insight into what a fractional brownian motion series is. Each percentage change in a fractional brownian motion time series is made up of an exponential average of n independent random numbers. Added to this average is a decaying weight of the last M observations. M represents the long memory effect in the system; theoretically, it is infinite. For the purposes of the simulation, we must limit it to an arbitrary large number. In the above examples, a series of 8,000 pseudo-random numbers is converted into 1,400 biased random

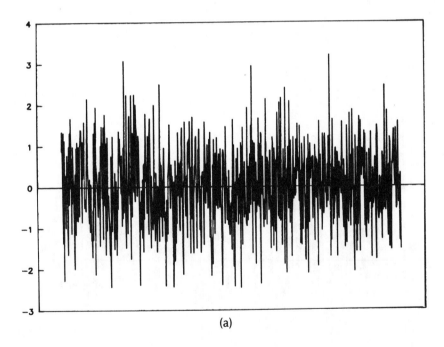

(a)

FIGURE 7.1a Fractal noise: Observations. H = 0.52. As H increases, there are more positive increments followed by positive increments, and negative increments followed by negative increments. The correlation of the signs in the series is increasing.

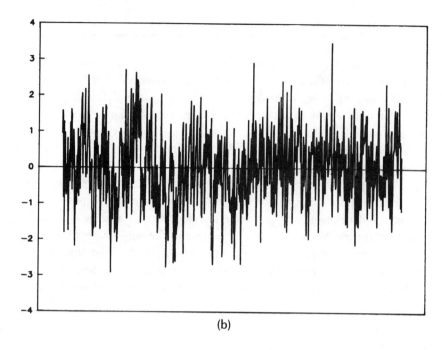

(b)

FIGURE 7.1b   Fractal noise: Observations. H = 0.72.

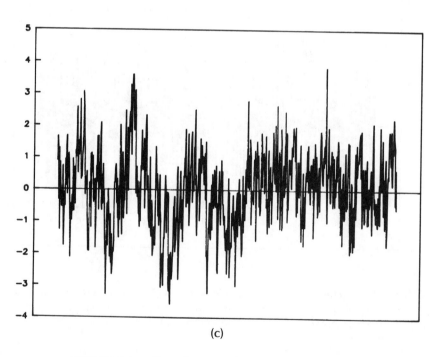

(c)

FIGURE 7.1c   Fractal noise: Observations. H = 0.90.

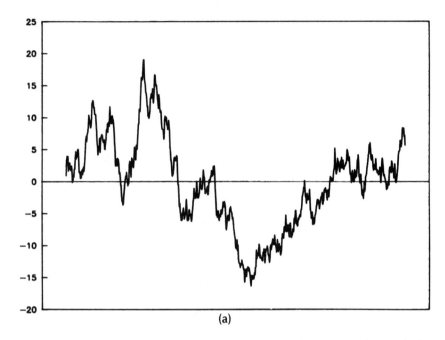

(a)

FIGURE 7.2a   Fractal noise: Cumulative observations. H = 0.50. The graphs become smoother and less jagged as H increases, and the range of cumulative values increases with H.

numbers by this method. Each biased increment consists of 5 random numbers and a memory of the last 200 biased random numbers. A brief review of the BASIC code indicates that the program is data-intensive. For each biased increment (which consists of 5 Gaussian numbers), we must evaluate the last 200 biased numbers (5*200 = 1,000 Gaussian numbers). The memory effect is caused by the inclusion of the previous numbers in calculations of the current number. If the market includes this memory effect, then each return is related to the last M returns. Measuring H turns out to be a straightforward, though data-intensive, exercise.

ESTIMATING THE HURST EXPONENT

By taking the log of equation (7.3), we obtain:

$$\log(R/S) = H*\log(N) + \log(a) \tag{7.5}$$

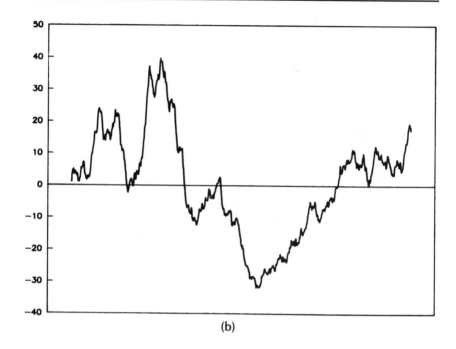

(b)

FIGURE 7.2b   Fractal noise: Cumulative observations. H = 0.72.

Finding the slope of the log/log graph of R/S versus N will therefore give us an estimate of H. This estimate of H makes no assumptions about the shape of the underlying distribution.

For very long N, we would expect the series to converge to the value H = 0.50, because the memory effect diminishes to a point where it becomes un-measurable. In other words, observations with long N can be expected to exhibit properties similar to regular brownian motion, or a pure random walk, as the memory effect dissipates. The regression referred to above would thus be performed on the data prior to the convergence of H to 0.50. The correlation measure in equation (7.4) does not apply to all increments.

It is important to remember that the correlation measure in equation (7.4) is not related to the Auto Correlation Function (ACF) of Gaussian random variables. The ACF assumes Gaussian, or near-Gaussian, properties in the underlying distribution; the distribution is the familiar bell-shaped curve. The ACF works well in determining short-run dependence, but tends to understate

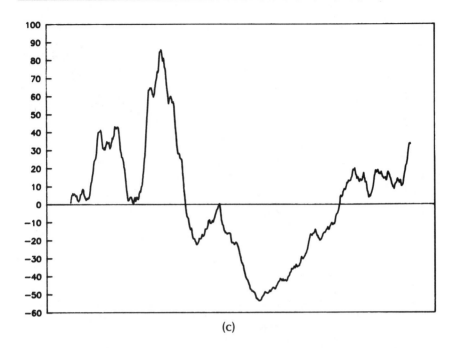

(c)

FIGURE 7.2c Fractal noise: Cumulative observations. H = 0.90.

long-run correlation for non-Gaussian series. Readers interested in a full mathematical explanation of why the ACF does not work well for long-memory processes are encouraged to read Mandelbrot (1972).

Figure 7.3 shows the log/log plot of R/S versus N for the H = 0.5 data generated for Figure 7.1. These data were generated using a pseudo-random number generator in the Gauss language system, and shows H = 0.55 ± 0.1. This estimate is a little higher than expected, but these are pseudo-random numbers generated by a deterministic algorithm. In this case, rescaled range analysis seems to have captured this bias. It is important to note that R/S analysis is an extremely robust tool. It does not assume that the underlying distribution is Gaussian. Finding H = 0.50 does not prove a Gaussian random walk; it only proves that there is no long memory process. In other words, any independent system, Gaussian or otherwise, would produce H = 0.5.

Figure 7.4 shows a similar plot for H = 0.72, a level that often shows up in nature. The data (which were used in Figure 7.1) were generated using the

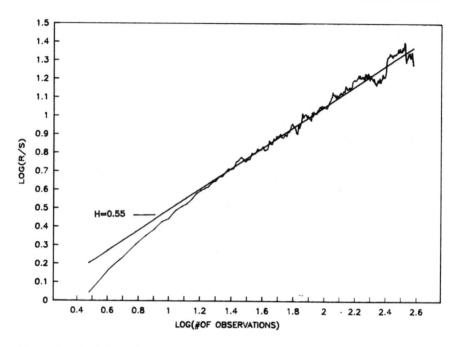

FIGURE 7.3   R/S analysis: Random Gaussian numbers. Actual H = 0.50; estimated H = 0.55.

fractional brownian motion approximation described in more detail in Appendix 3. This series was generated, as stated earlier, with a finite memory term of 200 observations. In the Hurst simulator, using a biased deck of 27 cards, the memory effect was modeled by the joker. The joker would arrive, on average, after 27 cuts of the deck, following a large number of simulations. The Hurst simulator had a finite memory term of 27 observations. Long-term correlations beyond 27 observations would drop to zero, and the system would begin to follow a random walk for increments of 27 observations or longer. Thus we could describe 27 observations as the average cycle, or period, of the system. The data used to generate Figures 7.1 and 7.2 simulate a natural cycle of 200 observations. When we cross N = 200 (log(200) = 2.3), the R/S observations begin to become erratic and random. This characteristic of R/S analysis allows us to determine the average cycle length of the system. In terms of nonlinear dynamic systems, the average cycle length is the length of time after

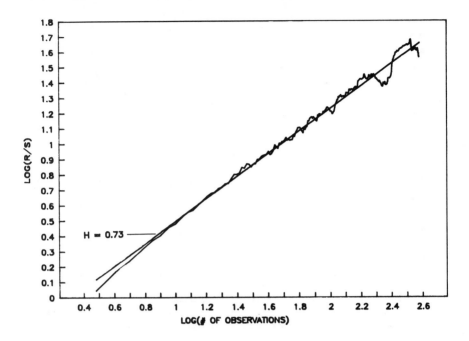

FIGURE 7.4 R/S analysis: Fractional Brownian motion. Actual H = 0.72; estimated H = 0.73.

which knowledge of initial conditions is lost. Figure 7.5 shows a similar
log/log plot for the H = 0.90 data. The effective H estimate was a little low at
H = 0.86, but well within reasonable bounds.

HURST'S EMPIRICAL LAW

Hurst (1951) also gave a formula for estimating the value of H from a single
R/S value:

$$H = \log(R/S)/\log(n/2) \tag{7.6}$$

Where n = the number of observations

This equation assumes that the constant, a, of equation (7.5) is equal to 0.50.
Feder (1988) shows that the empirical law tends to overstate H when it is

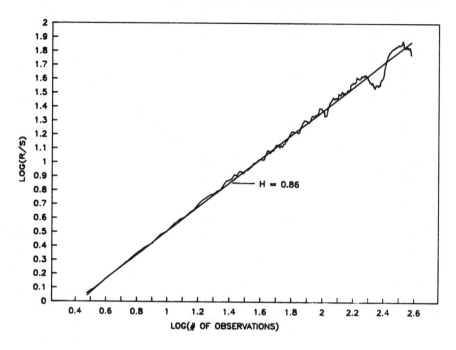

FIGURE 7.5   R/S analysis: Fractional Brownian motion. Actual H = 0.90; estimated H = 0.86.

greater than 0.70, and understate it when H ≤ 0.40. However, for short data sets, where regression is not possible, the empirical law can be used as a reasonable estimate.

FRACTAL DIMENSION AND H

The fractal dimension of the time series, or cumulative changes of a random walk is 1.50. The fractal dimension of a line is 1.0, and fractal dimension of a geometric plane is 2.0. Thus, the fractal dimension of a random walk would be half-way between a line and a plane, or 1.50.

The Hurst exponent (H) can be converted into a fractal dimension (D) using the following formula:

$$D = 2 - H \tag{7.7}$$

Thus, if H = 0.50, then D = 1.50. Both values are consistent with a random, independent system. A value of $1 < H \leq 0.50$ will result in a fractal dimension closer to a line. That is, a persistent time series, in the terminology of Hurst, would result in a smoother, less jagged line than a random walk, as we saw in Figures 7.2b and 7.2c. An antipersistent value of H $(0 < H < 0.50)$ would result in a higher fractal dimension, and a more jagged line than a random walk, that is, a system subject to more reversals. This, or course, precisely represents an antipersistent time series.

HOW VALID IS THE H ESTIMATE?

Even if a significantly anomalous value of H is found, there may still be a question as to whether the estimate itself is valid. Perhaps there were not enough data, or there may even be a question as to whether R/S analysis works at all. I suggest the following simple test, which is based on a test developed by Scheinkman and LeBaron (1989) for correlation dimension (which we shall study in Chapter 12).

Essentially, an estimate of H that is significantly different from 0.50 has two possible explanations:

1. There is a long memory component in the time series being studied. Each observation is correlated to some degree with the observations that follow.
2. The analysis itself is flawed, and an anomalous value of H does not mean that there is a long memory effect at work.

Perhaps we do not have enough data for a valid test, given that guidelines as to the correct amount of data are somewhat fuzzy. Still, the series being studied is an independent series of random variables, which happens to (1) scale according to a value different from 0.50, or (2) be an independent process with fat tails, as suggested by Cootner (1964a).

We can test the validity of our results by randomly scrambling the data so that the order of the observations is completely different from that of the original time series. Because the actual observations are all still there, the frequency distribution of the observations remains unchanged. Now we repeat the calculation of the Hurst exponent on the scrambled data. If the series is truly an independent series, then the Hurst exponent calculation should remain virtually unchanged, because there were no long memory effects, or correlations, between the observations. Therefore, scrambling the data would have no effect on the qualitative aspect of the data.

If there was a long memory effect in place, the order of the data is important. By scrambling the data, we should have destroyed the structure of the system. The H estimate we calculate should be much lower, and closer to 0.50, even though the frequency distribution of the observations remains unchanged.

I have done such a scrambling test for the simulated series discussed above. First, I scrambled the random series, which had an effective H value of 0.55. Figure 7.6 shows the log/log plot for the scrambled and unscrambled series. There is virtually no qualitative difference between the two. The scrambled series gives H = 0.58 as its estimate. Scrambling actually increased the Hurst exponent, showing that the original series did not truly have a long memory process in place.

Figure 7.7 shows the log/log plot for H = 0.90 of the scrambled and unscrambled series. Here, a qualitative difference appears. The original series gave an H estimate of 0.87. The scrambled series gives H = 0.52. This drop in

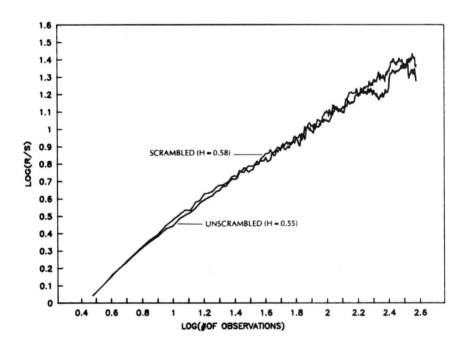

FIGURE 7.6   Scrambling test for R/S analysis: Random Gaussian numbers. Unscrambled H = 0.55; scrambled H = 0.58.

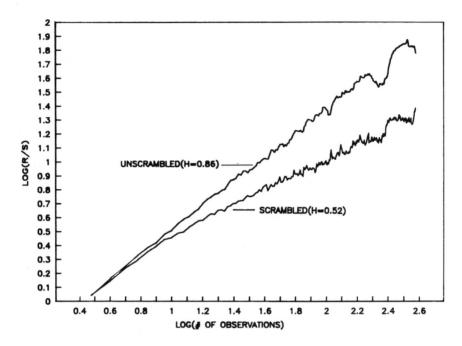

FIGURE 7.7 Scrambling test for R/S analysis: Fractional Brownian motion. Unscrambled H = 0.86; scrambled H = 0.52.

the value of H shows that the long memory process in the original time series was destroyed by the scrambling process. The scrambled series still has a nonnormal frequency distribution, but the scrambling process determined that the observations were independent. This proves Mandelbrot's assertion that R/S analysis is robust with respect to the distribution of the underlying series.

R/S ANALYSIS OF THE SUNSPOT CYCLE

Before we analyze the capital markets in the next chapter, it would be useful to apply R/S analysis to a time series of real data from a natural system.

Perhaps the most widely known natural system with a nonperiodic cycle is the sunspot cycle. Sunspot numbers have been recorded since the mid-18th century, when Wolf began a daily routine of examining the sun's face through his telescope and counting the number of black spots on its surface. When he died, the Zurich Observatory continued this practice, as it does to this very day. In one procedure inherited from Wolf, a cluster of closely spaced sunspots is counted as one large spot. Thus, five sunspots yesterday could become one large spot today. Combined with errors common in a manual procedure, this process lends itself to a certain degree of measurement error. Also, the number of sunspots is a highly asymmetric distribution: it can be as low as zero (which it has been at numerous times), but the maximum number can reach any level. In addition, the sunspot cycle is considered nonperiodic, with an average duration estimated at 11 years.

Sunspots offer a highly appropriate time series for R/S analysis, given their long recorded history. My local library carries an old book by Harlan True Stetson, *Sunspots and Their Effects,* which was published in 1938. It contains a table of monthly sunspot numbers from January 1749 through December 1937. Mandelbrot and Wallis (1969b) and Hurst analyzed sunspot data as well. However, it is useful to redo an analysis, incorporating the advances in technology since the last study. Please note that I am *not* making a connection

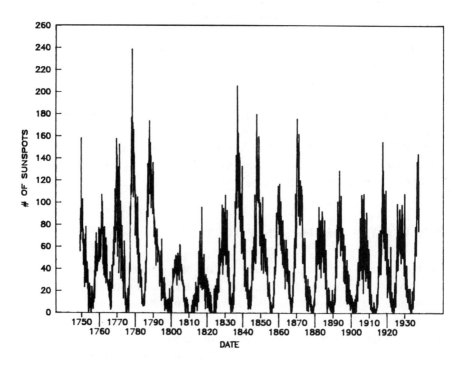

FIGURE 7.8   Wolf's monthly sunspot numbers, January 1749–December 1937.

between the sunspot cycle and capital market or economic cycles. I am analyzing sunspots as a cycle in their own right.

Figure 7.8 shows the monthly sunspot numbers as a time series. Note that, although its "cycles" are clearly apparent, the time series is very jagged. R/S analysis was applied to the logarithmic first difference in the monthly sunspot numbers.

Figure 7.9 shows the log/log plot of R/S versus time. We can see that periods shorter than 12 to 13 years have a Hurst exponent of 0.55. While not highly anomalous, it shows that sunspots do exhibit persistent behavior. Interestingly, the slope of the log/log plot drops drastically after this point, showing that the long memory effect has dissipated by 10 to 13 years. This is roughly equivalent to the estimated 11-year cycle accepted by scientists.

Figure 7.10 shows the result of the scramble test on the monthly sunspot numbers. The Hurst exponent is now measured at 0.50, and all trace of the memory length has been destroyed by the scrambling process.

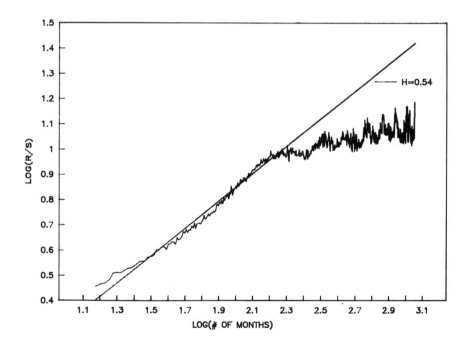

FIGURE 7.9 R/S analysis: Wolf's monthly sunspot numbers, January 1749–December 1937.

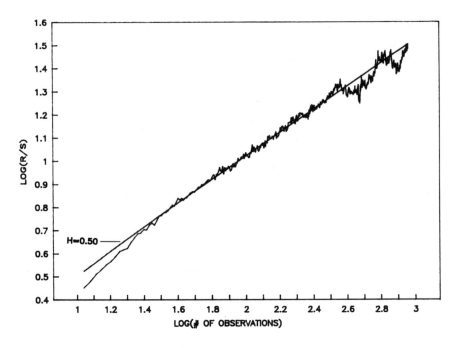

FIGURE 7.10   R/S analysis: Scrambled sunspot numbers, 1749–1937.

From this, we can see that natural systems may have long memories as postulated by the model of fractional brownian motion. However, the memory length is not infinite; it is long and finite. This result is similar to the relationship between natural and mathematical fractals. As we have seen, mathematical fractals scale forever, both infinitely small and large. However, natural fractals stop scaling after a point. Branches of our lungs, for instance, do not become infinitely small. In a similar manner, fractal time series have long, but finite memories. As we study the capital markets and economic time series, we will find similar characteristics. Economic and capital market time series are characterized by long but finite memories. We will also find that the length of these memory cycles varies from market to market, as well as from security to security.

SUMMARY

From R/S analysis, two important items of information can be determined: the Hurst exponent (H) and the average cycle length. The existence of a cycle length has important implications for momentum analysis. A value of H different from 0.5 means that the probability distribution is not normally distributed. If $0.5 < H < 1$, then the series is fractal. Fractal time series behave differently than random walks. We have already discussed persistence and long-term correlations, but there are other differences as well. These differences will be more closely examined in Chapter 9. First, we will do some capital market analysis.

8
R/S Analysis of the Capital Markets

Applying R/S analysis is simple and straightforward, but it requires a fair amount of data and number crunching. In this chapter, we will describe and show the results of applying R/S analysis to various capital markets. In all cases, we find fractal structure and nonperiodic cycles—conclusive evidence that the capital markets are nonlinear systems and that the EMH is questionable. The analysis presented in this chapter is an extension of Peters (1989, 1991).

METHODOLOGY

When analyzing markets, we use logarithmic returns, defined as follows:

$$S_t = \ln(P_t/P_{(t-1)}) \tag{8.1}$$

where S_t = logarithmic return at time t
P_t = price at time t

For R/S analysis, logarithmic returns are more appropriate than the more commonly used percentage change in prices. The range used in R/S analysis is the cumulative deviation from the average, and logarithmic returns sum to cumulative return, while percentage changes do not.

The first step is to convert the price or yield series into logarithmic returns. The second step is to apply equations (7.1) and (7.2) (page 63) for various increments of time, N. We do this by starting with a reasonable increment of time—say, a monthly time series covering 40 years of data, which is converted into 480 logarithmic returns. If we begin with six-month increments, we can divide the series into 80 independent six-month increments. Because these are nonoverlapping six-month periods, they should be independent observations. (They may not be independent observations if there is short-term Markovian-type dependence that lasts longer than six months. This situation is discussed later.) We can now apply equations (7.1) and (7.2) and calculate the range of each six-month period. We rescale each range by the standard deviation of the observations in each six-month period, to obtain 80 separate R/S observations. By averaging the 80 observations, we obtain the R/S estimate for the series with N = 6 months.

We continue this process for N = 7, 8, 9, . . ., 240. The stability of the estimate can be expected to decrease as N increases, because we have fewer observations to average. At this point, a number of studies run a regression of log(N) versus log(R/S) for the full range of N, taking the slope as the estimate of H, according to equation (7.3). However, doing so would be incorrect, if the series has a finite memory and begins to follow a random walk. In theory, long memory processes are supposed to last forever. However, as we will see in Chaos theory, there is a point in any nonlinear system where memory of initial conditions is lost. This point of loss corresponds to the end of the natural period of the system. It is important to visually inspect the data, to see whether such a transition is occurring. A regression can then be run over the range of the data, to show any evidence of a long memory process. Another way to view this problem corresponds to the discovery of fractal scaling in other natural systems. In theory, all fractals scale forever, like the Sierpinski triangle. However, natural fractals, like the human vascular system, do not scale forever. Physiologists have found that the change in the diameter of arteries and veins declines according to a fractal scale, as the arteries branch out. This fractal system has a limit, because the vascular system does not become infinitely small. In a similar way, I conjecture that the long memory process underlying most systems is not infinite, but finite. The length of the memory depends on the composition of the nonlinear dynamic system that produces the fractal time series. For this reason, visual inspection of the data in the log/log plot, before measuring H, is important.

A question now arises regarding data: How much is enough? Feder says that simulated data with less than 2,500 observations is questionable, but gives no indication of how many experimental data points are adequate. In the physical sciences, researchers can generate thousands of experimental data points under controlled conditions. In economics, because we are limited to relatively short data series that contain various market environments, we must be careful in our analysis.

I suggest that we have enough data when the natural period of the system can be easily discerned; we then have several cycles of data available for analysis, and that amount should be sufficient. In addition, Chaos theory suggests that data from 10 cycles are enough. If we can estimate the cycle length, we can use the 10-cycle guideline in collecting adequate data.

In this chapter, we will primarily be analyzing monthly data that are available from various sources dating back to the 1920s. In the next chapter, we will examine the behavior of H over different time increments, from daily to 90-day returns.

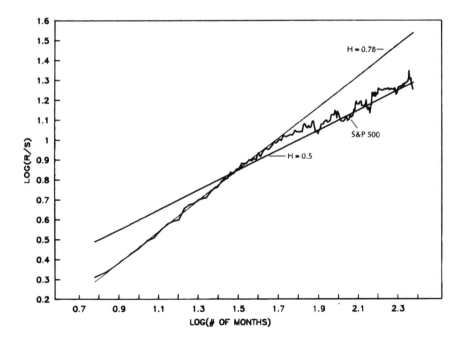

FIGURE 8.1   R/S analysis: S&P 500 monthly returns January 1950–July 1988. Estimated H = 0.78. (Reproduced with permission of *Financial Analysts Journal*.)

THE STOCK MARKET

We begin by applying R/S analysis to the S&P 500, for monthly data over a 38-year period, from January 1950 to July 1988. Figure 8.1 shows the log/log plot using the method described above. A long memory process is at work for N, for less than approximately 48 months. After that point, the graph begins to follow the random walk line of H = 0.50. Returns that are more than 48 months apart have little measurable correlation left, on the average. Figure 8.2 shows H values calculated by running the regressions for N less than or equal to 3, 3.5, 4, 4.5, and 5 years. The peak clearly occurs at N = 4 years, with H = 0.78, which we can say is the estimate for the Hurst exponent for the S&P 500. This high value for H shows that the stock market is clearly fractal, and not a random walk. It is, instead, a biased random walk, with an anomalous value of H = 0.78. Figure 8.1 graphs H = 0.78 and H = 0.50. Table 8.1 shows the results of the regression, using N less than or equal to 48 months. Regression results,

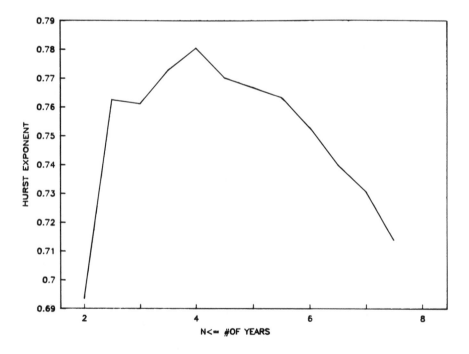

FIGURE 8.2   R/S analysis: Estimating the cycle length; S&P 500 monthly returns, January 1950–July 1988.

Table 8.1 R/S Analysis of Stock Returns, January 1950–July 1988

	Unscrambled	Scrambled
Constant	−0.32471	−0.04544
Standard error of Y (estimated)	0.01290	0.02005
R^2	0.99559	0.98564
X coefficient (H)	0.778	0.508
Standard error of X	0.008	0.004

using N ≥ 48 months, are H = 0.52 ± 0.02, confirming that the average cycle length, or period, of the S&P 500 is 48 months.

We can now apply the scrambling test to the series of monthly returns. Figure 8.3 shows the log/log plot of the scrambled and unscrambled series. The scrambled series, clearly different, gives H = 0.51. Scrambling destroyed the long memory structure of the original series and turned it into an independent series. There is also no drop in slope after 48 months, as there is in the original;

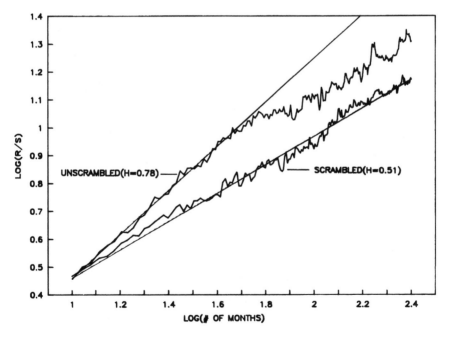

FIGURE 8.3 Scrambling test: S&P 500 monthly returns, January 1950–July 1988. Unscrambled H = 0.78; scrambled H = 0.51.

the series continues to scale as a random walk. The sequence of price changes is important in preserving the scaling feature of the series. Changing the sequence of returns by scrambling has changed the character of the time series.

These results are inconsistent with the Efficient Market Hypothesis. Roberts (1964) (as discussed in Chapter 2) described the market mechanism as a roulette wheel and asserted that "this roulette wheel has no memory." R/S analysis shows that the independence assumption, particularly regarding long memory effects, was and is seriously flawed. Market returns are persistent time series with an underlying fractal probability distribution, and they follow a biased random walk, as described by Hurst. The market exhibits trend-reinforcing behavior, not mean-reverting behavior. Because the system is persistent, it has cycles and trends with an average cycle length of 48 months. This length is average because the system is nonperiodic and fractal.

Figure 8.4 shows the log/log graphs of four representative stocks: IBM, Mobil, Coca-Cola, and Niagara Mohawk. Values of H are persistent, and

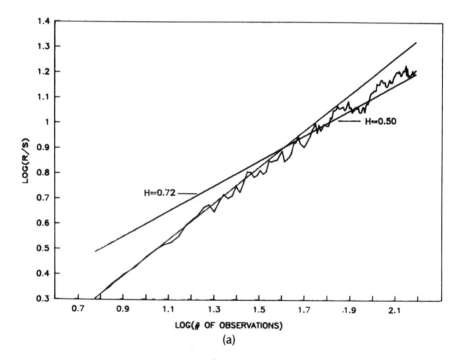

FIGURE 8.4a R/S analysis of individual stocks: Monthly returns, January 1963–December 1989. IBM: Estimated H = 0.72.

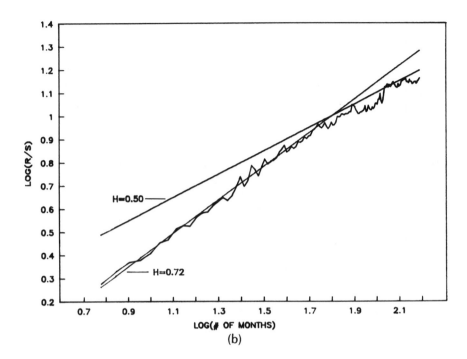

FIGURE 8.4b R/S analysis of individual stocks: Monthly returns, January 1963–December 1989. Mobil Oil: Estimated H = 0.72.

cycles are of various lengths. Table 8.2 shows the results for the S&P 500 and some individual stocks. In this limited study, stocks grouped by industry tend to have similar values of H and similar cycle lengths. Industries with high levels of innovation, such as the technology industry, tend to have high levels of H and short cycle lengths. In contrast, utilities, which have a low level of innovation, have lower levels of H and very long periods. The joker shows up less often for utilities than it does for technology stocks.

These results raise an interesting question about accepted definitions of risk. According to the Capital Asset Pricing Model (CAPM), a higher-beta stock, relative to the market index, is riskier than a lower-beta stock, because the volatility as measured by the standard deviation of returns is higher for high values of beta. Apple Computer, with its beta of 1.2 relative to the S&P 500, is riskier than Consolidated Edison (ConEd) with its beta of 0.60.

The Hurst exponent (H) measures how jagged the time series is. The lower the value of H, the more noise there is in the system and the more random-like

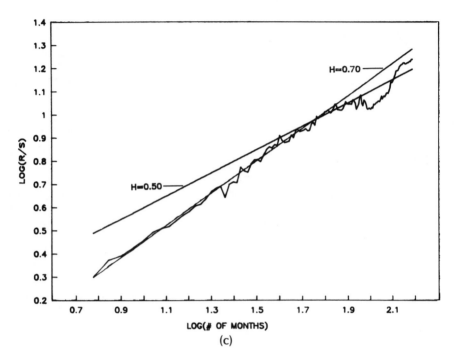

FIGURE 8.4c   R/S analysis of individual stocks: Monthly returns, January 1963–December 1989. Coca-Cola: Estimated H = 0.70.

Table 8.2   R/S Analysis of Individual Stocks

	Hurst Exponent (H)	Cycle (Months)
S&P 500	0.78	48
IBM	0.72	18
Xerox	0.73	18
Apple Computer	0.75	18
Coca-Cola	0.70	42
Anheuser-Busch	0.64	48
McDonald's	0.65	42
Niagara Mohawk	0.69	72
Texas State Utilities	0.54	90
Consolidated Edison	0.68	90

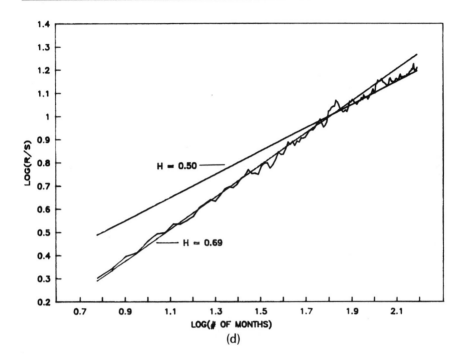

FIGURE 8.4d R/S analysis of individual stocks: Monthly returns, January 1963–December 1989. Niagara Mohawk: Estimated H = 0.69.

the series is. (Figure 7.1 and, particularly, Figure 7.2, the cumulative graph, illustrate the difference.) Apple Computer has an H value of 0.68; for ConEd, H = 0.58. ConEd's time series is less persistent and more jagged than Apple's time series. Which stock is riskier?

Because both stocks have H values greater than 0.5, they are both fractal, and application of standard statistical analysis becomes of questionable value. Variances are undefined, or infinite, which makes volatility a useless and possibly misleading estimate of risk. A high H value shows less noise, more persistence, and clearer trends than do lower values. I suggest that higher values of H mean less risk, because there is less noise in the data. This means that Apple Computer is less risky than ConEd, despite their betas. High H stocks do have a higher risk of abrupt changes, however.

A final observation is that the S&P 500 has a higher value of H than any of the individual stocks in Table 8.2. This higher value shows that diversification

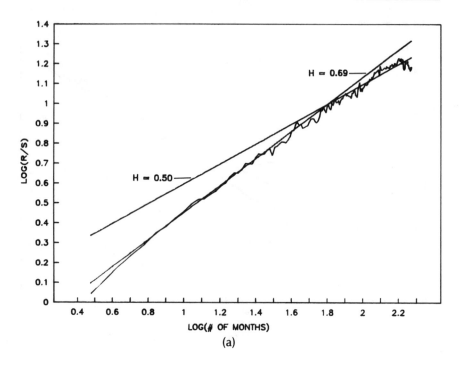

FIGURE 8.5a   R/S analysis of international stocks: Monthly returns, January 1959–
February 1990. MSCI U.K. index: Estimated H = 0.69.

in a portfolio reduces risk, by decreasing the noise factor and increasing the
value of H.

International markets also exhibit Hurst statistics. Figure 8.5 shows log/log
plots for the U.K., Japan, and Germany, as represented by each stock market's
Morgan Stanley Capital International (MSCI) index. The MSCI data used
were from January 1959 to February 1990. Table 8.3 lists the results.

Table 8.3   R/S Analysis of International Stock Indices

	Hurst Exponent (H)	Cycle (Months)
S&P 500	0.78	48
MSCI Germany	0.72	60
MSCI Japan	0.68	48
MSCI U.K.	0.68	30

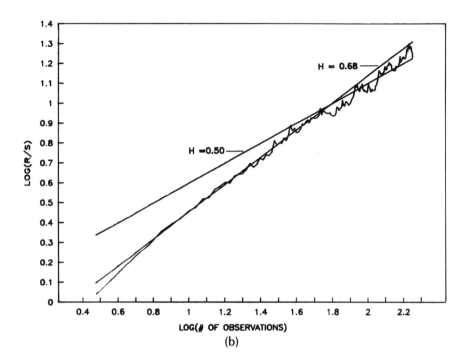

FIGURE 8.5b   R/S analysis of international stocks: Monthly returns, January 1959–February 1990. MSCI Japan index: Estimated H = 0.68.

If we include the S&P 500 as representative of the United States, all four countries have different H values and cycle lengths. The U.K. has the longest cycle (eight years). Germany has a six-year cycle, and the United States and Japan have four-year cycles. These cycle lengths are probably tied to economy cycles. We will examine this possibility later, for the U.S. market.

Market efficiency can be judged by the amount of noise in the data. Because the United States has the highest H value, it is the most "efficient" market: it has less noise than the others. It is followed by Germany, the U.K., and Japan.

THE BOND MARKET

R/S analysis of changes in 30-year Treasury Bond (T-Bond) yields also exhibits Hurst statistics. Bond yields were examined monthly from January 1950 through December 1989. The result was H = 0.68 with a cycle length of

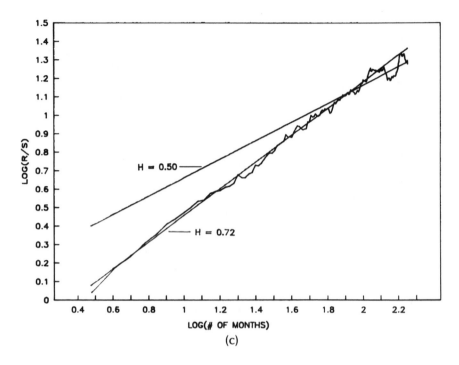

FIGURE 8.5c   R/S analysis of international stocks: Monthly returns, January 1959–February 1990. MSCI German index: Estimated H = 0.72.

five years, which coincides with the cycle length of U.S. industrial production, as we shall see later. Figure 8.6 shows this relationship.

A similar study was done for an average of 3-, 6-, and 12-month Treasury Bill (T-Bill) yields, as a proxy for the short end of the yield curve. Again, Hurst statistics result, with H = 0.65, slightly more noisy than the long bond. (See Figure 8.7.) Interestingly, no cycle length is apparent in the log/log plot. Either there are not enough data, or, perhaps, there is no cycle length and T-Bills do scale forever. Because T-Bill yields are an exception (the other series have cycles of four to five years), it is difficult to draw any conclusions.

CURRENCY

R/S analysis of selected currency rates also yields Hurst statistics. For this study, I have used currency exchange rates between the U.S. dollar and the

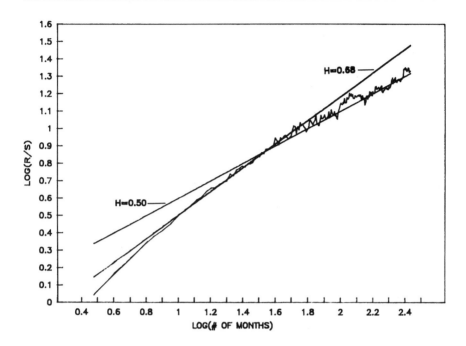

FIGURE 8.6   R/S analysis of 30-year Treasury Bond yields: Monthly, January 1950–
December 1989. Estimated H = 0.68.

Japanese yen, British pound, German mark, and Singapore dollar. The first three
exchange rates exhibit high levels of persistence. With the U.S. dollar/Singapore
dollar exchange rate, we encounter our first truly random series.

Figure 8.8 shows the log/log plots for the three primary currencies. All
three exchange rates have Hurst exponents at approximately 0.60. The
currency markets are not random walks, either. Table 8.4 summarizes the
results.

These results will come as no surprise to currency traders. Currency markets are characterized by abrupt changes traceable to central bank interven-
tions—attempts by the governments to control the value of each respective
currency, contrary to natural market forces. Currencies have a reputation as
"momentum trading" vehicles in which technical analysis has more validity
than usual. R/S analysis bears out the market lore that currencies have
trends, but the levels of the Hurst exponent for these currencies show that
they are not exceptionally persistent, when compared to equity markets.

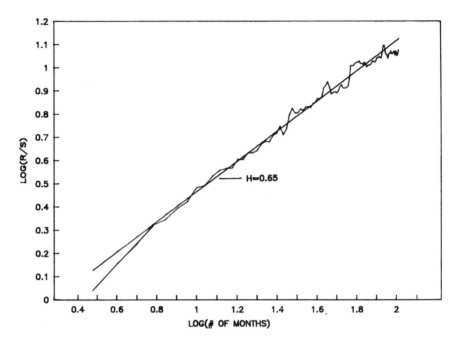

FIGURE 8.7   R/S analysis of Treasury Bill yields: Average of 3-, 6-, and 12-month T-Bill yields, January 1950–December 1989. Estimated H = 0.65.

This study was done on daily data from January 1973 through October 1990, almost 18 years' worth of daily observations. However, the natural cycle length is not apparent from the examination of any of the log/log plots. A flattening of the slope at the extreme end (about N = 100 months) could come from the sparseness of the data at that end. Apparently, 18 years' data do not cover enough cycles to make the cycle length visible. As we shall soon

Table 8.4   R/S Analysis of U.S. Dollar Exchange Rates:
Daily Changes, January 1973–December 1989

	Hurst Exponent (H)	Cycle
Japanese yen	0.64	Unknown
German mark	0.64	Unknown
U.K. pound	0.61	Unknown
Singapore dollar	0.50	None

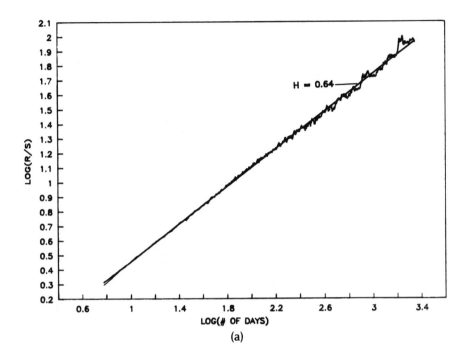

(a)

FIGURE 8.8a R/S analysis of currency exchange rates. Yen/dollar exchange rate: Daily rate, January 1973–December 1989. Estimated H = 0.64.

see, 30 years' stock market data are necessary for a well-defined period. Unfortunately, the United States did not go off the gold standard until 1973, so exchange rates prior to 1973 reflect an environment different from the current one. We may need another ten years' experience, to gather enough data to do a thorough analysis of the currency markets. As we shall see at the end of the chapter, more data points are not needed; tick-by-tick data will not yield more information. We need a longer time period. For that, we will have to wait.

The Singapore dollar is offered as an example of a capital market time series that does not exhibit Hurst statistics. The Singapore dollar/U.S. dollar exchange rate is a true random variable. This will be good news to the Singapore government, because the Singapore dollar is managed purposefully to track the U.S. dollar. Because of this conscious effort, any fluctuation in the exchange rate is due to random fluctuations in the timing of trades to fix the exchange rate.

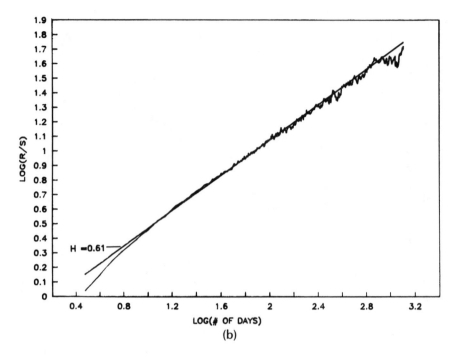

FIGURE 8.8b   R/S analysis of currency exchange rates. U.K. pound/dollar exchange rate: Daily rate, January 1973–December 1989. Estimated H = 0.61.

Figure 8.9 is the log/log plot that shows H = 0.50 for this time series. The Singapore bank appears to be doing its job. In other currencies, where the free market determines the exchange rate, persistent values of H continue to be found. Their presence confirms that currency markets also have a fractal structure.

ECONOMIC INDICATORS

R/S analysis also shows highly persistent values of H on the Index of Industrial Production, the Department of Commerce Leading Economic Index, the Index of New Business Formation, the Index of Housing Starts, and the Columbia

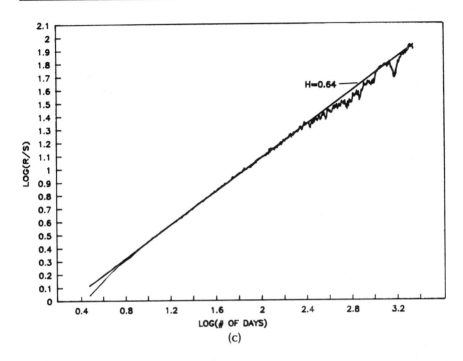

FIGURE 8.8c   R/S analysis of currency exchange rates. German mark/dollar exchange rate: Daily rate, January 1973–December 1989. Estimated H = 0.64.

University Leading Economic Index. These H levels finally prove that the economy follows a nonperiodic cycle.

Figure 8.10 shows R/S analysis for three economic indicators: Industrial Production, New Business Formation, and Housing Starts.

Industrial Production has H = 0.91 and a cycle length of about five years. Five years is a little longer than expected; most economists feel that the average economic cycle is about four years, to coincide with presidential elections. However, the log/log plot in Figure 8.10(a) clearly shows that the economic "joker" arrives every five years, on average. The other two indicators are also shown in Figure 8.10(b) and 8.10(c). New Business Formation has a high H value of 0.81; Housing Starts is at the more typical value of 0.73. Figure 8.11 plots the three time series together. The five-year cycle is evident for all three series. It has been suggested to me that seasonal adjustments might account for the high level of persistence in these series. When scrambled, however, each series dropped down into the random walk range, with H approximately

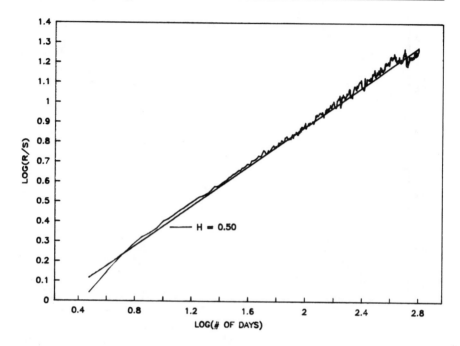

FIGURE 8.9   R/S analysis of Singapore/U.S. dollar exchange rate: Daily rate, January 1981–October 1990. Estimated H = 0.50.

equal to 0.50. Seasonal adjustment is not responsible for the persistence of these series.

The two leading economic indictors, shown in Figure 8.12, are remarkably similar. Their cycle lengths (about 4.5 years) are shorter than that of Industrial Production. This relationship confirms the "leading" nature of these indicators.

The existence of Hurst statistics for economic data should be especially troubling to economists who rely on econometric methods. Long memory effects severely inhibit the validity of econometric models, which explains the poor record economists have had in forecasting. Too much "subjective" art is still left in a discipline that is striving to be analytical.

IMPLICATIONS

Why do Hurst statistics arise in the capital markets? Prices change based on investors' perceptions of fair value. In the past, we have always judged "fair

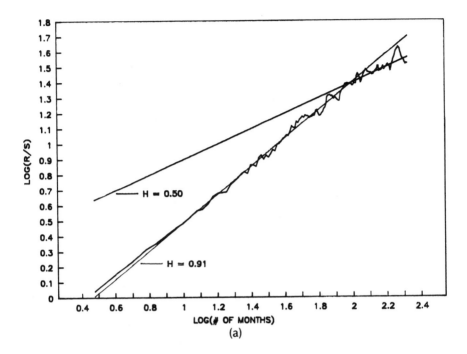

FIGURE 8.10a   R/S analysis of economic indicators, January 1950–January 1990. Industrial Production: Estimated H = 0.91.

value" to be a particular price. I postulate that investors actually value securities within a *range* of prices. This range is determined partly by fundamental information, such as earnings, management, new products, and the current economic environment. The information is often used to determine a single fair price by using fundamental analysis. The second component of the price range is what investors feel other investors will be willing to pay. This "sentiment component" is usually analyzed using technical analysis and sets a range around the "fair value." The combination of information and sentiment results in a bias in the assessment of a stock's value. If the fundamentals are good, the price will rise toward "fair value." As other investors see the trend confirming their positive outlook on the security, they will begin to buy as well. Yesterday's activity influences today; the market retains a memory of its recent trend. The bias will change when the price hits the upper range of its fair value. At that point, the bias will shift.

This model assumes that the "range" stays constant. In reality, it does not. New information about the specific security or the market as a whole can shift

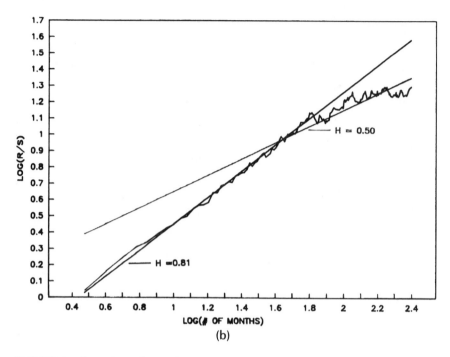

(b)

FIGURE 8.10b   R/S analysis of economic indicators, January 1950–January 1990.
New Business Formation: Estimated H = 0.81.

the range and cause dramatic reversals in either the broad market or an individual security.

Because broad market advances and declines are related to biases caused by economic factors, the S&P 500 and 30-year T-Bond yields have cycles similar to the economic cycle.

The Hurst exponent (H) measures the impact of information on the series. H = 0.50 implies a random walk, confirming the EMH. Yesterday's events do not impact today. Today's events do not impact tomorrow. The events are uncorrelated. Old news has already been absorbed and discounted by the market.

On the other hand, H greater than 0.50 implies that today's events do impact tomorrow. That is, information received today continues to be discounted by the market after it has been received. This is not simply serial correlation, where the impact of information quickly decays. It is a longer memory function; the information can impact the future for very long periods, and it goes across time scales. All six-month periods influence all following six-month

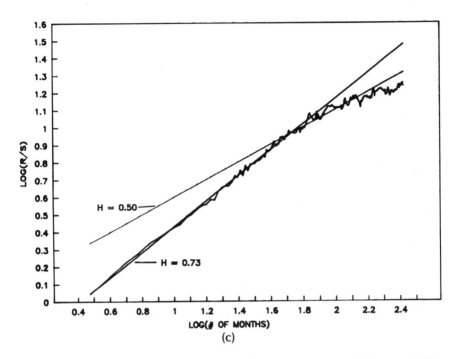

FIGURE 8.10c R/S analysis of economic indicators, January 1950–January 1990. Housing Starts: Estimated H = 0.73.

periods. All 12-month periods influence all subsequent 12-month periods. The impact does decay with time, but at a slower rate than short-term dependence. The cycle length, therefore, measures how long it takes for a single period's influence to reduce to unmeasurable amounts. In statistical terms, it is the decorrelation time of the series. For monthly S&P 500 data, this period, or cycle length, averaged 48 months. In terms of nonlinear dynamics (to be discussed in Part Three), memory of initial conditions is lost after approximately 48 months. The impact is still felt, however.

The 48-month cycle for the S&P 500 is an *average cycle,* because the series is nonperiodic. Nonperiodic cycles are characteristic of nonlinear dynamic systems. It is also a statistical cycle, not a "price" cycle that would interest technical analysts. Because the cycle is nonperiodic, spectral analysis would tend to miss this type of cycle as well.

The fractal nature of the capital markets contradicts the EMH and all the quantitative models that derive from it. These models include the Capital Asset Pricing Model (CAPM), the Arbitrage Pricing Theory (APT), and the

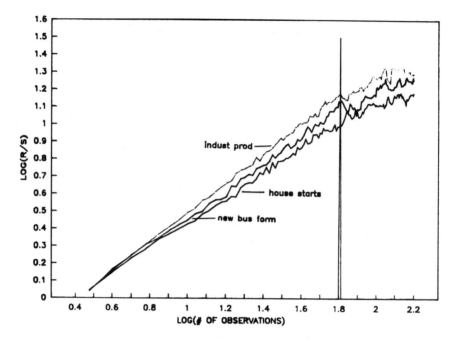

FIGURE 8.11   R/S analysis: Apparent five-year economic cycle.

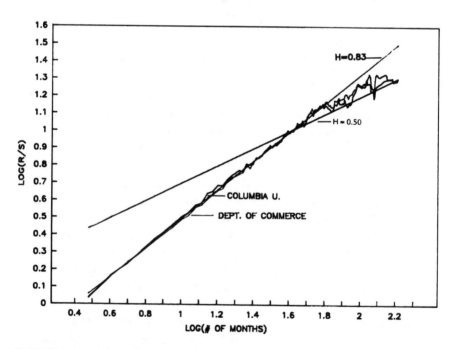

FIGURE 8.12   R/S analysis of leading economic indicators, January 1955–January 1990, Department of Commerce and Columbia University Index of Leading Indicators. Estimated H = 0.83.

Black-Scholes option pricing model, as well as numerous other models that depend on the normal distribution and/or finite variance.

Why do these models fail? They simplify reality by assuming random behavior, and they ignore the influence of time on decision making. By assuming randomness, the problem is simplified and made "neat"; the models can be optimized for a single optimal solution. Using random walk, we can find "optimal portfolios," "intrinsic value," and "fair price."

Fractal analysis makes the mathematics more complicated for the modeler, but it brings the results closer to those experienced by practitioners. Fractal structure in the capital markets gives us cycles, trends, and many possible "fair values." It returns the qualities that make the capital markets interesting, by returning the qualitative aspects that come from human decision making, and giving them measurable, quantitative attributes. Fractal statistics recognizes that life is messy and complex. There are many possibilities.

9
Fractal Statistics

This chapter deals with the difference between fractal and normal probability distributions. In particular, it generalizes the mathematics that underlies both, and shows that the normal form is a special case of fractal distributions. The technical nature of this chapter may not make it interesting to all readers. However, the implications of fractal distributions for modern capital market theory are profound. At a minimum, the chapter's final three expository sections and the conclusions should be examined.

PARETO (FRACTAL) DISTRIBUTIONS

Fractal distributions have actually been around for some time. In the economic literature, they have been called "Pareto," or "Pareto–Levy," or "Stable Paretian" distributions. The properties of these distributions were originally derived by Levy and published in 1925. His work was based on that of Pareto (1897), regarding the distribution of income. Pareto found that the distribution of income was well approximated by a log-normal distribution, except for approximately the upper 3 percent of wealthy individuals. For that segment, income began following an inverse-power law, which resulted in a fatter tail. Essentially, the probability of finding one person who is ten times taller than another person is relatively finite (and therefore follows a normal distribution), but the probability of finding a person with 100 times another's wealth is much higher than the normal probability would predict. Pareto speculated that this fatter tail probably occurs because the wealthy can more efficiently lever their wealth than the average individual, to create more wealth and achieve even higher levels of income. A similar inverse-power law was found by G. K. Zipf for the frequency with which words are used. Zipf found that long words are less frequently used than short words. A. J. Lotka found socio-logical examples of inverse-power laws; the publication of scientific papers in academia is one example. The more papers an academic has produced, the more he or she is likely to produce. Because the publication of papers can be leveraged through graduate students, the more well-known, and senior, members of the academic community can coauthor more papers. In this way, they lever their production of research. In all three cases, when the tails are investigated, a feedback mechanism enhances the production of whatever is being measured. This feedback effect levers the event and makes the tails even longer. Levy took these fat-tailed distributions and generalized all probability distributions to account for them.

Before we get to fractal distributions, let's review some of the characteristics of normal distributions. Most of us have encountered the normal distribution in some form. The familiar bell-shaped curve is used extensively; if nothing else, we were graded "on the curve" at some point in school. This curve has a formula, and the following is the log of the characteristic function of the normal distribution of a random variable, t:

$$\log f(t) = i*\mu*t - (\sigma^2/2)*t^2 \tag{9.1}$$

where μ = mean
        σ^2 = variance

For the "standard normal" distribution, the mean is zero and the standard deviation (the square root of the variance) is equal to one. Because the normal distribution applies when t is an independent, identically distributed (IID) random variable, it applies to brownian motion and random walks.

As stated in Chapter 2, Bachelier first advanced the idea that speculative markets follow a random walk and can be modeled like a game of chance. The Gaussian Hypothesis of Bachelier continues to be embraced, despite the fact that empirical evidence shows distinct anomalies from the random walk, as we discussed in Chapter 3. In particular, frequency distributions of returns have consistently found more large changes of outliers than there should be, as well as more observations around the mean (see Figure 3.1). The distribution has fatter tails and a higher peak than the normal distribution. Despite these characteristics, the distribution is often described as "approximately normal."

This fat-tailed, high-peak distribution is the characteristic shape of a Pareto distribution. Levy generalized the characteristic function of probability distributions to the following, somewhat complicated formula:

$$\log(f(t)) = i*\delta*t - \gamma*|t|^{\alpha}*(1 + i*\beta*(t/|t|)*\tan(\alpha*\pi/2)) \qquad (9.2)$$

This formula has four characteristic parameters: α, β, δ, and γ. δ is the location parameter of the mean. γ is a scale parameter to adjust, for example, the difference between daily and weekly data. β is a measure of skewness and can range from -1 to $+1$. When $\beta = 0$, the distribution is symmetric. When $\beta = +1$, the distribution is fat-tailed to the right, or skewed to the right. The degree of right skewness increases as β approaches $+1$. The converse occurs with $\beta < 0$. α measures the peakedness of the distribution as well as the fatness of the tails. α can take a range of values from 0 to 2 inclusive. Only when $\alpha = 2$ does the distribution become equivalent to the normal distribution. Taking equation (9.2), and setting $\alpha = 2$, $\beta = 0$, $\gamma = 1$, and $\delta = 1$, yields equation (9.1), the characteristic function of the normal distribution. The Efficient Market Hypothesis (EMH) essentially says that α must always equal 2. The Fractal Market Hypothesis (FMH) says that α can range between 1 and 2. That is the main difference between the two market hypotheses. However, changing the value of α changes the characteristics of the time series dramatically.

We consider Pareto distributions fractal because they are statistically self-similar with respect to time. If a distribution of daily prices has a mean(m) and $\alpha = a$, the distribution of five-day returns would have a mean of $5*m$ and still have $\alpha = a$. Once the adjustment for time scale is made, the series' probability distribution still has the same shape. The series is said to be scale invariant. The same description applies if $\alpha = 2$, and the distribution is the normal distribution, because the normal distribution is a special case of the family of fractal distributions. However, when does not equal 2, the characteristics of the distribution change.

First, when $1 \leq \alpha < 2$, variance becomes undefined, or infinite. Variance is finite and stable only if $\alpha = 2$. Therefore, sample variance is important information only if the system is a random walk. Otherwise, infinite variances are possible and, perhaps, typical. If α does not equal 2, sample variances are little better than meaningless as measures of dispersions or risk.

If $0 < \alpha \leq 1$, then there is also no stable mean. Alphas in this range are rare, but we will see an example of one later. However, if $1 < \alpha \leq 2$, then we do have a stable mean. Noninteger alphas in this range correspond to fractional brownian motions characterized by long-term correlations and statistical self-similarity. They are fractal. In addition, alpha is the fractal dimension of the probability space of the time series, and:

$$\alpha = \frac{1}{H} \tag{9.3}$$

where H = Hurst exponent

Note that while alpha is a fractal dimension, it is different from the fractal dimension, D, of equation (7.7). D is the fractal dimension of the time trace, while alpha is the fractal dimension of the probability space. D measures the "jaggedness" of the time series, while alpha measures the fatness of the tails in the probability density function.

Fractal distributions have two other interesting characteristics. Mandelbrot called the first one the "Joseph effect." As discussed earlier, the name refers to the tendency of fractal distributions to have trends and cycles. In the biblical story, Joseph interpreted Pharaoh's dream to mean seven years of plenty followed by seven years of famine.

Mandelbrot named the second characteristic the "Noah effect," after the biblical story of the Deluge. Its technical name is the *infinite variance syndrome*. These systems tend to have abrupt and dramatic reversals. In the normal distribution, a large change occurs because of a large number of small changes. Pricing is considered to be continuous. This assumption of continuous pricing which made Portfolio Insurance a possibility as a practical money management strategy. The idea was that, using the Black-Scholes option pricing model (or some variant thereof), an investor could synthetically replicate an option like a put by continuously rebalancing between the risky asset and cash. This method was plausible as long as pricing stayed continuous, or at least nearly so, which is usually the case. However, in a fractal distribution, large changes occur through a small number of large changes. Large price changes can be discontinuous and abrupt. A fractal distribution for the stock market would explain why the October events of 1987, or 1978, or 1929 could happen. In those markets, lack of liquidity caused abrupt and discontinuous pricing, as predicted by the fractal model. We saw evidence in Chapter 8 that the capital markets have fractal distributions.

"LOST" ECONOMICS

Mandelbrot conjectured that speculative markets were fractal, long before he developed fractal geometry. Mandelbrot had spent his life examining long-forgotten mathematical byways, and he continually found examples of nonrandom scaling. To Mandelbrot, Pareto distributions were yet another example of scaling, this time in economics rather than in nature. In the early 1960s, he argued in favor of infinite variance distributions, but lost the first round to the EMH. The Efficient Market Hypothesis was neater, and easier for academics to grasp intellectually. Risk defined as volatility was a cleaner concept. If two stocks have different volatilities, then the one with the higher volatility is the riskier one. The random walk model opened up an entire battery of analytical tools, which, in turn, offered the possibility of "optimal solutions," or one right answer. As data bases became more extensive, and computers became more powerful and plentiful, armies of graduate students and academics tested the EMH, the very bedrock of Capital Market Theory.

In pure mathematics, advances continued, and entire classifications of Pareto distributions were developed. The "infinite variance syndrome" was less popular in economics. Pareto distributions became largely forgotten, particularly in financial economics. Accepting Pareto distributions meant discarding a large body of work based on linear relationships and finite variances. Mandelbrot continued to publish. His work culminated in his rediscovery of R/S analysis in the late 1960s. At the end of one entirely theoretical paper with no empirical proof to back up its arguments, Mandelbrot (1972) promised to publish statistical results, but he never did. Mandelbrot largely left economics to go on to broader work, developing fractal geometry.

Interest in infinite variance distributions died because their implications were, mathematically, too messy. Quantitative analysts continued to keep the faith of the EMH because not enough anomalies had been found to point out the necessity for a new paradigm. The anomalies soon arrived, as discussed in Chapter 3. Prominent among them was the continued evidence that the distribution of stock market returns was non-normal. Consistently, it had a higher peak at the mean and fatter tails than the normal distribution, and it resembled a classical Pareto distribution. In addition, numerous anomalies to the EMH were found—the January effect, the small stock effect, and the low P/E effect, among others. All of these strategies have been shown to give excess returns without an increase in volatility at a statistically significant level.

Finally, the arrival of powerful personal computers and extensive data bases made R/S analysis of capital market data possible. In the previous chapter, we saw evidence that the capital markets were non-Gaussian. In this chapter, we will test the Fractal Market Hypothesis (FMH), which says that the markets follow a "Stable Paretian" distribution.

TESTS OF STABILITY

In Chapter 8, monthly data were used to calculate the Hurst exponent (H), so that economic data could be compared to international and domestic capital markets. Monthly data represent the best frequency available for most economic time series. For many international series, *only* monthly data are available. However, to test the stability of H, independent segments of time must be used. Because forty years' monthly data may not provide an adequate number of observations for a stability test, we turn to daily S&P 500 prices from January 2, 1928 to July 5, 1990, or 15,504 observations. In addition to the number of data items, we must also test how H scales over different frequencies of time. For that test, we need a long time series at the highest resolution that can be found. This long daily S&P 500 data series will fill the bill.

The first step is a Hurst analysis for the entire time period of daily data. If the stock market followed a classical Paretian distribution, we should obtain

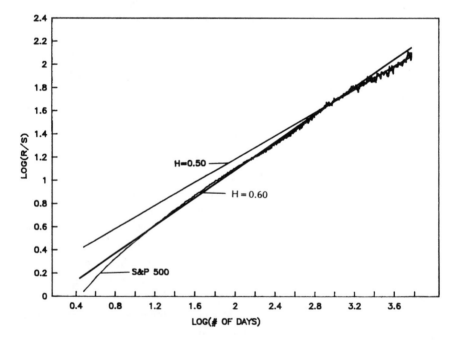

FIGURE 9.1   R/S analysis: S&P 500 daily returns, January 2, 1928–December 31, 1989. Estimated H = 0.60. Note the cycle length of 1,000 trading days, or about four years, which we also saw in the monthly analysis in Figure 8.3.

an H value of approximately 0.78, as we did for the monthly data. The results, shown in Figure 9.1, indicate that H came in at a much lower value (0.598) than predicted by the Fractal Hypothesis. The cycle length was, surprisingly, about 1,000 days, or roughly four years' daily trading days. This cycle corresponds to the 48-month cycle using the monthly data. R/S analysis is then performed on six independent contiguous increments of 2,600 days, to test the stability of H over different time periods and different economic conditions. Each 2,600-day increment is equal to roughly 10 years' daily data. As graphed in Figure 9.2, the Hurst exponent showed remarkable stability through 20-year periods that had radically different environments: three wars, the Great Depression, the social upheaval of the 1960s, the oil shocks of the 1970s, the leverage boom of the 1980s, and the stock market crashes of 1929, 1978, and 1987. The Hurst exponent varied from 0.57 to 0.62 for each of the decades. Interestingly, the four-year cycle is not easily discernible, which suggests that 10 years' data, even if gathered daily, are not enough for a full R/S analysis.

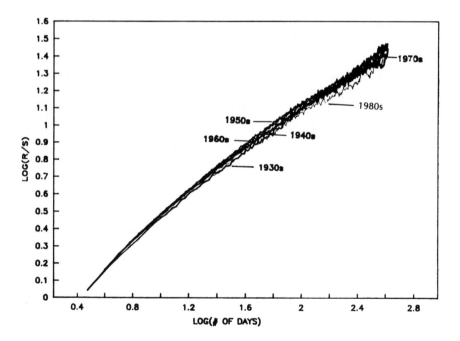

FIGURE 9.2   R/S analysis: S&P 500 daily returns by decade. Note that the slopes do not change much from decade to decade.

Still, H is lower than it should be, suggesting that there is more mean reversion in daily data than in monthly data. We shall investigate this further below. Regarding stability, however, the Hurst exponent is clearly one of the most stable statistics that can be calculated for the stock market. Mean and standard deviations of returns are displayed in Table 9.1, along with the Hurst exponent for each 2,600-day increment. Especially when compared to standard deviation, H is a very stable statistic. The intervals for this study are not the same as the Turner and Weigel study used in Chapter 3. These are even 2,600-day intervals starting on January 2, 1928. The Turner and Weigel numbers were calculated for calendar decades.

INVARIANCE UNDER ADDITION

Another property of stable distributions is that, after their adjustment for scale, they should retain their statistical properties if they are added together. For instance, if the series of daily price changes were normally distributed, with a mean (m) and a variance (s^2), then 10-day price changes should also be normally distributed, with mean 10*m and variance 10*s^2.

If the daily distribution were fractally distributed, then 10-day price changes would have a mean of 10*m, but the variance would be unstable. The value of H for 10-day returns would be the same as for daily returns.

To test this possibility, I created a series of one-day through 80-day logarithmic returns, using the daily S&P 500 price series. These are true and even increments of return. Calendar months are always treated as though they are $1/12$ of a year, even though the months have three different lengths of days, among other inconsistencies. For the test, trading-day increments were used.

Table 9.1   Stability of Statistics

Increment	Approximate Dates	Mean Return	Standard Deviation	H
1–2,600	1928–1939	−0.0598	0.3241	0.61
2,601–5,200	1939–1948	0.0474	0.1758	0.57
5,201–7,800	1948–1959	0.1228	0.1187	0.58
7,801–10,400	1959–1968	0.0661	0.0993	0.59
10,401–13,000	1968–1979	0.0036	0.1383	0.62
13,001–15,600	1979–1989	0.1157	0.1772	0.59

"Holes" from weekends and holidays were ignored and did not count as trading days. First, I checked how mean and variance scaled. The results for mean are in Figure 9.3, and those for variance are in Figure 9.4. Mean scaled almost exactly as predicted by theory; variance was usually higher. Variance was also more erratic than it should have been, which meant that there were some problems with the Gaussian Hypothesis.

Figure 9.5 shows the values of the above analysis for the Hurst exponent (H). Theoretically, H should be the same for all increments. Reality, once again, does not conform to theory. The value of H steadily rises from 0.59 for one-day increments to 0.78 for 30-day increments. Once there, it varies from 0.78 to 0.81 for each increment. This means that the noise in the system is present for periods shorter than 20 days. Somewhere between 20 and 30 days (or roughly one month), the noise is no longer a problem, and H converges to about 0.78, the measure for the calendar month data in Chapter 8. For less than 0.78, there is some noise, which we will attempt to explain later.

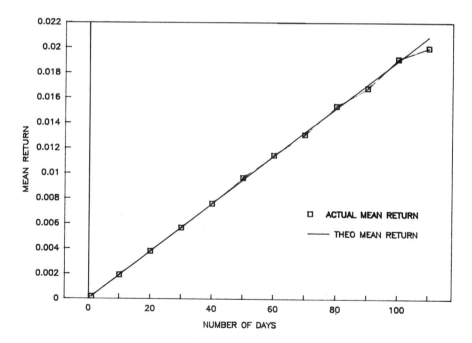

FIGURE 9.3 Stability of the mean return: S&P 500, January 1928–December 1989. Increments from daily to 110-day returns.

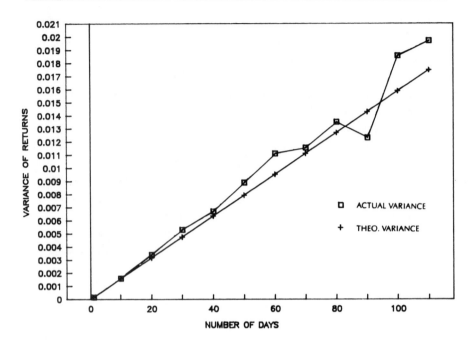

FIGURE 9.4   Stability of variance: S&P 500, January 1928–December 1989. Increments from daily to 110-day returns.

The cycle length is surprisingly consistent. It appears to be from 900 to 1100 days, or roughly four years. Figure 9.6 illustrates this for 20-day returns. This four-year cycle is not dependent on the resolution of the data. The "joker" shows up, on average, every four years, whether we are looking at daily or longer-interval data. In other words, what matters is not how many data points we have, but how many cycles the data encompass. This is quite different from a standard statistical analysis, where the number of data points is more important than the length of time being analyzed. Here, four years' daily data, or 1,040 observations, will not give as significant a result as 40 years' monthly data, or 480 observations.

The reason is that the daily data yield only one cycle; the monthly data yield 10 cycles. It is apparent that we must be very careful about the standards that we apply to nonlinear analysis. The standard method of finding many data points only helps the analysis when the observations are IID. Then, time does not matter; the number of observations does. However, nonlinear systems have a

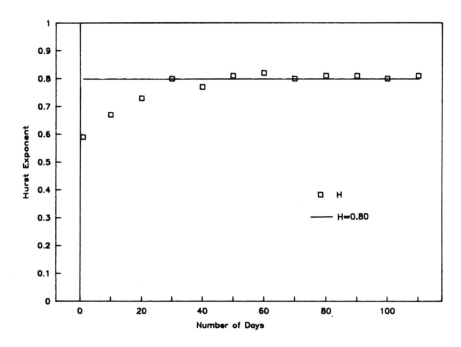

FIGURE 9.5 Stability of H: S&P 500, January 1928–December 1989. Increments from daily to 110-day returns.

time arrow. Time cannot be reversed, and the length of the time is more important than the resolution of the data. In fact, increasing the resolution often makes the analysis more difficult, without improving the validity of the results.

We have found two facts to support the Fractal Market Hypothesis:

1. The Hurst exponent (H), which is the inverse of the fractal dimension, is stable for independent periods of time. The four 10-year periods produced consistent values of H, an impressive result, considering how much the world has changed in the past 60 years.
2. For increments greater than or equal to 30 days, the FMH produced roughly equal values of H, varying between 0.78 and 0.81.

There were some surprises, however. At higher resolution than 30 days, we had lower values of H. The larger the increment, the higher the value, until we reached 30-day increments. Also, memory was found to be finite (four

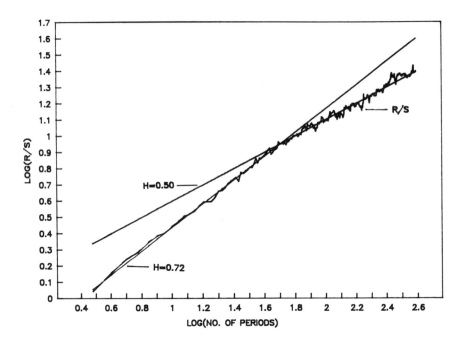

FIGURE 9.6   R/S analysis: S&P 500 20-day returns, January 1928–December 1989. Note that the apparent cycle length is 48 20-day increments, or 960 trading days. The cycle length of approximately four years is independent of the resolution of the data.

years), regardless of the resolution of the data. I would like to address these two inconsistencies.

A lower value of H would occur if there were more random noise in the data, or if there were more "mean reverting" behavior. That is, daily movements in stock prices are more likely to reverse than price movements in longer time periods. A third explanation is that price changes are not short-term independent, as the fractal model suggests, but contain some Markovian short-term dependence.

Mandelbrot, in a 1963 study of cotton prices, favored the third explanation. He noted that the cotton prices he was studying did not behave exactly as his theory predicted. In particular:

> ... large changes are not isolated between periods of slow change; they rather tend to be the result of several fluctuations which "overshoot" the final change. Similarly, the movement of prices in periods of tranquility [seems] to be smoother than predicted by ... [the fractal] process.

In other words, large price changes tended to be followed by large changes of either sign, but small changes were followed by small changes. Mandelbrot suggested that the individual price changes were not independent, as his original model suggested, but contained a Markovian short-term dependence. The occasional sharp changes predicted by the original model would be replaced by an oscillatory period. Likewise, periods without sharp changes would be smoother. This process might result in a level of H lower than the H level in a less Markovian process. Because Markovian dependence, being short-term, becomes weaker as the increments of time are increased, we would expect H to increase and stabilize. In roughly one month, the Markovian process seems to have dissipated, resulting in a stable H = 0.78.

This Markovian dependence should not be confused with the long-range dependence, or Joseph effect. The Joseph effect lasts forever, though it may not be measurable after a cycle, when initial conditions have become forgotten. Hurst dependence means that today's events change the future forever and cannot be undone. Markovian dependence decays rapidly and may be due to noise.

The second surprise, that the four-year "cycle" is independent of the resolution of the data, has exciting implications for quantitative analysis. First, it means that long-range dependence can and should be measured using monthly data. Some mathematical studies have determined the bias that would result from the use of small samples, or short time series. However, in applying this view to time-series analysis, we must remember that fractal distributions are additive. Each increment of time has all the individual transactions embedded in it. Thus, we should never need more observations. What we need are longer time series.

The implications for Chaos research are exciting. We will be able to use this information—the four-year cycle and the reduction in noise at 30-day increments—to help with nonlinear dynamic analysis.

Finally, these findings emphasize that we must let go of many of the statistical diagnostics that we have used in the past. Very few of them are valid in a nonlinear framework, where independence is rare and not to be expected.

HOW STABLE IS VOLATILITY?

We saw that variance does not scale as it should. But that does not mean that volatility itself is unstable. According to the Fractal Market Hypothesis, variance, or its square root, standard deviation, is undefined and therefore does not have a stable mean, or dispersion, of its own. Volatility should be antipersistent.

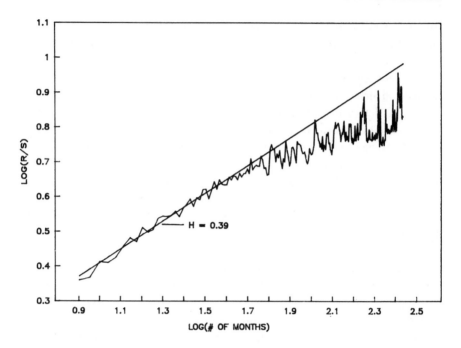

FIGURE 9.7   R/S analysis of S&P 500 daily volatility. Estimated H = 0.39. The only antipersistent economic time series yet found.

To check for antipersistence, I performed R/S analysis on volatility. For a time series, I used a monthly series of the standard deviation of daily returns, from January 1945 to July 1990, or roughly 45 years. Figure 9.7 shows the log/log plot of the changes in this series. It is highly antipersistent, with H = 0.39. This is one of the few antipersistent series that have been found in economics. If volatility has been up in the last month, it is more likely that it will be down in the next month. Since H is less than 0.50, there is no population mean for this distribution, or the distribution of variance is undefined, with no mean value. There is no population variance, as predicted by the Fractal Market Hypothesis.

SUMMARY

This chapter has brought together the elements of fractals covered thus far. We have found that most of the capital markets are, indeed, fractal. Fractal time series are characterized as long memory processes. They possess cycles and trends, and are the result of a nonlinear dynamic system, or deterministic chaos. Information is not immediately reflected in prices, as the EMH states, but is instead manifest as a bias in returns. This bias goes forward indefinitely, although the system can lose memory of initial conditions. In the U.S. equity market, the cycle lasts for four years; in the economy, five years. Each increment of time is correlated with all increments that follow it. All six-month periods are correlated with all subsequent six-month periods. All two-year periods are correlated with all subsequent two-year periods. Information biases the system, until the economic equivalent of "the joker" arrives to change the bias. This biased random walk seems to be descriptive of many capital markets.

Fractals describe, but do not explain. In Part Three, we will examine nonlinear dynamic theory, to explain why this fractal structure is present.

10
Fractals and Chaos

We have stated that fractals are generated by nonlinear dynamic systems, but we have not discussed what this means. In this chapter, we will make an intuitive link between the two concepts, which will lead into Part Three. This chapter will deal mostly with the Logistic Equation, a mathematical model that we discussed in Chapter 1. The Logistic Equation is a simple, one-dimensional model that exhibits a wealth of chaotic behavior, including a transition from orderly to chaotic behavior at an orderly rate. May (1976) studies this equation, and Feigenbaum (1983) found a new universal constant embedded in the system. In addition, a map of its possible solutions produces a statistical structure that is easily seen as fractal. For this reason, this chapter will deal mostly with the mathematical model rather than with investment finance and economics. In keeping with the rest of the book, the treatment will be intuitive. Those interested in a more mathematical treatment are encouraged to read the papers by May and Feigenbaum, as well as a complete treatment given in the textbook by Devaney (1989).

THE LOGISTIC EQUATION

As seen in Chapter 1, the following equation is the general form of the Logistic Equation:

$$x_{(t+1)} = 4*a*x_t*(1 - x_t) \tag{10.1}$$

where $0 < x \leq 1, 0 < a \leq 1$.

The Logistic Equation is a one-dimensional nonlinear feedback system. It is also a difference equation, as opposed to a continuous system, such as is obtained from partial differential equations. It is therefore a discrete system as well. As a difference equation, it lends itself to computer experiments with spreadsheets. One need only copy a formula down, in order to study its behavior.

We can create such a spreadsheet easily, using the following procedure:

1. In cell A1, place an initial value for the constant, a, between 0 and 1. Start with 0.50.
2. In cell B1, place an initial value for x of 0.10.
3. In cell B2, place the following formula:

    4*A1*B1*(1 − B1).

    Note that the value of a in cell A1 is treated as a constant.
4. Copy cell B2 down for at least 100 cells.

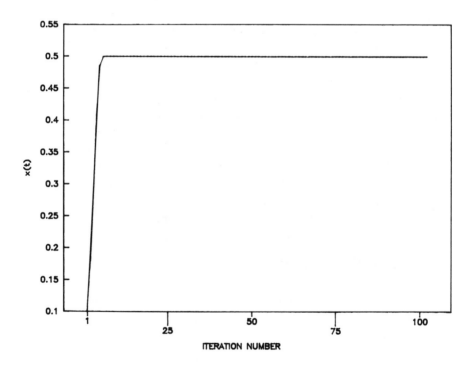

FIGURE 10.1   The Logistic Equation: Convergence of x(t); a = 0.50.

By plotting column B as a time series, we can study the transition of the system from stability to chaos.

THE ROUTE TO CHAOS

Viewing the time series with a = 0.50, we can see that, after an initial waviness the system settles down to one stable value (see Figure 10.1). Increasing the value of a to 0.60 results in convergence again, but to a slightly higher value.

Increasing the value of a does not seem that interesting, until we reach a = 0.75. Suddenly, the system does not settle down to one value, but oscillates between two values (see Figure 10.2). This split from one answer to two potential solutions is called a bifurcation.

If we again increase a, to about 0.87 (the actual value is 0.86237 . . .), the system once again loses stability, and four possible solutions appear, as shown

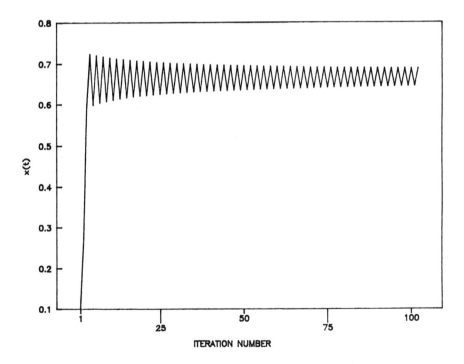

FIGURE 10.2   The Logistic Equation: 0.75 Period 2.

in Figure 10.3. As we continue to increase the value of a, the system continues to lose stability. Critical values of a come closer and closer together. At a = 0.886, we obtain eight solutions. At a = 0.8911, there are 16 solutions; at a = 0.8922, 32 solutions; at 0.892405, 64 solutions. This increase continues until a is approximately equal to 0.90 (actually 0.892486418). At that point, something amazing happens.

At a = 0.90, the system loses all stability. The number of solutions is infinite. Looking at the resulting time series, in Figure 10.4, we see chaos. The series looks random, and if a statistical analysis were run on the system, it would qualify as random. In fact, the Logistic Equation has been used as a random number generator.

An example of a physical system that behaves like the Logistic Equation is a public address system. If a microphone is placed next to a speaker system set at low volume, we can hear a low hum. If the speaker volume is turned up, the system will suddenly alternate between two tones. Continuing to increase the

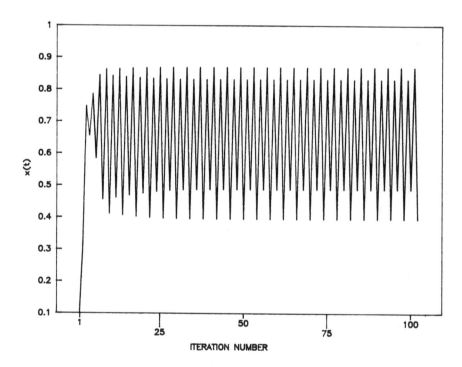

FIGURE 10.3 The Logistic Equation: Convergence of x(t); a = 0.87. This graph has Period 4 behavior, or four possible final values.

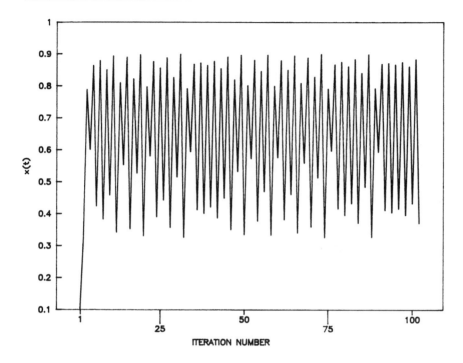

FIGURE 10.4 The Logistic Equation: Convergence of x(t); a = 0.90. This graph illustrates chaotic behavior, or an infinite number of possible values.

volume results in more bifurcations, until, at a critical level, we have uncontrolled feedback, the audio equivalent of chaos.

This simple equation has given us very complicated behavior. What is more, from a simple deterministic equation, we now have chaos. Let's examine the equation more closely.

BIRTH AND DEATH

The Logistic Equation was originally developed to model population dynamics in ecology. In the system, there will be a birth rate and a death rate. A nonlinear growth rate model would be a simple nonlinear equation:

$$x_{t+1} = a * x_t \tag{10.2}$$

In this system, the population grows indefinitely, and in an uncontrolled fashion, at the rate of a*x. The more the population grows, the fewer resources are available to sustain it. The system needs a death rate. The Logistic Equation adds a death rate tied to a*x². By subtracting this value from equation (10.2), we obtain the Logistic Equation (10.1). The Logistic Equation expands at a*x but contracts or folds into itself at a*x². As the constant (a) expands, the nonlinear feedback mechanism causes the population to have more than one possible steady state. In effect, as the population approaches the lower population size, enough resources become available to increase the population up to the larger potential population size. This interaction becomes more complex as the value of a is increased.

DISORDER AT AN ORDERLY RATE

We noted above that the critical points where the bifurcations occur come closer and closer together as the value of a is increased. Feigenbaum (1983) has shown that this occurs at a predetermined rate. Therefore, the system proceeds from order to disorder at an orderly rate. Feigenbaum conjectured, and Lanford (1982) proved, that this rate is a constant and is universal for all parabolic nonlinear systems. Its constancy allows us to predict when the next critical level of a is going to arrive. We can then classify different chaotic functions.

Feigenbaum found the following, as b, the values of a that cause bifurcation, get larger:

$$\frac{(b_n - b_{(n-1)})}{(b_{(n+1)} - b_n)} \rightarrow 4.669201609\ldots$$

The value 4.6692 . . . is usually called Feigenbaum's number and is labeled F. F is a new universal constant, like π and e.

THE FRACTAL NATURE OF THE LOGISTIC EQUATION

Formally, there has been no mathematical link between chaotic systems and fractals. However, we can easily observe the link by plotting the possible solutions to chaotic systems. Even a one-dimensional system like the Logistic Equation can be observed to be fractal.

Figure 10.5 is a bifurcation diagram for the Logistic Equation. It plots potential values of x versus the associated values of the constant (a). (A VBASIC

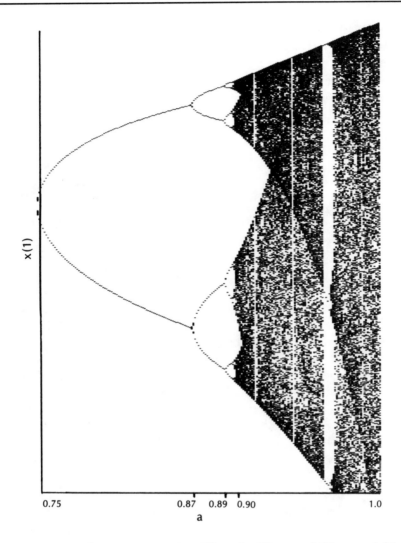

FIGURE 10.5   The Logistic Equation: Bifurcation diagram; $0.75 < a < 1.00$.

program for producing this diagram is given in Appendix 1.) In Figure 10.5, we can see that, although the system is considered chaotic, there is order in its possible solutions. At low levels of a are the single equilibrium solutions. We can also see the bifurcations, as they occur, and the chaotic region, when a crosses 0.90 and approaches 1. Even in the chaotic region, there is an inherent order in the system.

Figure 10.6 is a higher resolution graph that begins at a = 0.895. At this level of detail, we can see that the chaotic region is not just an area filled with points. There are "mountain ridges" that hang down like veils. At these ridges, there are more points, so the probabilities increase at those areas. There are also white bands, where order seems to come once again to the sys-

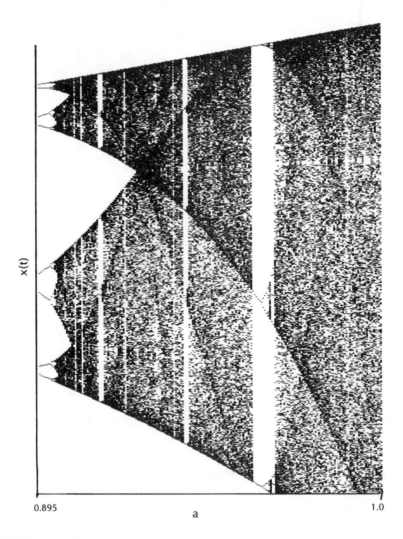

0.895   1.0

a

FIGURE 10.6   The Logistic Equation: Bifurcation diagram, chaotic region; 0.895 ≤ a ≤ 1.000.

tem. These bands show that, at certain areas of the chaotic region (a < 0.90), order reasserts itself.

These bands are of interest because they are illustrations of the fractal nature of the system. Figure 10.7 is a blow-up of the wide band region where 0.955 < a < 0.966. In the orderly region, we can see miniature versions of the larger bifurcation diagram. If we were to blow these up, we would again find

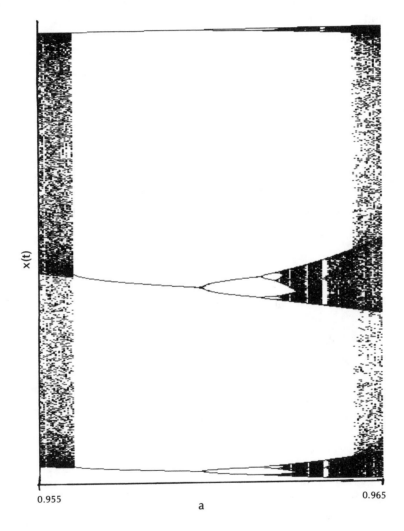

FIGURE 10.7   The Logistic Equation: Bifurcation diagram, semistable window; $0.955 \leq a \leq 0.965$.

smaller versions, and so on indefinitely. The small pieces are related to the whole, which ties in with our definition of fractals in Chapter 5.

The bifurcation diagram is the set of possible solutions in the equation. Statistically, in the chaotic region, all of the points are not equally likely to occur. The dark streaks, and the steadily widening potential solutions, show how the nature of the probabilities changes as the values of a are increased. Once again, at each value of a in the chaotic region, we have infinite solutions contained in a finite space, as in the Chaos Game. We can now conjecture that the fractal statistical structure for the capital markets that we have examined in Part Two is caused by nonlinear dynamic systems. We turn now to the study of those types of systems.

SUMMARY

I have attempted to draw an intuitive link between the world of fractals and the area of nonlinear dynamic systems. Higher-dimensional chaotic systems, which we will discuss in Part Three, share many similarities with the Logistic Equation; like the Logistic Equation, they are also related to fractals.

PART THREE
NONLINEAR DYNAMICS

"Chaos is the law of nature; order is the dream of man."
—Henry Adams

Chaos theory allows us to quantify the dynamics of uncertainty and find order in its irregularity. It has captured the imagination by showing how complex behavior can arise from simple deterministic equations. While the result is chaotic, the process is orderly. Chaos and order co-exist, but the "dream of man" Adams refers to above has been only partially realized. While there is order, a chaotic process cannot be predicted over the long-term. Prediction is the true dream of man. Chaos theory shows us the order in nature, but warns us that we must continue to live with uncertainty.

In this section we examine non-linear dynamic systems. We will learn what they mean, and how they are identified. We will see evidence that the capital markets can be characterized as non-linear dynamic systems *in the long-term*. This result is controversial, but thought-provoking. If true, the effects on capital market theory are profound and deep.

11
Introduction to Nonlinear Dynamic Systems

Fractals describe. We have seen that they describe very well. However, they do not explain. In Part Two, we examined the results of fractal statistics and postulated reasons for their existence. In Part Three, we will search for clues to the true nature of the capital markets and what determines price changes. To do this, we will use the mathematics of nonlinear dynamic systems, commonly called chaos theory. This research has a much shorter history than fractal analysis, particularly when applied to economics. It is hoped that the methods shown here, combined with research already completed, will lead to new models of the capital markets.

The statement that chaos theory has a short history is not completely true. Chaos theory dates from the work of Henri Poincaré, in the late 19th century. Economics and investment analysis have only recently begun to pay attention to chaos theory. The implications of chaos make the techniques controversial. In essence, a chaotic system can produce random-looking results that are not truly random. Long-term forecasting is impossible. In effect, both the EMH Quants and the Technicians are right. Chaos theory says that markets are not efficient, but they are not forecastable. Their status is similar to the "tromboon" of Peter Schickele, for his alter ego, P.D.Q. Bach. The tromboon is a trombone with a bassoon mouthpiece. As a composite of the bassoon and trombone, it manages to combine all the disadvantages of both instruments.

On closer examination, the picture is not that bleak. For one thing, knowing the truth, even if it makes life complicated, is better than hiding behind a convenient, but untrue, story. In addition, people are clever. Throughout history, we have been able to simplify complex problems enough to make them useful. Eventually, that resolution will come to chaos and the capital markets. As we said in Chapter 1, chaos theory recognizes that life is complicated and that there are many possibilities. We should not give up in the face of complexity, and chaos and complexity go hand in hand.

In this chapter, we will discuss the basics of nonlinear dynamic systems as they apply to systems with known equations. This is a necessary preliminary to introducing the analysis of real systems in Chapter 12. In real life, we end up knowing very little. In this chapter, we will learn the concepts necessary to understand dynamic systems. In Chapter 12, we will apply these concepts to time series, and, in Chapter 13, discuss actual analysis of capital market time series.

DYNAMIC SYSTEMS DEFINED

The study of nonlinear dynamic systems and of theories of complexity is the study of turbulence. More precisely, it is the study of the transition from stability to turbulence. This transition is all around us. We see it in a stream of cigarette smoke that breaks up in whirls of smoke and dissipates. It occurs when we put cream in our coffee. It happens when we boil water to make spaghetti. Yet, this common event of transition from a stable state to a turbulent state cannot be modeled by standard Newtonian physics. Newtonian physics can predict where Mars will be three centuries from now, but cannot predict the weather the day after tomorrow. How can this be?

Newtonian physics is based on linear relationships between variables. It assumes that:

- For every cause, there is a direct effect.
- All systems seek an equilibrium where the system is at rest.
- Nature is orderly.

The clock is the supreme symbol of Newtonian physics. The parts integrate precisely and in perfect harmony toward a predictable outcome. Newtonian physics was the ultimate achievement of the 18th-century "Age of Reason," the "classical" period in the arts, the era of Mozart and Haydn. Symmetry and balance defined the art, music, architecture, and science of the Age of Reason.

Newton gave us enormous knowledge. His physics and the calculus he developed to prove it remain one of humankind's ultimate achievements. Through mathematics, we were finally able to understand how nature acted on bodies in motion, and how these bodies interacted.

There were limits, however. Newtonian physics could explain how two bodies interacted, but it could not predict the interaction of three bodies. A vestige of this shortcoming is revealed when we send space probes to other planets. When the probe is launched, scientists set a trajectory for the probe to intercept its destination. If the target is the planet Mars, for example, they do not send the probe to where Mars is, but to where Mars will be, as predicted by astronomers using Newtonian physics. Along the way, a series of "midcourse corrections" is made. Why? If Newtonian physics worked perfectly, there would be no need for corrections, except to adjust for human error in the original calculations. But corrections are necessary, because Newtonian physics cannot predict with complete accuracy for more than two bodies, and the solar system is a many-bodied place.

The three-body problem occupied scientists for much of the 19th century. Finally, Poincaré said that the problem could not be solved for a single solution, because of the nonlinearities inherent in the system. Poincaré (1908) explained why these nonlinearities were important:

> A very small cause which escapes our notice determines a considerable effect that we cannot fail to see, and then we say that the effect is due to chance. . . . it may happen that small differences in the initial conditions produce very great ones in the final phenomena. A small error in the former will produce an enormous error in the latter. Prediction becomes impossible . . . .

This effect is now referred to as "sensitive dependence on initial conditions" and has become the important characteristic of dynamic systems. A dynamic system is inherently unpredictable in the long term.

The unpredictability occurs for two reasons. Dynamic systems are feedback systems. What comes out goes back in again, is transformed, and comes back out, endlessly. Feedback systems are much like compounding interest, except the transformation is exponential; it has a power higher than 1. Any differences in initial values will grow exponentially as well. We will see some examples later.

A second characteristic of complex systems involves the concept of critical levels. A classic example is "the straw that breaks the camel's back." When weight is added to the burden a camel is to carry, eventually a point is reached where the camel cannot handle any more weight. A straw placed on the camel's back will cause the camel to collapse. The camel's sudden collapse is a nonlinear reaction because there is no direct relationship between the camel's collapse and that particular straw. The cumulative effect of all the weight finally surpassed the camel's ability to stand (the camel's critical level) and caused the collapse.

The stream of cigarette smoke described earlier also has a critical level. In a draftless room, a column of smoke will rise from a cigarette and suddenly break into swirls and dissipate. What happens? The smoke rises and accelerates. Once its velocity passes a critical level, the smoke column can no longer overcome the density of air, and the column breaks up.

A dynamic system is a nonlinear feedback system. Crucial elements of chaotic dynamical systems include sensitive dependence on initial conditions, critical levels, and an old friend from Part Two, fractal dimensions. An important part of understanding nonlinear dynamic systems comes from looking at them. In chaos research, visual inspection becomes important, as we have already found in fractal analysis.

PHASE SPACE

Visual inspection of data becomes important in nonlinear dynamic systems, because, typically, these problems have no single solution. There are usually multiple—and perhaps infinite—solutions. As in real life, there are many possibilities. This characteristic has made nonlinear systems something to be avoided in the past. Now, with the extensive graphics capabilities available through personal computers, we can look at the numerous possible solutions. Many chaotic systems have an infinite number of solutions contained in a finite space. The system is attracted to a region of space, and the set of possible solutions often has a fractal dimension. (The similarity to Barnsley's Chaos Game, in Chapter 5, is entirely intentional.)

Looking at the data is easy, if we know all the variables in the system. We simply plot them together on a coordinate system. If there are two variables, we plot one variable as x, and the other as y, on a standard cartesian graph. We plot the value of each variable versus the other at the same instant in time. This is called the phase portrait of the system, and it is plotted in phase space. The dimensionality of the phase space depends on the number of variables in the system. If two or three variables are involved, we can visually inspect the data. If more than three dimensions are present, we inspect the data mathematically. The latter method is harder to relate to, but possible nonetheless.

Three basic classes of nonlinear systems are important to us. Each has its own type of "attractor" (a region where its solutions lie) in phase space.

The simplest type is a point attractor. A pendulum damped by friction is an example of a point attractor. When a pendulum is given initial energy, it swings back and forth, but each swing becomes shorter and slower, from the effects of friction, until the pendulum stops. The relevant variables for the pendulum are velocity and position. If velocity or position is plotted as a time series, the wavy line that results gradually drops in amplitude until it reaches zero and becomes a horizontal line. The pendulum has stopped. This is shown in Figure 11.1(b). If the phase space of the system is plotted as position versus velocity, we get a spiraling line that ends at the origin, where the pendulum has stopped (see Figure 11.1(a)). If we give the pendulum more initial energy, the times series and the phase space will show larger initial amplitude, but will again end at zero for the time series and at the origin for the phase space. In the phase space, we can say that the system is "attracted" to the origin. No

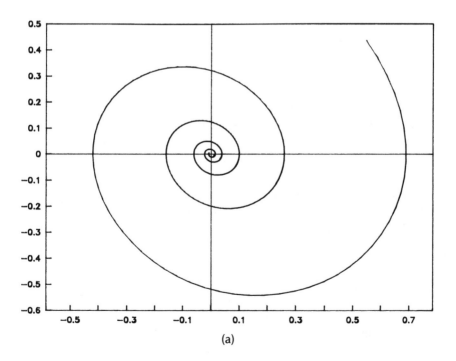

(a)

FIGURE 11.1a   Point attractor. Phase portrait.

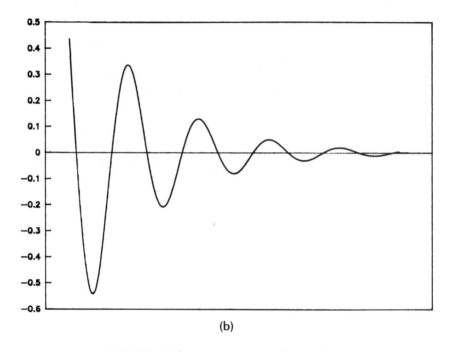

(b)

FIGURE 11.1b   Point attractor. Time series.

matter where one initializes the system, it ends up at the origin. The origin is the equilibrium state of the system.

Suppose the pendulum is not damped. Instead, we give it a kick of energy of exactly the same magnitude at exactly the same point in its swing. In Newtonian physics, this attractor is signified by a pendulum undamped by friction or gravity. The time series of velocity or position would now be a sine wave, as shown in Figure 11.2(a). The phase portrait would be a closed circle, as shown in Figure 11.2(b). The radius of the circle would depend on the size of the "kick" we give the pendulum, but it would still be a closed circle. This type of attractor, called a limit cycle, is a system of regular periodicity, as would be expected from a pendulum powered from the outside.

Classic econometrics tends to view economic systems as equilibrium systems (point attractors), or as varying around equilibrium in a periodic fashion (a limit cycle). Empirical evidence has not supported either view. Economic time series appear to be characterized by nonperiodic cycles (cycles that have no characteristic length or time scale). Nonperiodic cycles tend to appear in nonlinear dynamic systems.

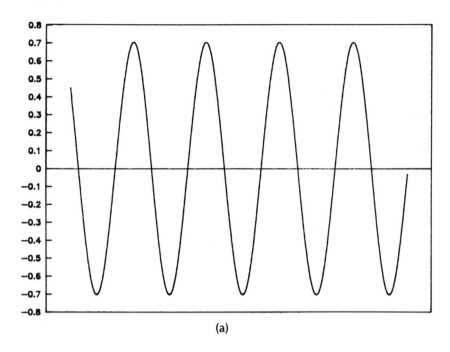

(a)

FIGURE 11.2a   Limit cycle attractor. Time series.

This brings us to the final type of attractor, a chaotic or "strange" attractor. Suppose we randomly vary the energy we give the pendulum, but the time between "kicks" remains the same. The impact of the energy will now vary, based on the magnitude of the previous kick, even though the magnitude of each kick is itself unrelated. Because we give the kick of random magnitude at the same time interval, the position and velocity of the pendulum will be different each time. If the pendulum is given a large kick the first time, it may already be headed downward when the second kick comes. If the second kick is small, the pendulum may be headed up when the third kick comes, which may slow it further. Even though we are still dealing with a pendulum given kicks of energy at regular intervals, its phase portrait will be different for each cycle. The cycle, from peak to peak of the swing, is an orbit. Because the pendulum will not be able to complete a cycle, its phase portrait will consist of orbits that are never the same and never periodic. The phase portrait will look random and chaotic, but it will be limited to a certain range (the maximum amplitude of the pendulum), and it will always rotate clockwise, though the size and time of the orbits will vary. This is a chaotic or "strange" attractor.

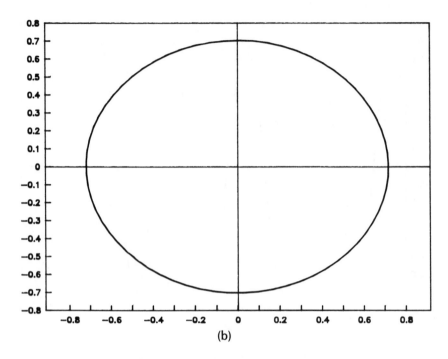

(b)

FIGURE 11.2b   Limit cycle attractor. Phase portrait.

Because chaotic attractors also have a fractal dimension (as we will see), Mandelbrot calls them "fractal attractors"—a better description than "strange," but the name has not caught on. The strange attractor encompasses all possibilities. Equilibrium becomes a region of phase space, a confined region with an infinite number of solutions. As with the Sierpinski triangle and the Koch snowflake, we have an infinite number of solutions in a finite space.

The phase space gives us a picture of the possibilities in the system. For systems where the equations are known, constructing a phase space is simple. For systems where the underlying system is not known but the effects can be observed, a phase space can be reconstructed. (We reserve that discussion for Chapter 12.) In the next section, we will study low-dimensional systems with known equations. They will allow us to examine the characteristics of these types of equations before tackling time-series analysis.

THE HENON MAP

The attractor of Henon (1976) is a good example of a two-dimensional iterative map. The equation itself is simple:

$$x_{(t+1)} = 1 + y_t - a*x_t^2$$
$$y_{(t+1)} = b*x_t \tag{11.1}$$

When $a = +1.40$ and $b = 0.30$, we achieve chaotic motion. Figure 11.3 shows the values of x and y as time series. Note the erratic movement apparent in both series. The phase space is shown in Figure 11.4. The structure is definitely not random. As in the Chaos Game, the points are plotted in a seemingly random way. The order is different, depending on the initial point, but the result is always the same: the Henon attractor.

This system has two degrees of freedom: x and y. Each value of x is tied to the previous values of x and y, and y is related to the previous value of x. Thus,

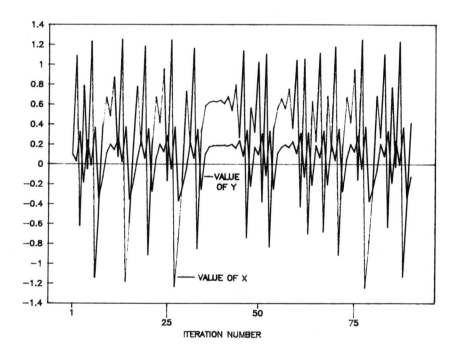

FIGURE 11.3 Henon attractor: Time series of X and Y.

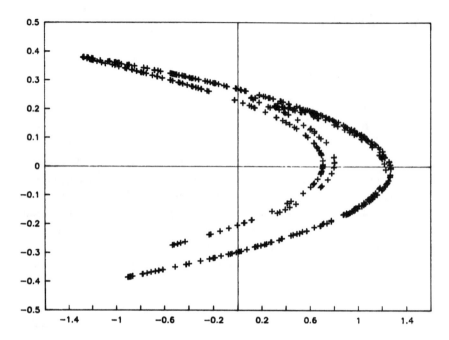

FIGURE 11.4 Henon attractor: Phase portrait; a = −1.4, b = 0.3.

each value is dependent on the previous value. The time series of values is dependent on the initial value used. However, no matter what initial value is used (or what time series is generated), the phase space always looks the same. The reader is encouraged to examine this personally. With any spreadsheet package, difference equations are easy to study in one or two dimensions. Here's how to do it:

1. In cells A1 and B1, place initial values of x and y between 0 and 1.
2. In cell A2, place the following equation:

    $1 + B1 - 1.4*A1^2$.

3. In cell B2, place this equation: $0.3*A1$.
4. Copy A2 and B2 down 300 rows or more (the more the better).
5. Do an xy plot, using symbols only (no lines), with column A as x and column B as y.

You will now see the Henon map. Change the initial values of x and y in cells A1 and B1. Note that all the values have changed. View the graph again. It looks exactly the same. No matter what initial values (or "initial conditions") you choose, the graph is always the same. The system is attracted to this shape. The shape is the strange attractor of the system.

Create a second Henon system in columns D and E, using initial values 0.01 different from the first set (columns A and B). Plot column A and column D through time, as a "line"-type graph. Figure 11.5 shows how they start out close to one another but rapidly diverge. This is sensitive dependence on initial conditions. The values diverge because x_t is squared in the x equation. Thus, the initial values of x used in cells A1 and D1, although they differ by only 0.01, will diverge in time as the 0.01 is squared with each iteration and fed back directly into the next value of x, and indirectly into the value of y two iterations further down.

If we blow up a portion of the Henon map (or attractor), we see more detail; increased enlargements reveal greater detail. The map is fractal, as most chaotic attractors are. Using the box-counting method, its fractal dimension

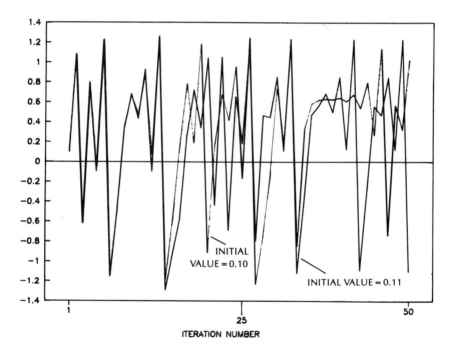

FIGURE 11.5   Henon attractor: Sensitive dependence on initial conditions.

is 1.26. It is more than a line, and less than a plane, like a time series of stock returns.

When the equations are known, we can do numerical experiments like the one just completed with the second column of numbers. Suppose we wish to forecast x, 30 iterations into the future. Our estimate of current conditions is off by 0.01, because our display terminal only prints to one decimal place. Figure 11.5 shows how wrong a forecast can be, if an estimate of current conditions is slightly wrong. The effect on the accuracy of the forecast could be substantial. In Figure 11.5, the initial values of x and y are really 0.11, 0.10, instead of 0.10, 0.10. By the 30th iteration, as a result of this 10 percent error in specifying x, our forecast is −0.17 when the actual value is 0.45. A small error in measuring current conditions becomes a large forecasting error. (Save this spreadsheet for use in Chapter 12.)

Numerical experiments, like the ones we have been doing with the Henon equation, are very enlightening. They give us an intuitive feel for the motion in a nonlinear system, by empirically testing the system. To a pure mathematician, however, they prove nothing. This type of mathematical experiment is not something a pure mathematician would even approve of. Only when a problem is proven for the general case is it truly solved, to a mathematician.

Many nonlinear systems have been proven in the classical sense (like the existence of Feigenbaum's number in Chapter 10), but many others have not. Henon's map is still "awaiting proof." For practitioners who do not require a mathematical proof, numerical experiments offer a "hands-on" way of understanding nonlinear systems and achieving the intuitive feel necessary to make chaos useful. I encourage experimentation. For chaos, the computer becomes a laboratory. Experiment with different attractors. Change parameters and examine the results. Devise your own attractors. Computers offer the ability to see what Poincaré could only imagine.

THE LOGISTIC DELAY EQUATION

Henon's map offers a two-dimensional system that lends itself to spreadsheets. Another map that exhibits a different behavior is the Logistic Delay Equation:

$$x_t = a * x_{(t-1)} * (1 - x_{(t-2)}) \qquad (11.2)$$

where x_t = a variable
         a = a constant

The Logistic Delay Equation is interesting because it exhibits a behavior called a Hopf bifurcation, a change from a point attractor to a limit cycle. In the Logistic Delay Equation, the current value of x depends on the two previous values of x; in the Logistic Equation, it depends only on x in the previous period.

Create a spreadsheet similar to the one used for the Henon attractor:

1. In cell A1, place the value of the constant, a. Start with 1.50.
2. In cells B1 and B2, place the initial value of x, 0.10.
3. In cell B3, place the following equation:

    A1*B2*(1 − B1).

4. Copy cell B3 down 300 or more times.
5. In cell C1, insert "+B2" (the value in B2) so that the C column is the B column lagged one observation. Copy this down so that it is the same length as B.
6. Do an xy plot, with column B as x and column C as y. Use a line plot this time, rather than symbols.

When you observe the graph, you will see the value spiral into a final value. This is a classic point attractor. If you increase the constant (a) in cell A1, the spiral becomes wider and wider. When it passes the critical value 2.58, the plot becomes the shape of a closed egg. The attractor is now a limit cycle. This transition is the Hopf bifurcation.

THE CONTROL PARAMETER

The Logistic Delay Equation is important because it shows how the behavior of a nonlinear dynamic system varies because of its control parameter, the constant a. In our computer experiments, we held the value of the control parameter constant while we examined the system's behavior. In the physical sciences, researchers can perform such controlled experiments. If the control parameter is the equivalent of temperature, then the temperature is held constant while the behavior of the system is observed in the laboratory. In economics and investment finance, we are unable to hold a control parameter constant and perform a controlled experiment. If the ratio of advancing to declining value is the "heat" that drives the stock market, we are unable to run an experiment and observe behavior at different levels. We can only examine historical data where the control parameter can vary from moment to moment. Therefore, in examining time-series data in economics and investments, we must realize that the data may contain all possible states jumbled together: point attractors, limit cycles, and strange attractors.

LYAPUNOV EXPONENTS

We have said that an important characteristic of chaotic systems is "sensitive dependence on initial conditions." There are two ways of viewing this concept. In the first view, the concept describes difficulty in specifying the problem. The model builder knows the proper equations of motion, but the accuracy of the predictions generated by the model depends on the quality of the inputs. The further out in time we go, the less accurate our forecasts become. This classic modelers' problem is made real by the nature of nonlinear systems, which amplify errors. This is a "forward looking" interpretation of sensitive dependence on initial conditions.

The second view is that the system itself generates randomness through a mixing process, and, after a certain point, all knowledge of initial conditions becomes lost. This interpretation is "backward looking." Where we are is dependent on where we have been. The evolutionary process may be so complex, however, as amplified by the nonlinearities, that we cannot retrace out steps and "unmix" the system. A common metaphor for this type of behavior is a taffy-pulling machine, which consists of two mechanical arms that work in a circular motion in a bowl, pulling the taffy and folding it back on itself. Suppose the machine is working, pulling taffy, and a drop of dye is dropped at a random spot in the taffy. The dye would be stretched and folded until elaborate striations appeared in the taffy. However, because of the sensitive dependence on initial conditions, we could never unmix the taffy so that we could return to the initial drop of dye.

This is a historian's view of sensitive dependence on initial conditions. We can never unwind a system with enough precision to find out where we have come from.

These two views can be combined into a continuum. Where we are is dependent on where we have been, and how accurately we forecast the future depends on how much we understand about where we are. One event can influence the future indefinitely, even though the system may remember the event for only a finite length of time.

The susceptibility of a system to sensitive dependence on initial conditions can be measured by numbers called Lyapunov exponents, which measure how quickly nearby orbits diverge in phase space. There is one Lyapunov exponent for each dimension in phase space.

A positive Lyapunov exponent measures stretching in phase space; that is, it measures how rapidly nearby points diverge from one another. A negative Lyapunov exponent measures contraction—how long it takes for a system to reestablish itself after it has been perturbed. Imagine an undamped pendulum placed on a table and swinging in regular motion. Someone bumps the table and causes the pendulum to lose its rhythm. However, if there is no other disturbance, the pendulum will settle back to a steady rhythm with a new amplitude. In phase space, the pendulum's orbit is characterized by a closed circle, or limit cycle. If we were to plot the action when the table is bumped, we would see some orbits swing wildly away from the limit cycle, before settling into a new limit cycle. The negative Lyapunov exponent measures the number of orbits, or the amount of time, it takes for the phase plot to return to its attractor, which in this case is a limit cycle.

Lyapunov exponents offer a way to classify attractors. Point attractors always converge to a fixed point. Therefore, a three-dimensional point attractor is characterized by three negative Lyapunov exponents $(-, -, -)$. All three dimensions contract into the fixed point.

Three-dimensional limit cycles have two negative exponents and one exponent equal to zero $(0, -, -)$. Limit cycles have two dimensions that converge into one another and one in which no change in the relative position of the points occurs. This causes the closed orbits.

Finally, three-dimensional strange attractors have one positive exponent, one negative, and one equal to zero $(+, 0, -)$. The positive exponent shows sensitive dependence on initial conditions, or the tendency for small changes in initial conditions to change forecasts. The negative exponent causes the diverging points to remain within the range of the attractor. For a strange attractor, equilibrium is defined by how far values can diverge before they are brought back into a reasonable range. One possible explanation for a strange attractor for the capital markets, for instance, is that stretching is caused by sentiment or technical factors, but fundamental value brings the prices back into a reasonable range.

In phase space, we measure Lyapunov exponents by measuring how the volume of a sphere changes over time. If we start with a three-dimensional phase space, and a sphere of nearby points representing slightly different initial conditions, the sphere will, after time, become an ellipsoid. After a long enough time, it will be stretched and folded so much that it could represent someone's small intestine. The exponential growth rate of the volume of the sphere is a measure of the Lyapunov exponent. The formal equation for the ith Lyapunov exponent (L_i) for the ith dimension $(p_i(t))$ is:

$$L1 = \lim_{t \to \infty} (1/t)\log_2 \left(\frac{p_i(t)}{p_i(0)} \right) \tag{11.3}$$

The linear part of the sphere grows at the rate $2^{L_1 t}$. The area of the first two dimensions grows at $2^{(L_1 + L_2)t}$. The volume of the three-dimensional sphere grows at $2^{(L_1 + L_2 + L_3)t}$. Higher than three dimensions, the expression of growth continues on in the same way.

Wolf, et al. (1985) published a FORTRAN program for calculating a full spectrum of Lyapunov exponents when the equations of motion are known. Using this program, the Henon attractor is found to have Lyapunov exponents equal to $(0.42, -1.6)$ bits per iteration when $a = -1.4$ and $b = 0.30$.

These results mean that we lose 0.42 bit of predictive power with each iteration. Therefore, if we could measure current conditions to 2 bits of accuracy, we would lose all predictive power 4.8 iterations $(4.8 = 2/0.42)$ into the future.

What do we mean by "bits" of information? Lyapunov exponents was originally created for the information theory developed by Shannon (1963). Information theory measured the effectiveness of computers. Because most computers are digital computers, their data are stored in binary format (zeros and ones) and recorded in base two. These binary digits are called bits. Because they are binary, equation (11.3) uses $\log_2$, not $\log_e$, or "nats." Shannon developed a communication theory to measure the uncertainty that a message will be correctly received. He used the thermodynamic concept of entropy, and measured entropy in bits. Therefore, the more bits of information coming into the system, the higher the entropy, or uncertainty, of the system. Rather than uncertainty, I like to describe entropy using forecasting ability, which is more relevant to capital market analysis.

"Bits of accuracy" measure how much we know about current conditions. Suppose the largest positive Lyapunov exponent were 0.05 bit per day (in a time series, we use bits per day or month rather than bits per iteration or orbit). This means that we lose 0.05 bit of predictive power every day going forward. Therefore, if we can measure current conditions to one bit of precision, that information becomes useless after 1/0.05, or 20 days. If we knew exactly what today's stock market return was going to be, we still would have 0 percent accuracy forecasting returns 20 days into the future. From another viewpoint, the impact of that one bit of information dissipates after 20 days, and the system no longer remembers it.

Knowing the largest Lyapunov exponents tells us how reliable our forecasts are for what future time period. We can only measure reliability for a system for which we know the equations of motion. In real life, we never know all of the variables involved with certainty, let alone the equations of motion.

In the next chapter, we will apply the concepts of phase space construction and analysis to a time series. In Chapter 13, we can apply this analysis to some capital market time series.

12
Dynamic Analysis of Time Series

The techniques outlined in Chapter 11 are useful when the equations of motion are known. However, in real life, we rarely know all the relevant variables in a system, let alone the equations of motion. We can postulate models and use the analysis of Chapter 11 to study effects, but most of those data are generated using the equations. The techniques for known equations are not very useful in determining whether a real system is truly chaotic, or nonlinear. They are, however, a starting point.

The analyses for systems of known equations are pure mathematical experiments. Because the systems are run without the noisy interference of real life, we can learn about feedbacks, critical levels, and bifurcations. Among the creations of the science of chaos, they are the closest match to the pure forms so dear to the ancient Greeks.

Empirical analysis is never clean. It remains messy. The clean, orderly, strange attractors of theory rarely show up in real life. However, we can still determine whether a system is a nonlinear dynamic system. If we find that this is the case, we can develop models of known equations to study relationships. Proving a system to be nonlinear is not easy, but it is possible. It requires patience and the willingness to try any idea, no matter how outlandish.

Empirical work requires numerical experiments. Reality rarely conforms to theory.

RECONSTRUCTING A PHASE SPACE

In Chapter 11, the phase space of the system was the starting point for all measurement. To construct the true phase space, we needed to know all of the variables relevant to the system. In real life, we usually begin with one known dynamic variable.

Packard et al. (1980) outline a simple method developed by David Ruelle for reconstructing a phase space from one dynamic variable. The method fills the other dimensions with lagged versions of one observable. Suppose time series A in Table 12.1 is an original time series. Time series B is A lagged one period, and time series C is A lagged two periods.

Why does this work? Packard et al. give a mathematical explanation; I will give an intuitive one. Nonlinear dynamic systems are interdependent simultaneous systems. Current values of each variable are transformations of past values. Recall equation (11.1) for the Henon map:

$$X_{t+1} = 1 + Y_t - a*X_t^2$$
$$Y_{t+1} = b*X_t$$

Both X_{t+1} and Y_{t+1} contain the previous value of X and Y. The exponent makes the system nonlinear, but the simultaneous nature of the equation makes it dynamic.

Examine the spreadsheet created in Chapter 11 for the Henon attractor. (If you erased it, see page 144 for how to recreate it.) In column C, place values of X lagged one iteration (in cell C1, place the value of cell A2), and copy these down to the bottom of column A. The values in columns B and C will be

Table 12.1   Phase Space Reconstruction with Logged Values

A	B	C
10	5	14
5	14	21
14	21	2
•	•	•
•	•	•
•	•	•

different. In the xy plot of the Henon attractor, replace column B with column C as the y values of the scatterplot. View the graph.

As Figure 12.1 shows, the result is a duplicate of the Henon map, rotated 90 degrees. If someone had given you the column A values only, without giving you equation (11.1) or telling you that it was the Henon map, you still could have produced a map of the Henon attractor. Ruelle has proven mathematically that this reconstructed phase space has the same fractal dimension and spectrum of Lyapunov exponents as the "true" phase space of two variables. The reconstructed phase space can be calculated with just one observable, and no equations of motion.

We knew the Henon attractor was two-dimensional, because we knew the equations of motion. Having a single observable, and no other information, is much more limiting. How do we know how many dimensions to use? We don't. How do we know what the appropriate time lag is? We don't. We must perform experiments to fix the data and reconstruct the phase space.

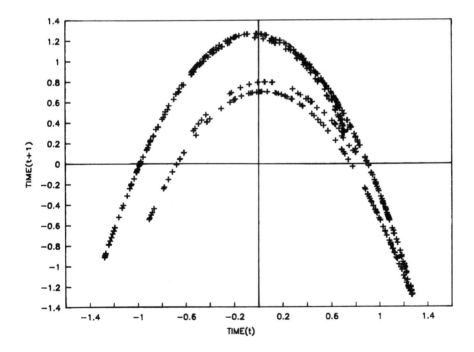

FIGURE 12.1 Henon attractor: Reconstructed phase portrait using X value only, lagged one iteration.

First, the dimensionality of the attractor does not change, as long as we embed it in a dimension higher than its own. A plane plotted in a three-dimensional space is still a two-dimensional object. A line plotted in a two- or three-dimensional space is still one-dimensional. An attractor, if it is truly a nonlinear dynamic system, will retain its dimension as we increase the embedding dimension beyond the fractal dimension. Why? Because the points are correlated and remain clumped together no matter what the dimensionality. In a true random walk, the points are uncorrelated and fill up whatever space they are placed in, because they move around at random.

Think of a random time series as a gas, and a correlated series as a solid. A gas placed in a larger space spreads itself out until it fills the larger volume. In a gas, the individual molecules are not correlated; they simply fly apart if placed in a larger space. The position of a solid's molecules are fixed, or correlated; its volume does not change. In a similar manner, a random time series fills its embedding dimension because its points are uncorrelated. A series of long-run correlations will bind together like a solid and retain its shape no matter what dimension it is placed in, as long as the embedding dimension is higher than the series dimension.

As long as we reconstruct the attractor in a dimension higher than the dimension of the "true" attractor, dimensionality is not a problem.

The appropriate time lag turns out to be a relatively simple problem as well. Wolf et al. (1985) have determined that a good estimate comes from the relation:

$$m*t = Q \qquad\qquad\qquad (12.1)$$

where m = embedding dimension
        t = time lag
       Q = mean orbital period

The time lag is the ratio of the mean orbital period and the embedding dimension, or the percent of an orbit within each dimension. This ratio ensures that the orbital period does not change in the higher dimension. For instance, if the period is 48 iterations, 2-points-lagged 24 iterations would be used in a two-dimensional space, and 3-points-lagged 16 observations would be used in a three-dimensional space. Either way, once all dimensions have been crossed in the reconstructed phase space, one orbit of 48 months has been used for the analysis.

The next question is: How do we know what the mean orbital period is? Rescaled range (R/S) analysis has already shown us, in Part Two, how to estimate the period of a time series as the length of time until observations become uncorrelated. If the mean orbital period is not readily apparent using R/S analysis, we probably do not have enough data.

Reconstructing a phase space becomes relatively easy. It is important to remember, however, that the above rule is a rule of thumb, not a law. In the experiments, variations of the rule can be tried, to see what works. Using this reconstructed phase space, we can calculate the fractal dimension and measure sensitive dependence on initial conditions.

THE FRACTAL DIMENSION

The fractal dimension of the phase space is a little different from the fractal dimension of a time series. A time series will have a dimension between 1 and 2, because we are dealing with a single variable. The phase space includes all of the variables in the system. Its dimensionality is dependent on the complexity of the system being studied.

As we stated in Chapter 6, the fractal dimension gives us important information about the underlying system. The next higher integer to the fractal dimension tells us the minimum number of dynamic variables we need, in order to model the dynamics of the system. It places a lower bound on the number of possible degrees of freedom. We also stated that the fractal dimension (D) could be approximated by covering the fractal with circles and taking the following measure:

$$D = \frac{\log N}{\log(1/R)}$$

where N = number of circles of diameter R
        R = diameter

This measure worked for a fractal embedded in two-dimensional space, like the Koch snowflake. For a higher-dimensional attractor, we need to use hyperspheres of dimensionality 3 or higher.

A similar, more practical method developed by Grassberger and Procaccia (1983) is the correlation dimension, an approximation of the fractal dimension that uses the correlation integral Cm(R). The correlation integral is the probability that a pair of points in the attractor is within a distance R of one another.

We count the number of pairs of points in the following manner. First, we reconstruct our time series as a phase space, starting with a low embedding dimension of m = 2, as outlined in the previous section. Then, starting with a small distance R, we calculate the correlation integral $C_m(R)$ for this distance, according to the following equation:

$$C_m(R) = (1/N^2)* \sum_{i,j = 1;\ i\ \text{not equal to}\ j}^{N} Z(R - |X_i - X_j|) \tag{12.2}$$

where $Z(x)$ = 1 if $R - |X_i - X_j| > 0$; 0 otherwise
$\quad\quad\quad$ N = number of observations
$\quad\quad\quad$ R = distance
$\quad\quad\quad$ C_m = correlation integral for dimension m

$Z(x)$ is called a Heaviside Function because it is valued at 0 if the distance between the two points, X_i and X_j, is less than R, and at 1 if the distance is greater. The correlation integral is the probability that two points chosen at random are less than R units apart. If we increase the value of R, C_m should increase at the rate of R^D. This gives the following relation:

$$C_m = R^D$$

or

$$\log(C_m) = D*\log(R) + \text{constant} \tag{12.3}$$

For a dimension (m), we can calculate C_m for increasing values of R. By finding the slope of a graph of the log (C_m) with the log (R), through a linear regression, we can estimate the correlation dimension (D) for the embedding dimension (m). By increasing m, D will eventually converge to its true value. This same result occurs as the embedding dimension (m) becomes greater than the fractal dimension (D), for the reasons stated earlier. Usually, convergence occurs when the embedding dimension is three or more integer levels above the fractal dimension. A fractal embedded in a higher dimension retains its true dimension because of the correlations between the points. Hence, the correlation dimension of Grassberger and Procaccia is a good estimate for the fractal dimension. The two are directly related, as Grassberger and Procaccia illustrate.

Appendix 4 provides a VBASIC program for calculating correlation integrals for a time series. Because it must calculate the distance of every point from every other point a number of times, this BASIC program is slow, but it works.

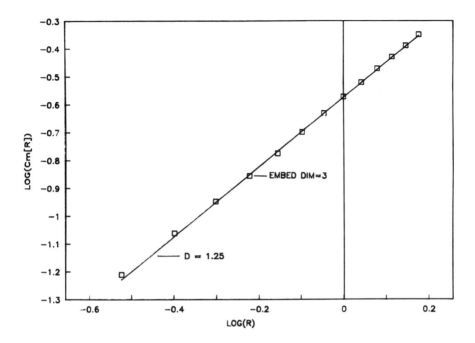

FIGURE 12.2 Correlation integral: Henon attractor; estimated fractal dimension of 1.25.

Figure 12.2 shows correlation integrals for the Henon attractor, using the reconstructed phase space from a variable that we examined earlier. The graph is a log/log plot between C_m and R for an embedding dimension of 3. A regression was run over the linear region in the plot. D is estimated as 1.25, versus 1.26 when measured using the box-counting method.

The Grassberger and Procaccia method offers a reliable, relatively simple method for estimating fractal dimensions when only one dynamical observable is known. This method is data-intensive and requires a fair amount of computer time, but the results are reliable.

LYAPUNOV EXPONENTS

We cannot calculate the full spectrum of Lyapunov exponents using experimental data, because the equations of motion are not known. However, a method has been developed by Wolf et al. (1985) for calculating the largest

Lyapunov exponent, L_1, using experimental data. L_1 greater than zero would signify that sensitive dependence on initial conditions exists, and that there is a strange attractor for the system. This method measures the divergence of nearby points in the reconstructed phase space, and indicates how the rate of divergence scales over fixed intervals of time.

First, two points are chosen, at least one mean orbital period apart. After a fixed interval of time (the "evolution period"), the distance between the two points is measured. If the distance becomes too long, a replacement point with an angle of orientation similar to that of the original point is found. The orientation between the new pair of points should be as close as possible to that of the original pair.

A replacement point is necessary so that we measure only the stretching or divergence in phase space. If the points are too far apart, they will fold into one another, which would measure convergence. Convergence is not part of L_1. Figure 12.3 is an artist's sketch of the algorithm. The formal equation of the algorithm is as follows:

$$L_1 = (1/t) * \sum_{j=1}^{m} \log_2 \left(\frac{L'(t_{j+1})}{L(t_j)} \right) \tag{12.4}$$

In theory, with an infinite amount of noise-free data, equation (12.4) is equivalent to equation (11.3). In reality, we must deal with a limited amount of noisy data, which means that the embedding dimension (m), the time lag (t), and the maximum and minimum allowable distances must be chosen with care.

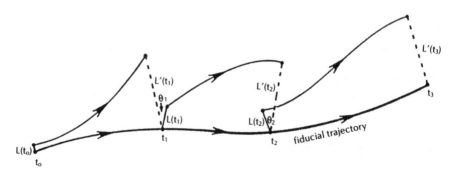

FIGURE 12.3 Artist's sketch of Wolf algorithm for estimating the largest Lyapunov exponent from a time series. (Reproduced with permission of *Financial Analysts Journal.*)

Luckily Wolf et al. give a number of "rules of thumb" in dealing with experimental data. First, the embedding dimension should be larger than the phase space of the underlying attractor—no surprise, given our earlier discussions relating to fractal dimensions. What is new, however, is that the embedding dimension should be more than just the next higher integer, because a rough surface often looks smoother at a higher dimension. The dimensionality should not be too high, however, or the data becomes too sparse when we reconstruct the phase space. The result would be too few candidates for replacement points.

The time lag can be calculated from equation (12.1). Wolf et al. state that the evolution length should not be greater than 10 percent of the attractor's length in phase space. Essentially, the maximum length should not be greater than 10 percent of the difference between the maximum and minimum values of the time series. Wolf et al. arrived at this number through experimentation, so there seems to be no quantifiable logic behind their guideline. I have found it to work in general. The evolution time should be long enough to measure stretching, but not folds. Again, there is no rule, but the shorter the better. The tradeoff is that, although short evolution periods require more calculations, they require fewer replacements and result in more stable convergence.

When completed, the calculation over a long time series should converge to a stable value of L_1. If stable convergence does not occur, the parameters have not been well chosen, or there are insufficient cycles of data for the analysis, or the system is not truly nonlinear.

The data requirements necessary for using the Wolf algorithm vary according to the complexity of the system. At a minimum, we need 10^D data points and $10^{(D-1)}$ orbital periods. Therefore, if the dimensionality of the attractor is 2, we need only 100 points of data; if it is 6, we need 1 million points. Determining the dimensionality is crucial, before Lyapunov exponent estimation can be attempted.

A BASIC program for calculating L_1 from a time series is supplied in Appendix 5.

Figure 12.4 shows the convergence of L_1 to 0.45 for the Henon attractors, which has been shown to have a Lyapunov spectrum of $(0.4, -1.6)$, using the equations of motion.

A final word is required about the nature of "experimental data" in investments and economics and in the physical sciences. In the physical sciences, experimental data are derived from a controlled experiment. In fluid convection, for instance, data are collected only when the temperature is high enough to induce a turbulent state. The data analysis determines whether the turbulent state is truly chaotic with a strange attractor, or merely random.

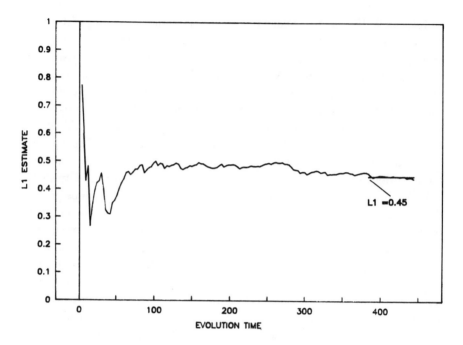

FIGURE 12.4 Convergence of the largest Lyapunov exponent: Henon attractor; estimated $L_1 = 0.45$.

In economic time series, such as stock market prices, stable and turbulent multiple states are mixed together. For scientists, this situation would be comparable to having the temperature in a fluid fluctuate out of the control of the experiment. The scientist would be measuring states where the fluid is simmering or boiling, with the level of the heat changing at random.

The largest Lyapunov exponent calculated over an economic time series will always be lower than the turbulent value, because the data will also include random walk phases and chaotic regimes. A positive value of L_1 is symptomatic of a chaotic system, but, using economic data, we may be calculating the *average* divergence, which would lower the value. The real value may never be known.

This possibility would not be present if the market were always in a critical state, or far from equilibrium. There is no proof of this statement, however, and it conflicts with the Coherent Market Hypothesis, which we will discuss in Chapter 14.

13
Dynamic Analysis of the Capital Markets

In this chapter we will show the results of applying the analysis described in Chapter 12 to a few capital markets. This methodology, still in its infancy, has given us new insights into the functioning of the markets, but it does not yet offer forecasting ability. It is hoped that as the dynamic nature of the capital markets becomes better understood, new capital market theories will evolve. In Chapter 14, we will examine two new approaches currently being used to illustrate that practical market analysis is possible at this early stage. Before we evaluate those new approaches, we will examine further evidence that the markets are nonlinear dynamic systems. Combined with the results of R/S analysis shown in Chapter 9, this evidence gives a convincing picture of the capital markets as nonlinear dynamic systems.

DETRENDING DATA

In the quantitative analysis of the capital markets, we have always used returns; that is, we have used the percent of change in prices instead of the prices themselves. Prices are inappropriate for linear regression because they are serially correlated. Each price is related to the price before it, in violation of the assumptions necessary for Gaussian, linear-based analysis to work. We attempt to forecast returns, but we should not forget that the objective is to forecast the behavior of prices. Returns simply make the data appropriate for linear analysis and for the independence requirements that go with it.

Percent of change may not be the appropriate time series for nonlinear dynamic systems analysis. It whitens the data by eliminating serial dependence which may be evidence through the noise of a nonlinear dependent structure. When scientists study turbulence in natural systems, the phase space consists of observed data, not the rates of change of the variables. Finance and economics have a long tradition of using returns. In studying markets as nonlinear dynamic systems, we need to set new standards. Returns are not an appropriate transformation of prices for research of nonlinear dynamic systems.

Previous studies of the equity market as a nonlinear dynamic system have centered on returns. The findings were not encouraging. Scheinkman and LeBaron (1986) found slim evidence of a nonlinear dynamic structure, including a positive Lyapunov exponent and a fractal dimension. However, they found that their daily stock return series of 5,000 observations had a fractal dimension of between 5 and 6. The fractal dimension is particularly disheartening because it implies a dynamic system of six variables. A six-variable system would be virtually impossible to deduce or model, because of its extreme complexity. The study is commendable, but its findings are questionable because its use of 5,000 daily returns may not have been adequate. As we said in Chapter 12, a minimum of 10^6 data points would be needed for a system with a fractal dimension of that magnitude. Combined with the high embedding dimension that Scheinkman and LeBaron used for the reconstructed phase space ($m = 14$), the data set may have been too sparse for reliable results. In addition, R/S analysis has already shown us that the mean orbital period of the U.S. equity market is four years. This means that 10 orbital periods, or 40 years' data (roughly, 10,400 daily returns), would be needed for this analysis. These authors did show that using returns complicates the problem dramatically, and that an alternative that does not use rates of change should be considered for analysis. In imitation of the natural sciences, it would seem reasonable to use the actual object under study—prices.

Using prices involves a different problem. The value of assets grows with the economy and inflation. Prices would continue to grow because of inflation alone, even if there were no real growth prospects. Prices can and will grow without bound. A phase space of nominal prices (that is, unadjusted for inflation) would simply spiral upward. Analyzing such a time series would be a useless exercise.

Therefore, we must detrend prices for economic growth, because the motion of prices concerns us, not inflationary growth. Chen (1988) detrended monetary aggregates by subtracting out the internal rate of growth. He found that the money supply, as measured by Divisia indices, did have a strange attractor with a fractal dimension of 1.24 and a cycle length of 42 months. The cycle length is similar to the T-Bond cycle we found in Chapter 9, using R/S analysis. Chen detrended according to the following formula:

$$S_i = \log_e(P_i) - (a*i + \text{constant}) \tag{13.1}$$

where S_i = detrended price series
P_i = original price series
i = observation number

By regressing the log of price against time and subtracting the two series, we obtain a new series detrended for exponential growth over time.

This method has appeal, but it assumes that economic growth occurs at a constant rate. Because we know that this is not true, it would be preferable to detrend through a variable more directly related to economic growth.

A preferred variable would be growth in GNP, but those data are available only quarterly. We need a series that is available at least monthly. The next choice would be a measure of inflation, because assets grow with inflation. By subtracting out inflation, we can obtain a series of real prices and attempt to model that motion.

We can modify equation (13.1) to the following inflation-adjusted form:

$$S_i = \log_e(P_i) - (a*\log_e(\text{CPI}) + \text{constant}) \tag{13.2}$$

where CPI = Consumer Price Index

In the United States, consumer price information has been recorded for many years. In other countries, this is not the case. Therefore, we will use equation (13.2) when inflation data are available, and equation (13.1) when they are not.

Inflation-detrended S&P 500 data from January 1950 to July 1989 are shown in Figure 13.1(a). The time series has a wave-like motion. The S&P 500 appears to be characterized by periods where it stays high, on an inflation-adjusted basis, or low. A two-dimensional phase space is shown in Figure 13.1(b). The time lag is 15 months. While plotting, the graph moves in a clockwise manner, like spiral chaos. It also has two "lobes." One, located in

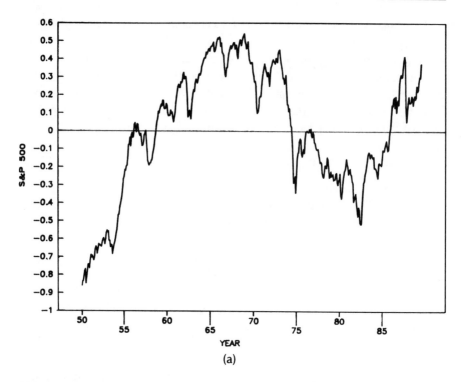

FIGURE 13.1a   S&P 500 detrended by CPI: January 1950–July 1989. Time series. (Reproduced with permission of *Financial Analysts Journal.*)

the second quadrant, covers periods when stock prices are higher than their inflation-adjusted values. The second lobe is located in the fourth quadrant, and corresponds to the below-inflation trend. These two regions are connected by arms that reflect the transition from one lobe to the other. Figure 13.1(c) is a three-dimensional phase space with a time lag of 16 months. The same basic structure—two attracting basins connected by arms—still exists.

Figures 13.2 through 13.4 continue this analysis for U.K., German, and Japanese markets detrended for growth (no inflation numbers were available). Morgan Stanley Capital International (MSCI) indices were used, from January 1959 to February 1990, in local currency. Each country has its own dynamics, but the graphs continue to plot in a clockwise manner.

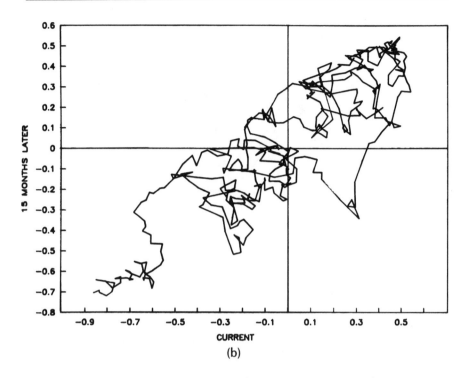

FIGURE 13.1b S&P 500 detrended by CPI: January 1950–July 1989. Two-dimensional phase portrait. (Reproduced with permission of *Financial Analysts Journal*.)

The U.K. market was dominated by a large drop in the early 1970s, when the British economy was falling apart and the pound was taking a beating. Aside from that period, the U.K. market tended to oscillate around its internal growth rate. The German market showed remarkable stability over the whole period.

The Japanese market had periods of stable growth followed by accelerated stock values and a collapse back to steady growth. This pattern of behavior occurred in the late 1950s, the late 1960s, and the mid- to late 1980s. As of 1990, the Japanese hypergrowth phase appeared to have once again corrected itself.

These phase space reconstructions are not "technical" graphs related to technical analysis (point and figure charts and the like). Instead, they are the basic data for finding the characteristics necessary to define the markets as

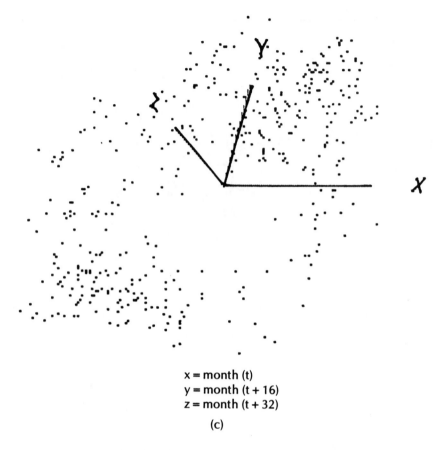

x = month (t)
y = month (t + 16)
z = month (t + 32)

(c)

FIGURE 13.1c   S&P 500 detrended by CPI: January 1950–July 1989. Three-dimensional phase portrait.

nonlinear dynamic systems. We can now use these detrended data to reconstruct phase spaces, in order to calculate fractal dimensions and Lyapunov exponents.

FRACTAL DIMENSIONS

We calculate the fractal dimensions in the manner discussed in Chapter 12. First, correlation integrals are calculated, according to equation (12.2), for increasing embedding dimensions. Then, regressions are run over the linear

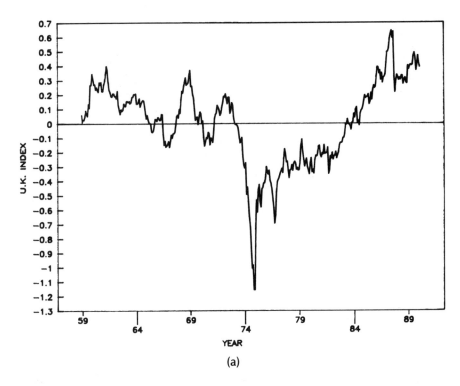

FIGURE 13.2a   MSCI U.K. equity index, loglinear detrended: January 1959–February 1990. Time series.

regions of the log/log plots. The fractal dimension should eventually converge to its true value as the embedding dimension is increased.

Figures 13.5 through 13.8 show correlation integral plots for the four markets. The linear regions in each plot can be used to run regressions. Figures 13.9 through 13.12 show the convergence of the fractal dimension. Table 13.1 summarizes the results.

The United States, the U.K., and Germany all have fractal dimensions between 2 and 3. This is good news, because it means that we should be able to model the dynamics of these markets with three variables. Again, we do not know what the three variables are, but plotting three variables is a solvable problem.

Japan is different. Its fractal dimension of 3.05 suggests that four variables are needed. The Japanese market is more complex than the other three markets.

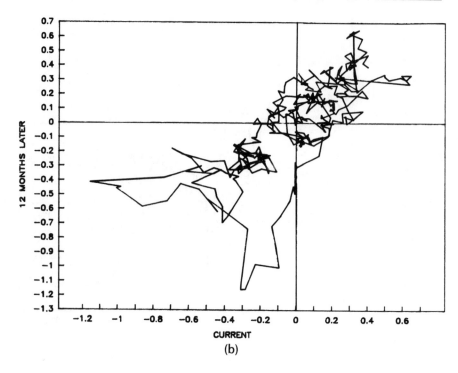

FIGURE 13.2b MSCI U.K. equity index, loglinear detrended: January 1959–February 1990. Two-dimensional phase portrait.

The high fractal dimension also suggests that we need more data for the analysis—1,000 points rather than 500. However, as we will see later, this is not so.

The actual analysis is quite convincing; it shows the stable convergence of fractal dimension estimates as predicted by theory. It is also encouraging

Table 13.1 Fractal Dimensions: Equity Indices

Index	Fractal Dimension
S&P 500	2.33
MSCI Japan	3.05
MSCI Germany	2.41
MSCI U.K.	2.94

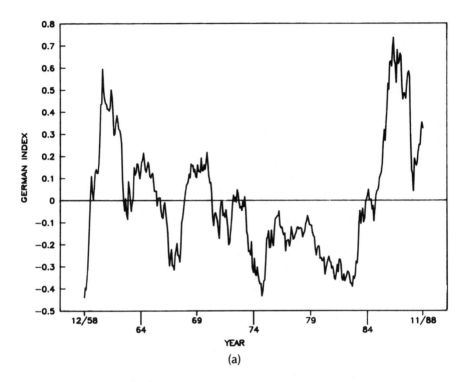

FIGURE 13.3a MSCI German equity index, loglinear detrended: January 1959–
February 1990. Time series.

because, with the exception of Japan, these are low-dimensional systems. As
such, they are solvable, and we can hope that they will be solved in the near
future.

LYAPUNOV EXPONENTS

Calculating Lyapunov exponents is time-consuming. Theoretically, the Lyapunov exponents remain constant, regardless of the parameters chosen to
measure them. Alas, real life once again makes this a less than precise process. Economic time series contain all the phases of the system, not just the
chaotic ones. Our parameters must be chosen to maximize the measurement
of the "stretching" of points in phase space while minimizing the "folding,"
or contractions, that can occur when market activity is truly random or when
market activity is low.

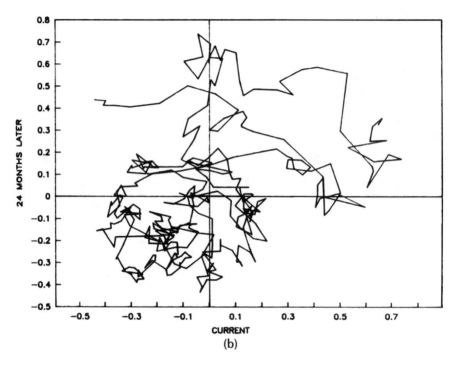

FIGURE 13.3b MSCI German equity index, loglinear detrended: January 1959–February 1990. Two-dimensional phase portrait.

The "rules of thumb" suggested by Wolf et al. are exactly that—suggestions. Actual results depend on many numerical experiments, with varying test parameters. If this sounds unscientific, it is. A fruitful area of research would be to develop a method less subject to experimentation that can be confused with "data mining," or torturing the data until it confesses. Fortunately, the effects of incorrect specification are easily seen and corrected, but the process is a long one.

The program supplied in Appendix 5 prints out each iteration. By examining each iteration, we can see whether a particular point in time causes the methodology to collapse.

For the S&P 500, the existence of the two "lobes" in the second and fourth quadrants (see Figure 13.1(b)) causes particular problems regarding replacement points. The Wolf algorithm works by starting with two nearby points (at least one mean orbital period apart) in the phase space, and following their evolution over time. If the points become too far apart, a replacement point is

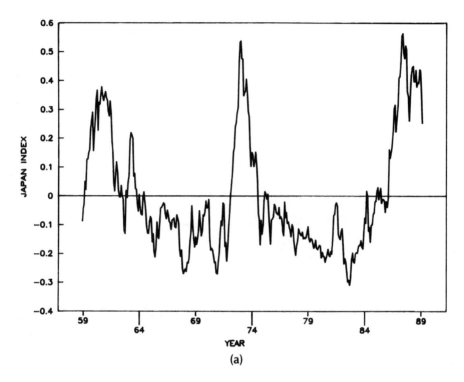

FIGURE 13.4a   MSCI Japanese equity index, loglinear detrended: January 1959–
February 1990. Time series.

found, to avoid folding. The largest Lyapunov exponents measures stretching,
or divergence, of points in phase space, not convergence. If one of the two
points leaves one lobe and travels to the other, an exceptional inflation in the
calculation of the Lyapunov exponent will occur.

A final point concerns the number of data points. Having more data points
for a short time period is not necessarily better than having fewer data points
over a longer time period. Unlike statistical analysis, having four years' daily
data (approximately 1,000 data points) is *not* better than 40 years' monthly
data, or 480 data points. As we shall see, having more data is not necessarily
better in chaos analysis.

Suppose we take a natural system, like the well-documented sunspot cycle
of 11 years, as an example. The Lyapunov exponent can be approximated as $\frac{1}{11}$
or .09 bit per year. If we increase the resolution to 11 years' daily data, or
3,872 days, the Lyapunov exponent will be $\frac{1}{3872}$ of .00002 bit per day. Either

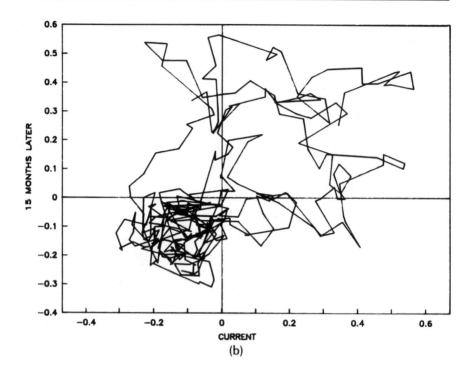

FIGURE 13.4b   MSCI Japanese equity index, loglinear detrended: January 1959–February 1990. Two-dimensional phase portrait.

way, the 11-year cycle asserts itself. Increasing the data points per cycle increases the computation time needed, without improving the accuracy of the result.

An additional problem with time series analysis, particularly with capital market returns, is noise. At higher resolution, such as daily returns, we are likely to have more random fluctuations than at lower resolutions. We can see why the Scheinkman and LeBaron (1989) study gave marginal results. It contained only five cycles of data at a high resolution, where, as we have seen from R/S analysis, there is a high level of noise and/or Markovian short-term dependence.

This view of data sufficiency is quite different from the one used by most statisticians. In standard statistics, the more data points the better, because the observations are assumed to be independent. Nonlinear dynamic systems are characterized by long memory processes; more time is needed, not more data. Wolf et al. supply another rule of thumb: approximately 10 cycles are necessary.

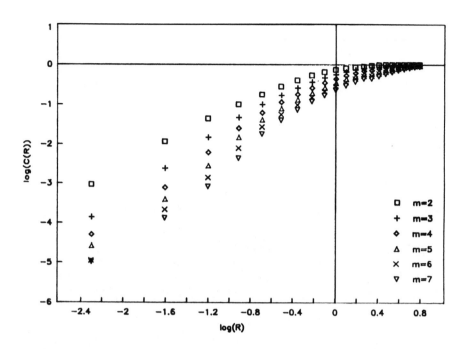

FIGURE 13.5 Correlation integrals: CPI detrended S&P 500. (Reproduced with permission of *Financial Analysts Journal*.)

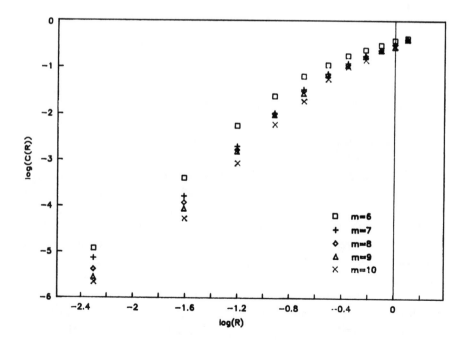

FIGURE 13.6 Correlation integrals: Loglinear detrended MSCI U.K. equity index.

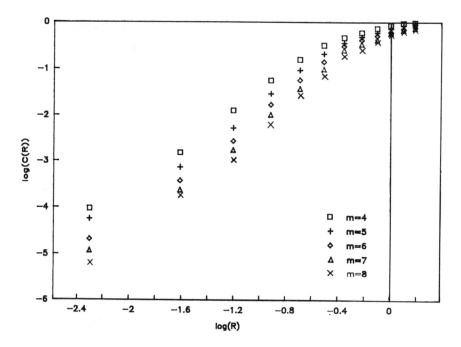

FIGURE 13.7   Correlation integrals: Loglinear detrended MSCI German equity index.

In Chapter 9, we found, using R/S analysis, that the S&P 500 had a long memory cycle of approximately four years. This cycle length was clear for all time increments of returns, which made it independent of the resolution of the data. We also found that the Hurst exponent for daily returns was 0.60, but it rose as we increased the increments of time used for the returns, and it stabilized at 0.80 for 30-day returns and higher. From this information, we can determine that daily data are much noisier than monthly data, because of the low Hurst exponent. Data increments monthly and higher have removed the noise, as shown by their stable Hurst exponents. Also, the structure of the long memory effect stabilized after we reached monthly increments. Because we have a four-year cycle, we should use 40 years' data in order to calculate the Lyapunov exponent.

Finally, we have to decide what resolution is important. Should we use monthly, quarterly, or semiannual data? Lower resolution decreases the computation time needed, but may not supply enough data points to find good

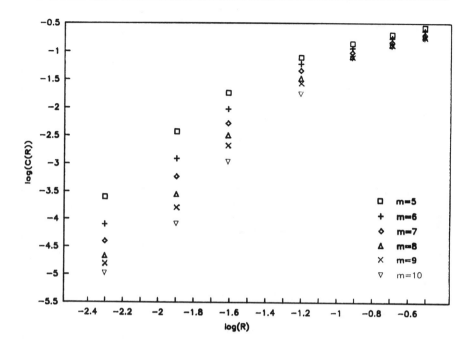

FIGURE 13.8 Correlation integrals: Loglinear detrended MSCI Japanese equity index.

replacement points. There must be a balance. This balance is usually found, unfortunately, through trial and error.

For evaluation of the S&P 500, monthly data supplied the lowest resolution and the most replacement candidates. Applying equation (12.4) to our detrended S&P 500 time series finally requires choosing the embedding dimension of the reconstructed phase space, an evolution time, and a maximum divergence of points before replacement.

Wolf et al. give additional rules of thumb for performing the final analysis, as we discussed in Chapter 12. First, the embedding dimension should be higher than the fractal dimension, because a rough surface often looks smoother when placed in a higher dimension. We have already found the fractal dimension of the S&P 500 to be 2.33; the embedding dimension should be 3 or higher. The time lag can be calculated from equation (12.1). Because we have a cycle of about 48 months, an embedding dimension of 3 would require a time lag of 16 months. The maximum length of growth between the two points should be no

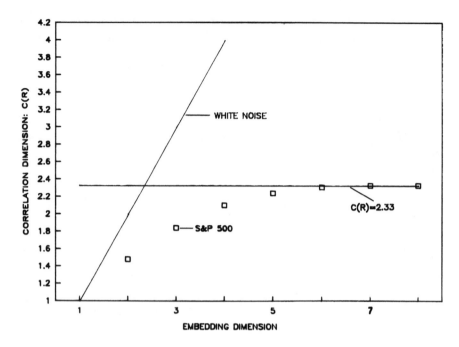

FIGURE 13.9 Convergence of the fractal dimension: CPI detrended S&P 500; D = 2.33. (Reproduced with permission of *Financial Analysts Journal.*)

more than 10 percent of the extent of the attractor. Finally, the evolution time should be long enough to measure stretching without including folds.

Once the calculation is done, it should converge to a stable value of the largest Lyapunov exponent, L_1. If convergence does not occur, then the specifications need to be redone, or the system is not chaotic.

Stable convergence was found for the detrended S&P 500 data series (monthly data from January 1950 to July 1990), using an embedding dimension of 4, a time lag of 12 months, and an evolution time of six months. Figure 13.13 shows stable convergence of L_1 to a value of 0.0241 bit/month.

This means that we lose predictive power at the rate of 0.0241 bit/month. If we knew exactly what next month's return would be (if we could measure initial conditions to one bit of precision), we would still lose all predictive power after 1/0.0241, or 42 months' time. This 42-month cycle is roughly equal to the 1,000-day trading cycle obtained using R/S analysis in Chapter 8 confirming that the cycle length for the S&P 500 is approximately four years.

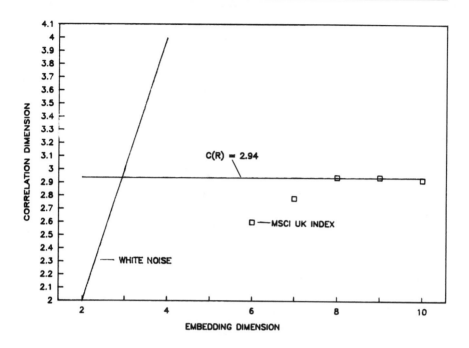

FIGURE 13.10   Convergence of the fractal dimension: Loglinear detrended MSCI U.K. equity index; D = 2.94.

To perform an additional test, I calculated the Lyapunov exponent for the 90-day trading data used in Chapter 9, detrended for internal growth from equation (13.1). These data extended from January 1928 to June 1990, or over 60 years. Figure 13.14 shows that stable convergence was attained at 0.09883 bit per 90-day period. The cycle length is again 1/0.09883, or about ten 90-day periods—roughly, four years.

Tests of the three international indices yielded encouraging but less conclusive results for Germany. The reason is, once again, data insufficiency. The MSCI data covered the 41-year period from January 1959 to February 1990. Germany has been shown, from R/S analysis, to have a cycle length of about 60 months. Therefore, our rule of thumb says that we should have about 50 years' data, and we fall short of that amount. Japan exactly meets it requirement of 40 years, and the U.K. is well over its requirement of 30 years.

As a result, the U.K. gives the smoothest convergence. L_1 is estimated to be 0.028 bit/month, as shown in Figure 13.15. The inverse is about 36 months. Japan also converges, though more erratically, to L_1 = 0.0228, as shown in

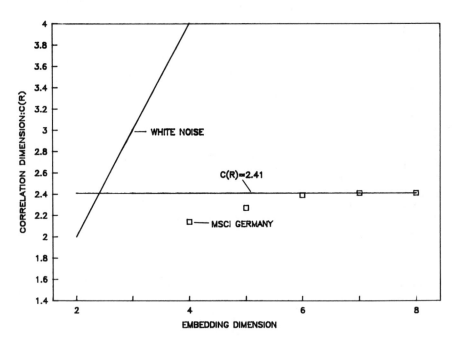

FIGURE 13.11   Convergence of the fractal dimension: Loglinear detrended MSCI
German equity index; D = 2.41.

Figure 13.16. Again, the inverse of the largest Lyapunov exponent implies a
cycle of 44 months, similar to the cycle derived using R/S analysis. The German market gives L_1 = 0.0168 bit/month, with a resulting decorrelation time
of 60 months. However, the convergence, as shown in Figure 13.17, is less
convincing, and more data appear to be necessary for stable convergence.

This shows, again, that the number of points is not as important as the number of cycles, when running this type of analysis. We must reorient our think-
ing when using non-Gaussian data and methods.

IMPLICATIONS

The long memory effect in equity prices has now been confirmed by two separate types of nonlinear analysis. R/S analysis on monthly S&P 500 stock returns found a biased random walk with a memory length of about four years.
The Lyapunov exponent for monthly inflation-detrended S&P 500 prices

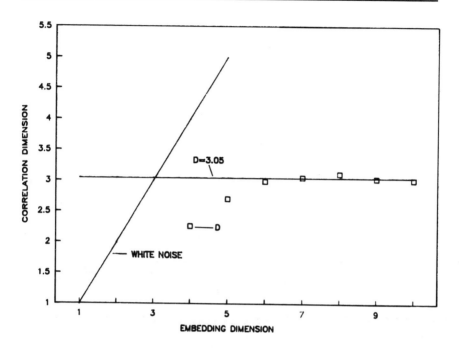

FIGURE 13.12 Convergence of the fractal dimension: Loglinear detrended MSCI Japanese equity index; D = 3.05.

found a 42-month cycle. A similar relationship was found for the U.K., Japan, and Germany, using MSCI equity index numbers.

The Lyapunov exponent can be interpreted in two ways. We lose predictive power at the rate of 0.0241 bit/month in the United States. If we could measure initial conditions to one bit of precision, we would lose all predictive power after 42 months. That is the "forward looking" interpretation from Chapter 12. But there is also the "backward looking" interpretation. The system loses all memory of initial conditions after 42 months. On the average, market activities 42 months apart (or longer) are no longer related or correlated. This interpretation of the Lyapunov exponent is similar to the decorrelation time, or cycle, found in R/S analysis. In R/S analysis, the crossover to random walk behavior at four years implies that the long memory effect dissipates after four years, or returns become independent. The similarities in concept and result are striking.

It is important to note that the cycle length is nonperiodic. It is an average cycle length that will not be visible to standard cyclical analysis, like spectral

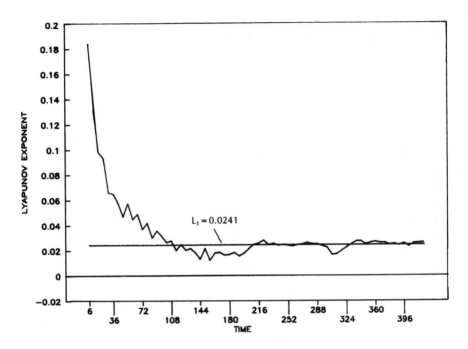

FIGURE 13.13 Convergence of the largest Lyapunov exponent: CPI detrended S&P 500, monthly returns; $L_1 = 0.0241$ bit/month.

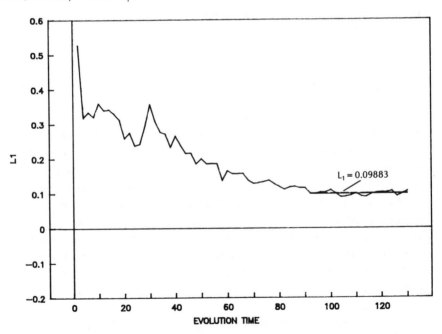

FIGURE 13.14 Convergence of the largest Lyapunov exponent: CPI detrended S&P 500, 90-day returns; $L_1 = 0.09883$ bit/90 days.

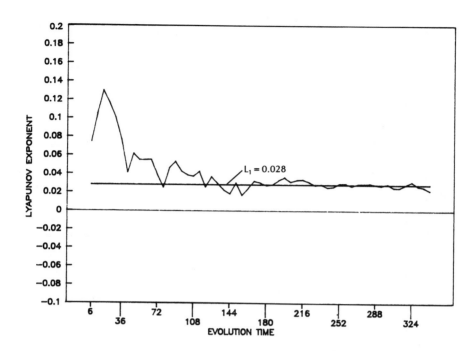

FIGURE 13.15 Convergence of the largest Lyapunov exponent: Loglinear detrended MSCI U.K. equity index; $L_1 = 0.028$ bit/month.

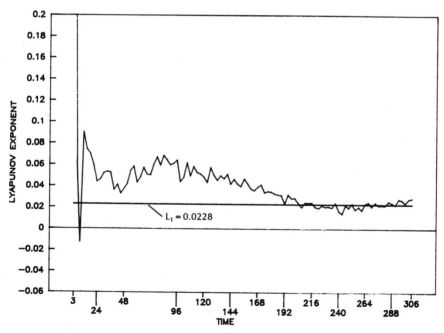

FIGURE 13.16 Convergence of the largest Lyapunov exponent: Loglinear detrended MSCI Japanese equity index; $L_1 = 0.0228$ bit/month.

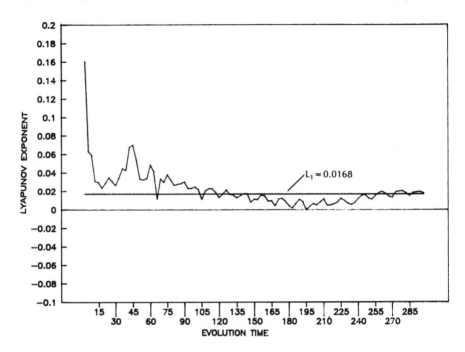

FIGURE 13.17 Convergence of the largest Lyapunov exponent: Loglinear detrended MSCI German equity index; $L_1 = 0.0168$ bit/month.

analysis, because it does not have a characteristic scale. It is also not a "charted" or "peak to trough" cycle in prices, so dear to the heart of technical analysts. It is a statistical cycle; it measures how information impacts the market, and how memory of those events affects future behavior of the markets.

SCRAMBLING TEST

In Part Two, we scrambled time series data and reran R/S analysis to test whether a long memory effect was present. This test was based on a similar test of correlation dimension developed by Scheinkman and LeBaron. As a final confirmation of the results already shown in this chapter, I applied the scrambling test to all detrended time series. If the series is not part of a chaotic attractor, the correlation dimension should not change. If, however, there is a strange attractor present, then scrambling the data should destroy the structure of the attractor, and the correlation dimension should rise. In all cases, the fractal dimension rose, showing that scrambling had a material effect on the analysis. Figures 13.18 and 13.19 show results of the scrambling test for the U.S. and German equity markets, for an embedding dimension of 6. In the unscrambled tests, the correlation dimension had been achieved for this embedding dimension. In both cases, the correlation dimension rose to about 4. The same was true for the other two markets. Thus, we can reject the null hypothesis that there is no chaotic system present.

WHAT DOES THIS MEAN?

In this chapter we have tested the S&P 500 for the two characteristics of a chaotic system: existence of a fractal dimension, and evidence of sensitive dependence on initial conditions.

We found that the S&P 500 has a fractal dimension of approximately 2.33. This means that we should be able to model the motion of the system with a minimum of three dynamic variables. We also found that the market has a

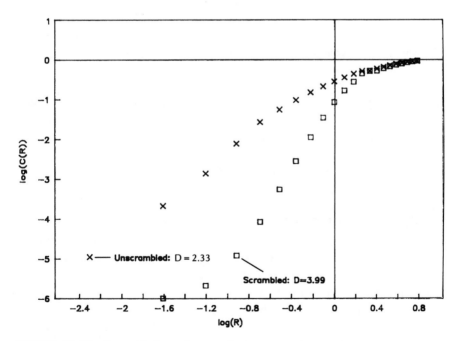

FIGURE 13.18 Scrambled test for correlation integrals: CPI detrended S&P 500; unscrambled D = 2.33, scrambled D = 3.99.

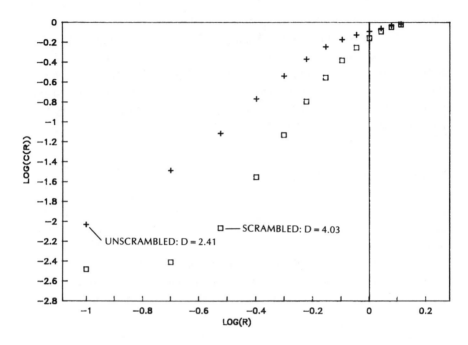

FIGURE 13.19 Scrambled test for correlation integrals: Loglinear detrended MSCI German index; unscrambled D = 2.41; scrambled D = 4.03.

positive Lyapunov exponent, implying that its cycle is about 42 months, similar to the four-year cycle found using R/S analysis in Chapter 8. A similar relationship was found for the U.K., German, and Japanese equity markets.

Combined with R/S analysis we now have strong evidence that the world equity market is a nonlinear dynamic system. In the end we are left asking, what does this mean? Are we close to determining *the* market equation (something like the Lorenz attractor)?

In physical models, like the Lorenz attractor, there are specific measurable variables that define their state. For many nonlinear systems these variables include concepts such as temperature, air pressure, or density. Such factors summarize how the system under study reacts to other, outside forces. Temperature, after all, does not come into being on its own. Instead it is a measurement of the impact of other forces that produce heat. The physical sciences are lucky. They can measure the impact of these exogenous variables. For markets we face a different environment. The markets, after all, are affected by less measurable forces. Therefore, the three dynamic variables implied by a fractal dimension of 2.33 for the U.S. stock market will not be easily identifiable, *local factors* such as P/E or GNP. Instead, the driving forces in the markets are more likely to be *global characteristics* that are a combination of the fundamental/technical schools of thought. My own conviction is that the stretching in phase space is caused by market sentiment, or technical factors. The folding, which brings prices back into the attractor is caused by valuation, or fundamental factors. Thus, expectation (or sentiment) is the "heat" behind the market, while value defines the limit of the attractor. The third factor, which would be a form of fluid density, could be market liquidity. Liquidity, after all, is the reason that markets exist.

Note that the field has tried to measure these factors from the beginning, yet no foolproof method has ever been found. Why? The market is a complex dynamical system, similar to an ecosystem. It evolves to ensure its own survival. If any one set of factors could define the market, one investor, like a parasite invading an organism, could destroy the market by cornering the world's wealth. Thus, the market evolves. Cycles come and go, but each market cycle is different in detail, though similar in its global characteristics. That is, each bull and bear market consists of rising and falling prices, during rising and falling business cycles. However, the causes or circumstances around each cycle are never exactly the same. Like the Sierpinski triangle, they are locally random and globally deterministic.

It is also important to point out that the market attractor appears to be tied to the business cycle, not to trading per se. This is due to the similarity in the cycles found with R/S analysis of economic indicators. While the market is made up of many traders, in the aggregate it is a long-term economic entity. Viewing it as a large number of short-term traders is like viewing a complex organism as a collection of cells. Understanding how a cell works will not explain how the organism as a whole functions. In this context, the low-dimensional attractor that has been identified in this chapter will not help the day-trader. It will only help the investor with a long-term investment horizon. Even the long-term investor cannot depend on a *regular* four-year cycle.

What does this mean for investors? It means that there will always be opportunity for profit, but no single simple system for doing so. Systems that depend on a repeating set of specific rules are doomed to eventually fail. Such systems either are not adaptable, or do not measure the global characteristics of the market.

So, despite the fact that we have found evidence of a low-dimensional attractor for the stock market, it does not mean that it will be easier for anyone to develop *the* system. By understanding the markets we should be able to develop consistent investment disciplines that accumulate wealth over the long term. Short-term gains are lucky, educated guesses usually offset later by "bad luck."

PART FOUR
LIVING WITH COMPLEXITY

Part Four deals with developments in applying nonlinear ideas as ways to cope with complexity. It is not, however, a cookbook on making a fortune in the markets. Readers who have gotten this far in the text can see that I am not saying that we now have the potential to unleash the inner workings of the markets. Instead, we have learned that markets are evolving complex systems. Markets exists in this form for one purpose: survival. Like other adaptive complex systems, the market evolves to ensure its survival. In the case of the markets, survival ensures that no one can corner the world's wealth. If that were done, the need for the market would cease to exist. The markets exist to give us liquidity in which to trade, not to give us a fair price, and certainly not to make any one trading system work all the time.

What we have examined so far is *science,* that is, analysis with the purpose of understanding. It is not *technology,* or the practical application of science. In this section we will examine some attempts at technology that have come to the forefront since the first edition of this book. Nonlinear technology has largely been centered on artificial intelligence (AI). It has become clearer to cognitive scientists that human intelligence and decision making are nonlinear processes. So AI is the attempt to create models that mimic the human brain. Much of what follows is closely tied to AI.

Chapter 14 is not tied to AI. It is the nonlinear statistical model of Vaga (1991). This model, however, is an attempt to install the psychology of crowds upon markets in a quantitative way. Chapter 15 covers the relationship between two fields of study. *Behavioral finance* examines empirically the way investors make decisions. *Fuzzy logic* mathematically models the way people make decisions. The two fields complement each other, but there has been no apparent attempt to formally link them. Chapter 15 attempts to do that. Chapter 16 examines a number of practitioners who are applying nonlinear concepts to actual investment strategies.

14
The Coherent Market Hypothesis

VAGA'S NONLINEAR STATISTICAL MODEL

Vaga (1991) has developed a unique approach. His Coherent Market Hypothesis (CMH) is a nonlinear *statistical* model, as opposed to the nonlinear deterministic models we discussed in Chapters 11, 12, and 13. It is related to the Fractal Hypothesis of Part Two, but it is a dynamic statistical model. Its basic premise is that the probability distribution of the market changes over time, based on:

- The fundamental, or economic, environment, and
- The amount of sentiment bias, or the level of "groupthink," that exists in the market.

As combinations of these two factors change, the state of the market changes. The phase transitions that occur are changes in the shape of the probability density function.

The market can attain four distinct phases:

1. *Random walk.* According to Vaga, true random walk states do exist: investors act independently of one another, and information is quickly reflected in prices.

2. *Transition markets.* As the level of "groupthink" rises, biases in investor sentiment can cause the impact of information to extend for long periods of time.

3. *Chaotic markets.* Investor sentiment is highly conducive to groupthink, but fundamentals are neutral, or uncertain. Wide swings in group sentiment can result.

4. *Coherent markets.* Strong positive (negative) fundamentals combined with strong investor sentiment can result in coherent markets, where the trend can be strongly positive (negative) and risk is low (high).

These states are a result of the nonlinear statistical model, which we will now discuss.

COHERENT SYSTEMS

Coherent behavioral models have already been developed for natural systems that have a large number of degrees of freedom, or influences, that can be combined into "order parameters." An order parameter summarizes the external influences on the system. Fluctuations in the order parameter determine the state of the system. Temperature is an example of an order parameter. Temperature summarizes all the atmospheric variables that are relevant to some weather systems, without examining them directly or even knowing what they are. Order parameters are different from the control parameters we discussed in Chapter 11. The control parameters reflect the influence of the order parameters. In equations of motion, control parameters are the coefficients and order parameters are the variables.

Vaga found a Theory of Social Imitation, developed by Callan and Shapiro (1974) to model the polarization of public opinion. Their model was, in turn, developed from the Ising model of coherent molecular behavior in a magnetized bar of iron.

The Ising model said that the level of the magnetic field of a bar of iron depends on the coupling between adjacent molecules and an external field factor. In a bar of iron, magnetization depends on whether the molecules have a positive or negative spin, that is, on whether the molecules are pointing "up" or "down."

If a bar of iron is hot, the molecules are not coupled with one another. The number of molecules pointing up or down will fluctuate randomly over time, and the average difference between the number of molecules pointing up or down will be zero. This will result in a normal probability distribution, as is usual with random behavior.

As the temperature is lowered, the relationship between adjacent molecules increases. When it passes a critical level, this interaction begins to dominate the random thermal forces. A group of molecules forming a positive-oriented cluster will cause adjacent molecules to also become positive. Soon, large clusters, both positive and negative, will form, causing long-lasting magnetic field fluctuations. The average will still be zero, but the fluctuations from the mean can become large and will last for long periods. In the absence of an external bias, the mean will remain zero, however.

An external magnetic field applied at this time will result in most of the clusters aligning in one direction. Random thermal forces, or fluctuations in temperature, will still have some short-term impact, but, as long as the external field remains in place and the temperature remains below its critical level, most of the molecules will remain aligned toward the external force.

The relationship between this phenomenon and the biased random walk of fractal statistics is readily apparent. In fractal statistics, the level of the Hurst exponent governs the coherence of the trends and the impact of random noise on the system. In the Ising model, the coherence between the individual molecules depends on the temperature level and on the existence of external influences that mitigate the impact of noise, or random thermal forces. The fractal model says that this process depends on one variable, the fractal dimension. The Ising model includes two parameters, internal clustering and external forces. The Ising model is a richer model; nonetheless, it appears to measure the same thing as the fractal model. In essence, the Ising model is concerned with systems in which there can be correlations between the components of the system, but the relationship can also be influenced by outside forces. This coupling of the level of internal correlation and the strength of outside influences determines the state of the system.

THE THEORY OF SOCIAL IMITATION

Callan and Shapiro (1974) applied the Ising model to the social sciences. They postulated that the interaction of social groups, like birds flying in flocks and fish swimming in schools, could be represented using the Ising model. Their main purpose was to examine how people follow the dictates of fashions and fads. They called this the Theory of Social Imitation.

The Theory of Social Imitation assumes that there is a strong similarity between the behavior of individuals and the behavior of the molecules in a magnetized bar of iron. The positive and negative polarization of the iron molecules is translated into positive and negative sentiment. At times, there is no consensus of public opinion, and individuals react independently of one another. At other times, there can be strong coherent sentiment. A third possibility is that public opinion polarizes into two opposing camps, resulting in a chaotic social environment.

Vaga has translated the "public opinion" of Callan and Shapiro into "market sentiment." The external force, which was an external magnetic force in the Ising model, becomes the economic environment. The risk/return tradeoff of the market becomes a combination of market sentiment and the fundamental environment. Once again, we have a combination of the points of view of technical and fundamental analysts.

THE COHERENT MARKET HYPOTHESIS

The probability density function, as developed by Callan and Shapiro and restated by Vaga, is the following, somewhat complicated formula:

$$f(q) = c^{-1}*Q(q)*\exp(2*\int_{-1/2}^{q}(K(y)/Q(y))dy) \tag{14.1}$$

where $f(q)$ = probability of an annualized return, q
$K(q)$ = $\sinh(k*q + h) - 2*q*\cosh(k*q + h)$
$Q(q)$ = $(1/n)*(\cosh(k*q + h) - 2*q*\sinh(k*q + h))$
n = number of degrees of freedom
k = degree of crowd behavior
h = fundamental bias
c^{-1} = $\int_{-1/2}^{1/2} Q^{-1}(q)*\exp(2\int_{-1/2}^{q}(K(y)/Q(y))dy)dq$

This formidable formula can be solved numerically, using a computer. Its solutions depend on the level of crowd behavior (k), the degree of fundamental bias (h), and the number of degrees of freedom (or number of market participants) (n). These are the order parameters of the system.

Figure 14.1, reproduced from Vaga (1991), shows how varying the control parameters changes the shape of the probability density function of equation (14.1). The right-hand scale reflects the density function. The left-hand scale

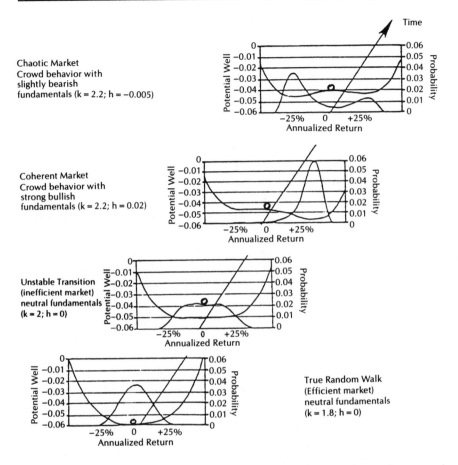

FIGURE 14.1   Coherent Market Hypothesis: Transition from random walk to crowd behavior. (Reproduced with permission of *Financial Analysts Journal.*)

refers to the "potential well," which looks like a flattened mirror image of the probability function.

The potential well reflects the possible effects of random forces on a particle caught in the well. The concept is borrowed from "catastrophe theory," a subset of chaos theory. The circle represents the particle in a two-dimensional environment, where a force can push it from the right (negative information, or bad news), or left (positive information, or good news).

At the bottom of Figure 14.1, we see that setting k = 1.8 and h = 0 transforms equation (14.1) into the normal distribution, reflecting a true random walk state. The potential well is a symmetric bowl shape. Random forces pushing the particle are quickly damped, so the particle returns to zero. In other words, information is quickly discounted by the market.

As k approaches 2, with h remaining at zero, the density function widens and becomes flatter, and we achieve the next higher graph, labeled "Unstable Transition." The potential well has flattened. If the particle is pushed in one direction, it is likely to stay there until a new force pushes it again. Information is undamped, and trends persist until new information changes them. Results from R/S analysis in Chapter 9 seem to confirm that this is the most common state of the markets.

As k becomes greater than 2 (its critical level), the probability function develops a double bottom. This is a bifurcation of the probability density function. If h remains at zero, reflecting the lack of a fundamental bias, we have a very unstable system. The particle sits on a cusp in its potential well. Information from the right or the left can use drastic changes. This would be a classic chaotic market: a high level of crowd behavior, but no fundamental information to firmly place the bias in either positive or negative territory. Rumors or misinterpreted information can cause panics, as investors watch each other's behavior, hoping to outguess one another. Once movement begins, it can rapidly stampede, or opposite information can cause wide swings in the other direction. A recent example of a chaotic market was stock market behavior on January 9, 1991, when Secretary of State James Baker met with Iraqi Foreign Minister Aziz to discuss the positions of the two countries regarding the Iraqi invasion of Kuwait. In an environment where a possible political event, in this case, an impending war, could drastically change the economic environment, economic news has a much lower weight in investors' minds than usual. Early in the day, the fact that the meeting was lasting longer than expected caused investors to speculate that a peace treaty was possible. The Dow Jones Industrials soared 40 points. When the meeting was over and both sides reported no progress, the Dow immediately reversed and closed down 39 points on the day. That day's roller-coaster trading had little to do with fundamental information. It was pure crowd behavior.

However, a shift in the fundamental environment will shift the density function to strongly negative or strongly positive territory. Increasing h to +0.02 results in a coherent bull market. The density function is drastically skewed to the right but retains a long negative tail, showing that losses are still possible, even if the probabilities are quite small. The potential well shows a dip into positive territory with a flat well on the negative side. Negative information would have a smaller effect in this environment than positive information of the same magnitude. The long negative tail remains, however, showing that enough negative information can still cause losses. However, in coherent bull markets, the risk of loss is low, and overall volatility declines. This inverts the CAPM risk/return tradeoff. Examples of coherent bull markets include January 1975 and August 1982.

Coherent bear markets are also likely if h becomes negative. Vaga feels that coherent bear markets are rare, but the bear market of 1973–1974 is a recent example. The crash of October 1987 and the "October Massacre" of 1978 (which prompted Vaga's studies) were chaotic markets, not coherent bear markets.

CONTROL PARAMETERS

We have seen that the Ising model depends on three control parameters, which Vaga has defined in the Coherent Market Hypothesis in the following manner:

1. k = market sentiment; can range from 1.8 (random), to 2.0 (unstable transition); to 2.2 (crowd behavior).
2. h = fundamental environment; can range from −0.02 (bearish), to 0.0 (neutral), to +0.02 (bullish).
3. n = number of degrees of freedom or number of market participants.

k and h assumed to vary; n is fixed. For his purposes, Vaga assumes that n = 186 (the number of industry groups). Although this seems a bit of a simplification, n is a constant. Assuming n = 186, or some other number, is relatively unimportant.

k and h, on the other hand, are very important. How do we estimate their values? Standard estimation techniques are totally inadequate, because the dynamic nature of the CMH is what makes it unique. However, if we cannot estimate k and h, how can we make this very appealing theory useful?

VAGA'S IMPLEMENTATION

Vaga feels that we can never know exactly what k and h are, so knowing whether they are positive, negative, or neutral is good enough. He examines a number of sentiment indicators and decides which of the three possible states of k are currently reflected in the marketplace.

For fundamentals, he examines Fed policy to see whether h should be negative (reflecting a tight monetary environment), neutral, or stimulative. He follows some simple rules in setting the levels. A positive fundamental environment can occur when the Fed eases monetary policy twice in six months; a negative environment can arise from two tightening actions within six months.

Vaga uses sentiment signals based on up/down volume and advancing/declining issue ratio extremes for the New York Stock Exchange. He defines a buy signal as two or more 1:9 downside extremes followed by a 9:1 upside reversal. On average, Vaga says, the market returns +23.6 percent for the six months after such a buy signal. A sell signal would be three or more 1:9 downside extremes. In the six months following such a sell signal, the return of the S&P 500 averages −21.87 percent. (The period studied was January 1962 to December 1983.) Each signal lasts for six months unless a contrary signal arrives sooner.

Using these indicators, Vaga has tested his theory since April 1983 by comparing a buy and hold strategy with an S&P 500 index fund with a stock/cash switching scheme adding a money market fund. Through October 31, 1989, Vaga's strategy had produced an annualized return of 17.67 percent with an annualized risk of 5.1. By contrast, the buy and hold strategy produced 16.0 percent in annualized return with 8.1 percent annualized risk. In this limited time frame, Vaga has produced an efficient return.

CRITIQUE OF THE COHERENT MARKET HYPOTHESIS

The CMH is a very appealing model because it is a nonlinear statistical theory. We have already seen evidence in Chapter 13 that the markets are chaotic, with sensitive dependence on initial conditions. Forecasting becomes difficult, and a statistical description becomes even more necessary. This statistical description cannot be based on a Gaussian distribution and random walks. The CMH offers a rich theoretical framework for assessing market risk and how it changes over time in response to fundamental and technical factors.

However, the empirical evidence supporting the CMH is weak as of this time. Vaga's investment strategy experience is rather short and basically covers the bull market phase since 1982, including the crash of 1987. Primary supporting evidence comes from the R/S analysis of Chapter 9. The Fractal Hypothesis implies that the market is primarily in the unstable transition phase, when we have an inefficient market; it does not lend support to coherent phases or random walk phases. However, R/S analysis finds the average state of the market which, according to the CMH, may well be the unstable transition phase.

The lack of empirical evidence does not deny the validity of the theory. Although it has not yet been widely studied, the theory seems to fit in with experience. The market environment does seem different at different times. Further empirical study is essential and, I believe, will be done in the future.

15
Fractional Truth: Fuzzy Logic and Behavioral Finance

Complex objects and situations are all around us. We recognize the qualitative aspects of complex objects without being able to precisely measure them. Trees, handwriting, and chairs are all objects that are individual, yet have global characteristics. Complexity assures that they are different in detail while similar in concept. That is, they are locally random and globally deterministic. Like the Sierpinski Triangle, they are also fractal. Decision making depends on being able to classify these complex objects according to their global characteristics. Is that a bear we see? If so, what should we do? Are we in a bear market? If so, what should we do? As we know, each bear and each bear market is different, but if we recognize the global characteristics we can make a decision, that is, run or sell.

A great deal of research on complex decision making has been done in two separate areas: fuzzy logic, and behavioral psychology. In behavioral psychology (and its subset behavioral finance), we have a wealth of empirical evidence that people make decisions based on rules of thumb called *heuristics*. However, behavioralists have no mathematical model that would allow us to use this knowledge. In addition, the behavioralists claim that individuals make suboptimal decisions when comparing what people actually do with what they should do based on good Baysian analysis. In fuzzy logic, we have, ironically, a rigorous branch of mathematics that has been able to quantitatively formulate decision making, but there is no empirical evidence to support its validity as a cognitive model. There is also little work distinguishing between optimal fuzzy decisions and optimal probabilistic ones. The two groups do not seem to communicate with each other. Each group also has different ideas of what is rational.

In this chapter, we will examine each school of thought and compare their similarities. We will conclude with an examination of how this complex behavior can result in the fractal statistics that we have observed. We cannot delve into these topics in great detail here. Those interested should consult the bibliographical references that will be given throughout the text.

FUZZY LOGIC

Fuzzy logic recognizes that humans classify objects in order to recognize them. Likewise, humans often classify situations according to past experience in order to make decisions. Since the nineteenth century, it was assumed that people should make decisions in a *rational* manner. That is, we should assess the probabilities surrounding the outcome of each situation. Unfortunately, our brains are too limited to achieve this ideal of rational thought. That is why there was much excitement when the computer was developed. Here was a machine that could make a "rational" assessment when enough information was presented. It was assumed that this would be true even for the early computer when limited problems were used.

Early on, computers were applied to chess problems. In the early pre–Artificial Intelligence (AI) days, computers went through *all* the possibilities and selected the best move based on statistical assumptions. Since humans could not calculate all the possible combinations (let alone evaluate the probabilities of success), it was assumed that no human could beat a computer at chess. Yet, no computer using this "brute force" method could achieve Grand Master status. Human Grand Masters consistently won. While Grand Masters did not have the raw calculating power of the computer, they did have an interesting capability of their own. Grand Masters had played and studied thousands of games. While playing, they would typically recognize the similarity between the current stage of a game and other games they knew. Of course, the other games would not be identical to the current game, but they would be *similar* enough to learn from. This would limit their "search" to the games that had favorable outcomes. By adapting the strategy from those games to the current situation, a Grand Master could formulate a new course of action. The "brute force" computer programs could not learn from the past and adapt. Thus, they were always at a disadvantage.

The Grand Masters use similarity with the past to make their judgment. Note that they do not copy the past. Instead, they use their knowledge to classify the situation into one where, say, attack is the best solution rather than defense. Then they formulate a precise strategy for their own game. It is this process of classification and similarity that is at the heart of fuzzy logic.

The name *fuzzy logic* is a bit misleading. There is an area called "fuzzy logic" that deals with multivalued forms of logic. We are not dealing with that area here. Instead, fuzzy logic has come to mean a broad range of fuzzy set theory applications. *Fuzzy sets* are what most people think of as fuzzy logic.

Fuzzy sets deal with the problem of classification. However, before we deal with fuzzy sets, we should briefly review classical, or *crisp* set theory.

Classical set theory was, like classical geometry, formulated by the ancient Greeks and also derived from Plato. A *set* is a collection of objects. In crisp sets an individual item either belongs to a set, or it does not. That is, a cocker spaniel belongs to the set of all dogs, while a Persian cat does not. Two different sets can have items in common. These are the *intersection* of the two sets. For instance, the *intersection* of the set of all pets and the set of all fish, would be all pet fish, like guppies. The *union* of the two sets is all the objects put together. In this case, it would be all pets and all fish.

The *complement* of a set is the set of all items that do not belong in a set. Thus, the complement of the set of all animals that are pets would be the set of all animals that are not pets. By definition, the intersection of a crisp set and its complement is the empty set. There is no intersection. This is called the *Law of Contradiction*. An animal cannot be both a pet and not a pet. The union of a set and its complement is the entire universe of discourse. So the complement of the set of all animals that are pets and the set of all animals that are not pets is the set of all animals. This is called the *Law of the Excluded Middle*. That is, an animal must be either a pet or not be a pet.

Paradox

For simple sets, this works fine. We can definitely draw the line between animals that are pets and animals that are not. However, this reliance on firm definitions can lead to problems called *paradoxes*. Take the following example, called the *paradox of the heap:*

> Start with a heap of sand. Remove one grain of sand and you still have a heap. Remove another grain, and another. Eventually you have one grain left. Is it still a heap? If not, when did it stop being a heap?

This gets to the heart of fuzzy sets. Is two grains of sand a heap? is one? Let's take a different example. Suppose we have the set of tall men. How do we define such a set? Is someone six feet tall considered tall? then how about 5'11"? If that is tall, how about 5'10"? When do we decide someone is tall, and not-tall? Where do we apply the Law of the Excluded Middle?

With crisp sets, we have to set a limit. We have to decide that people six feet tall or taller are "tall." An individual shorter than that belongs to the complement set of not-tall. So someone 5'11" is "not-tall." But that seems silly. How can one inch make the difference between tall and not tall? Certainly, when we see someone who is 5'11" we don't classify that person as short. He is "tall, but not too tall." Here lies the crux of the problem. *The concept of tall is too complex for a crisp set to handle.* Deciding that someone is tall is largely a matter of perspective. We can, of course, extend this to more important concepts such as what is fair and what is not fair, or what is just and what is not just. Even in military actions, what is war and what is not war? Technically, Vietnam and Korea were not wars since there was no formal declaration of war. However, they certainly felt like wars to the people who fought them.

Crisp sets cannot handle these concepts. They are too complex. Lotfi Zadeh (1965) created fuzzy sets in order to adapt set theory for complex situations. The need for fuzzy sets is stated in his *Law of Incompatibility,* which was paraphrased by McNeill and Freiberger (1994) in the following manner:

> As complexity rises, precise statements lose meaning and meaningful statements lose precision.

So when faced with complex situations, the precision required of crisp sets becomes counterproductive. In particular, the Law of the Excluded Middle and the Law of Contradiction are too precise to be useful. In language, we get around these problems by using "hedges" such as *almost, around,* and *near.* We also use "qualifiers" like *green, big,* or *fast.*

Zadeh developed a set theory that generalized the meaning of a set. In crisp sets, an object is either in the set or not in the set. In a binary representation, the object has a value of 0 or 1. Zadeh incorporated partial belonging to a set, represented by a membership function. The membership function defines how *similar* an object is to the concept of the set. In a crisp set the membership function is either 0 or 1. It's either completely similar or completely different from the set. In a fuzzy set the membership function could range from 0 to 1, and incorporate all of the fractional values in between. Thus, a man who is 6 feet tall has a membership value of 1.0 in the set of tall men, while someone 5'11" may have a membership value of 0.9, and someone 5'4" may have a membership value of 0.1. Set theory had been generalized, and suddenly all of the paradoxes went away. In addition, we could rigorously define vague concepts such as a "heap." A pile of 1,000 grains has a membership function of 1.0 with the set "heap." A pile of 20 grains has a membership function of 0.4. As we found with fractals, generalizing a concept to include fractional values improved its usefulness and its ties to reality.

Fuzzy Sets

A fuzzy set, as we stated, is a way of describing a complex concept. The more complex it is, the fuzzier it becomes. For instance, the set of integers from 1 to 10 is a simple, crisp set. However, suppose the set is the "numbers around 6." Five is near 6. So is 7 and 8. But what about 11, or 16? Fuzzy sets give us a precise way of defining this concept of "around 6," but it is subjective. Graphically, we can see it in Figure 15.1.

In a crisp set, we would have to decide exactly what "around 6" means. If we decide that the numbers 5 to 7 are "around 6" we get Figure 15.2. That is,

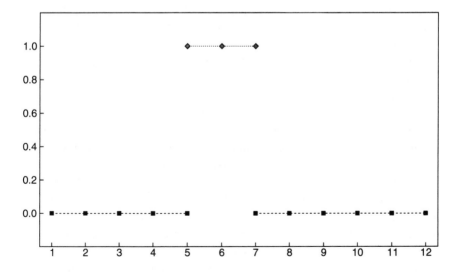

FIGURE 15.1 Crisp set: Numbers around six.

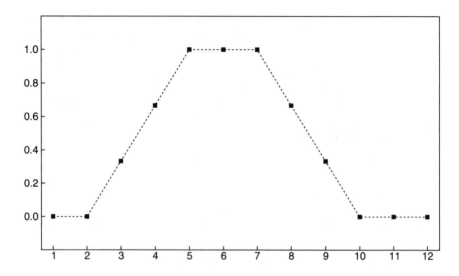

FIGURE 15.2   Fuzzy membership function: Numbers around six.

how *similar* a number is to the concept "around 6." The y-axis contains the membership function. As you can see, in the usual crisp set tradition, values less than 5 or greater than 7 receive a value of zero. They are not "around 6." Only the numbers 5, 6, and 7 are "around 6," and they are also equal in being "around 6."

In a fuzzy set, we must decide on values that are definitely not "around 6" and on a membership function for the numbers that are. For the purposes of this example, we will say that a number less than 2 or greater than 10 is definitely not around 6. Values five to seven are definitely around 6, and so receive a membership value of 1.0. From 2 to 5, we draw a line from y = 0 to 1. From 7 to 10 we also draw a downward-sloping line from y = 1 to 0. Values on the y-axis along these lines describe their membership values in the set of "numbers around 6." Thus, the number 4 has a membership value of 0.67, while 5 has a membership function of 1.0. Five is more "around 6" than 4, but 4 is still "around 6." We could have set the boundaries as well as the shape of the membership function in any of a variety of ways. How do we decide what to do? Here is the strength and weakness of fuzzy sets. The parameters are set subjectively depending on the nature of the problem. The validity of the model is only as good as the modeler's understanding of the problem. A well-understood problem will result in a good fuzzy model. However, the results of a model developed with a mistaken understanding of the problem will result in a model with all the limitations and mistakes the modeler might make.

In addition, there are various definitions for the complement, union, and intersection of fuzzy sets. These are similar to crisp set rules. We will state the basic definitions here; the generalized definitions can be examined more closely in Zadeh and Kacprzyk (1992).

A	= Membership in set A, $0 \leq A \leq 1$	(15.1)
$1 - A$	= Complement of A	(15.2)
Min(A,B)	= Intersection of sets A and B	(15.3)
Max(A,B)	= Union of sets A and B	(15.4)

As you can see, the complement of a fuzzy set is one minus the membership function. Thus, if 4 belongs 0.67 to the set of numbers around 6, it also belongs 0.33 to the set of numbers not around 6. The Law of the Excluded Middle was one of the first things to go in the theory of fuzzy sets. In fuzzy sets, an object can belong to both the set and its complement. This can be examined graphically in Figure 15.3.

For instance, suppose that someone is 5'7" tall and belongs 0.5 to the set of tall people, and 0.5 to the set of short people. In this definition of tall and

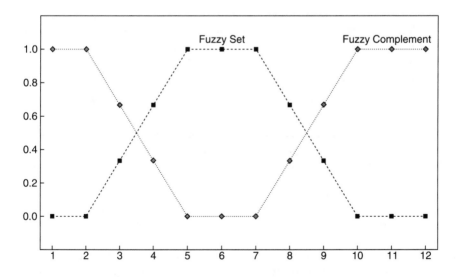

FIGURE 15.3 Fuzzy complement: Numbers around six.

short, someone 5'7" tall is in between, neither tall nor short. On a more realistic note, suppose we were rating stocks, and we had a set of criteria of what constituted a good buy. There is one stock that fits all the criteria but one. It has a P/E ratio of 20 rather than 15. Using fuzzy sets, it would be possible to come up with a quantitative measure saying that the stock belongs 0.8 to the set of buys, that is, almost a buy but not quite.

Fuzzy Sets and Probability

Fuzzy set theory is often confused with probability. Indeed, its detractors have said that there is no problem that fuzzy set theory can solve that cannot be stated in probabilistic terms. This misunderstanding seems to stem from the similarity of the membership function, which ranges from 0 to 1, with probabilities, which also range from 0 to 1. Aside from the values, the two measures are quite different though both can be described as measures of uncertainty. Each measures a different aspect of uncertainty.

A fuzzy membership function is a description of a complex state. Additional data or sampling will not change its value. Probabilities, on the other hand, depend on frequency and chance. Further sampling can change the probability.

Take the following classic fuzzy example. Suppose you have two bottles of liquid. Bottle A has a membership function of 0.9 with the set of potable liquids, while bottle B has a 90 percent chance of being potable. If you were forced to drink from one bottle, which would you choose?

Bottle A is not completely potable, according to its membership function, but it is similar. It may be dirty water. Bottle B, on the other hand, has a 90 percent chance of being completely potable, *and* a 10 percent chance of being deadly. Once sampled, bottle B will either be 100 percent drinkable, or 100 percent deadly. You won't know until you try. However, we know that bottle A is mostly drinkable, so we would pick bottle A. Note that when we drink from bottle A, its membership function with the fuzzy set of potable liquids will not change. It is still dirty water, and its membership value is still 0.90. The fact that fuzzy sets do not depend on frequency has important implications when we examine behavioral finance.

Fractional Truth

Fuzzy logic is a system where fractional values improve the ability of set theory to model reality. Fuzzy set applications are the AI success story. In Japan, a whole subway system runs on fuzzy concepts. Fuzzy controllers for everything from electric razors to automatic transmissions, as well as industrial machinery, have worked with great efficiency and adaptability. In AI, hybrids of fuzzy rules and neural networks have resulted in systems with faster learning ability and greater adaptability.

In statistical analysis there has been less emphasis, even though fuzzy sets have been shown to have great success in the area of pattern recognition. Here we should see what fuzzy sets imply about how people make decisions.

Fuzzy sets are archetypes of complex concepts. For full membership, there is a set of criteria that everyone agrees fits the definition of the set. However, around that there is a vague area, where objects partially belong to the set. The further we get from this core, the less the object belongs to, or is similar to, the set.

This membership function does not depend on frequency. It is a measure of state, and how the object compares with or is similar to the ideal member of the fuzzy set, that is, the item with a membership function of 1.0. This degree of similarity does not change as we continue sampling.

We have examined in a brief manner an area that seems to have accurately quantified how most people think and make decisions. Interestingly, there is little empirical work being done to support the contention of Zadeh and his followers that people really use fuzzy sets in this manner. In another area, behavioral psychology, there is much empirical evidence. Much of it has been directed at economics and markets.

BEHAVIORAL PSYCHOLOGY

Behavioral psychology looks at how people actually make decisions. This differs from the conventional "rational" model, which describes how people *should* make decisions. The rational model led to the EMH as we discussed in Chapter 2. In Chapter 2 we briefly examined the work of Amos Tversky (1990). In this section, we will more fully discuss the work of Kahneman and Tversky (1974) and their followers.

Kahneman and Tversky were interested in how people actually make decisions. Their results have shown that the rational model of human behavior usually does not hold up, except under certain, very specific circumstances. In the following section we will examine some of their findings. Once again, my purpose is to focus on the relationship between their findings, fuzzy logic, and the behavior of markets. Those interested in more detailed information are encouraged to consult the bibliography.

Heuristics

Kahneman and Tversky found that people generally approach problem making, not by probabilities, but by applying rules of thumb called heuristics. These heuristics are simplified strategies for dealing with complex problems and limited descriptive information. Sometimes this approach to decision making is optimal, but at other times it is not. Kahneman and Tversky found that people cannot distinguish between the best time to apply the heuristics, and the best time to use probability. This results in seemingly irrational behavior.

There are three basic categories of heuristics: The *availability* heuristic assesses probability based on how easily examples are pulled out of memory. We use the *representative* heuristic to make decisions based on similarity with archetypal situations we have learned from in the past. People also use *anchoring and adjustment* to make decisions. That is, we often choose a reference point and adjust our decision based on current information.

Each of these heuristics has a direct relationship with the theory of fuzzy sets. Indeed, we shall see that the confusion between fuzzy membership functions and probability has been rediscovered by Kahneman, Tversky, and their followers. Much of the "irrational" behavior found by the behavioralists is the difference between using probability theory and fuzzy set theory. The following section reveals *biases* that result from the use of heuristics in decision making. The list is taken from Bazerman (1994) and Kahneman and Tversky (1973). We will discuss them here in the context of fuzzy sets and market inefficiency.

BIAS FROM THE AVAILABILITY HEURISTIC

Ease of Recall

Individuals tend to assign higher probability to familiar events. For instance, Russo and Shoemaker (1989) found that most people think that more deaths result from automobile accidents than stomach cancer even though the reverse is true by a factor of 2:1. This misjudgment results from the fact that automobile accidents receive much more publicity from the media than deaths from stomach cancer. Likewise, in the market investors are more likely to think that large companies that they know are less risky than small companies, though that is not necessarily true, as holders of Wang Labs found out, for instance. In addition, investors are more wary of the stock market after a big correction than after a long runup, even though the likelihood of a correction increases as time passes from the last one.

BIASES FROM THE REPRESENTATION HEURISTIC

As you would expect, the representation heuristic has the most direct relationship with fuzzy sets. It is the heuristic that is based primarily on similarity. Also, most of the biases found by the behavioralists mirror the differences between fuzzy set theory and probability. There needs to be more discussion as to which is more "rational," however.

Insensitivity to Base Rates

Suppose you are facing a lineup of ten individuals. You are told that eight of the ten are truck drivers, and two are accountants. You are asked to guess the occupation of one individual who is burly, but wearing a suit and glasses. Most people would guess that he is an accountant, despite the fact that the odds are 4:5 against. Not only that, they would assign high odds to the person being an accountant, completely ignoring the stated probability. This bias shows that on the basis of descriptive information, people will typically ignore the base rate probability and go with the description. Interestingly, Kahneman and Tversky (1972, 1973) found that when given no descriptive information, we do make decisions based on the probability.

Of course, this deviation from "rational" behavior comes about because we are making a decision based on a fuzzy set, rather than a probabilistic assessment. The burly man wearing a suit has more *similarity* to the set of accountants than the set of truck drivers, so we set a higher membership function with the fuzzy set of accountants than the fuzzy set of truck drivers. Not only that, we will state the membership value as a "probability" that he is an accountant. Kahneman and Tversky (1974) state, "people order the occupations by probability and similarity in exactly the same way." This is not to say that this is the correct way to make a decision, but it is what is behind the behavior.

The question arises, why do we do this? Why do we ignore probabilities, even when we know them in advance, if descriptive information is available? The reason is tied to the survival instinct. Suppose we were to ask, what is the probability that a dangerous animal will turn up in your backyard? For most of us, the probability is very low. However, suppose you walk into your backyard and you find a large animal, with large teeth, who is growling? What would you say is the probability that this animal is dangerous? Most would say very high, yet we just said that the probability of finding a dangerous animal is very low. We now say that it is high because this animal has a high membership function with the fuzzy set of dangerous animals, due to its description. In this case, knowing the probability density function will not help us escape injury. In many ways this is similar to the old joke about how an economist would not pick up a five-dollar bill lying on the street because he knows that in an efficient market someone else would have already picked it up.

In these two examples, the heuristic is the optimal way to make the decision. We err when we use this method at inappropriate times.

Insensitivity to Sample Size

People rarely seem to consider small sample bias when evaluating probabilities. If the sample is drawn from a specified population, people will assume that the statistical structure of the population will apply to the sample. Ninety-five subjects were presented with two hospitals: a large one with 45 births a day, and a smaller one with 15 births a day. They were asked which hospital, over a year's time, would record more days with at least 60 percent boys born. Twenty-one said the larger hospital. An equal number said the smaller hospital. Fifty-three said about the same. Of course, probability would favor the smaller hospital because of the small sample bias (the small hospital would also be more likely to record less than 40 percent boys as well). Evidently, since both hospitals were considered representative, the population statistics were considered appropriate in both cases.

Kahneman and Tversky (1973) note that we normally face more general questions than these examples. Realistic questions would include, "Will there be a recession within the next six months?" or "What are the chances that the Fed will raise interest rates?" These questions have no real answers. Kahneman and Tversky say:

> These problems differ from those discussed earlier in the paper in that, due to their unique character, they cannot be readily answered either in terms of frequency of occurrence in the past, or in terms of some well-defined sampling process.

In other words, the answer does not depend on frequency. As we saw earlier, fuzzy membership functions also do not depend on frequency. If we say that "there is a 70 percent chance that a recession has already started" we are not really stating a probability since there is no way to sample that kind of data. What we are really saying is that current conditions have a 0.7 membership value with the fuzzy set of recessions. It is 70 percent *similar* to past recessions. This kind of assessment is perfectly rational, given the information we have. The behavioralists have found that we apply similar reasoning even when we can sample the process and accurately evaluate the probabilities. That *is* irrational.

Misconceptions of Chance

Suppose you are confronted with the following two sequences of coin flips:

> A: TTTTT
> B: THHTTT

Which one is more likely? Surprisingly, most people choose B even though both have the same probability of occurring. Kahneman and Tversky (1972) believe that this is another sampling problem, coupled with a belief that random processes have a self-correcting tendency to restore equilibrium. A simpler explanation incorporates fuzzy sets. Each of us have an ideal of what a truly random sequence of events is, and it should include no discernible pattern. Sequence B is more similar to that ideal, hence it is more likely than sequence A. That is, sequence B has a higher membership value with the fuzzy set of random sequences than sequence A. Sequence A has a higher value with the fuzzy set of lucky runs, and so is less likely to occur. This, again, relates to the fact that fuzzy membership functions do not depend on frequency, but with similarity with some ideal, or representative set.

Of course, this is completely wrong. This instance shows that misapplying the representativeness heuristic, or the theory of fuzzy sets, can result in a silly answer. The likelihood of a purely statistical process should not be evaluated this way, but many of us do it anyway.

Overconfidence

This bias may reflect overconfident stock market predictions more than any other. We have seen that people often predict outcomes by selecting the answer that is most representative of the information they have. In the selection of occupations, we rely on the descriptive information available. If more descriptive information confirms the choice, we become more confident, even if the new information is highly correlated with the evidence already in hand.

However, we know that a model based on highly correlated variables is less robust than a smaller model with uncorrelated variables. Thus, a stock market guru will become more confident based on data that is actually reducing the accuracy of his forecast.

Once again, investors are basing their judgment on fuzzy sets. The more confirming information is received, the higher the membership function will become. However, you can overfit a fuzzy model as well as a conventional one.

The Conjunction Fallacy

The conjunction fallacy is one of the more celebrated findings of the behavioralists. It also is directly related to a well-known criticism of fuzzy sets.

Subjects were presented with the following description of a hypothetical woman named Linda. Linda was presented as outspoken and involved in social protest as a student. The subjects were asked to rate possible descriptions of Linda according to likelihood. Subjects said that it was less likely that Linda would be a bank teller, than a bank teller who is active in the feminist movement. Clearly a feminist bank teller is a subset of the set of bank tellers, so how could it be more likely that Linda be the former than the latter? The answer is simple. The description created by Kahneman and Tversky was more representative of a feminist than a bank teller. Hence, Linda had a higher fuzzy membership function in the set of feminist bank tellers than just in the set of bank tellers. The behavioralists have labeled this the Conjunction Fallacy because it gets the probabilities wrong. Yet, it is perfectly consistent with fuzzy theory.

McNeill and Freiberger (1994) bring up the following relationship with fuzzy sets. It is, in fact, one of the few times that a relationship has been drawn between the two. Osherson and Smith (1981) criticized fuzzy set theory by examining a discrepancy in the concept of a fuzzy intersection. They looked at the concept of "pet fish." Pet fish is clearly the intersection of the set of pets, and the set of fish. A guppy is also a pet fish, and its membership value in the fuzzy set of pet fish must be high. However, according to the laws of fuzzy intersection (eq. 15.3) it must have a value that is the lesser of its membership value in the fuzzy set of pets and in the fuzzy set of fish. Clearly, a guppy's value in those two sets must be low since it is not very representative of either category. So, a guppy is more a pet fish than it is either a pet or a fish, but according to the rule of fuzzy intersection it must be less. This anomaly, according to Osherson and Smith, destroys the fuzzy set concept.

The conjunction fallacy points to the answer. People will sometimes convert an intersection into a full fuzzy set. Hence, with the example of Linda, feminist bank tellers becomes a set of its own. Likewise, pet fish becomes its own set. Zadeh calls this "normalizing" because it changes the scale for comparison.

BIASES FROM THE ANCHORING AND ADJUSTMENT HEURISTIC

This heuristic is closely related to the formation of fuzzy sets. The biases shown in the following section show how misconstructing a fuzzy set can result in a silly process.

Insufficient Adjustment

People often base their valuations from a beginning value. Once they start from this value, they do not tend to readjust even when additional information is obtained. For instance, it is often difficult to obtain a fair price for a used personal computer (PC) from individuals. The price of PCs has not increased much, even as the capability has increased. Thus, in 1992, a 486-33 IBM-compatible PC with 4 megabytes of memory and a 100-meg hard drive would have cost about $3,000. By late 1995, the same price got you a Pentium 100 with 8 meg of memory and a 850-meg hard drive. Yet, it is not unusual to see the old system advertised for $1,500 even though it is worth only half that. Why? The seller has anchored on the price he or she paid for the system, rather than adjusted to market value. The same often happens with automobiles.

Anchoring serves an important function in fuzzy sets. It is usually the full membership value in the fuzzy set. As such, the anchored value is extremely important and should be selected with care.

A FUZZY-BEHAVIORAL-FRACTAL SYNTHESIS

In fuzzy sets we've seen yet another example of how fractional values can greatly expand the usefulness of an already well-known concept. Fuzzy sets can accurately model the human decision-making process. Its success in modeling behavior when precision is not necessary is almost legendary. Behavioral psychology has shown empirically that the fuzzy model of human decision making has validity in the real world. At the same time, the behavioralists have also shown that there are times when such an approach to decision making is suboptimal. It can lead to evaluations that can be better made with other more statistical methods.

DeBondt and Thaler (1986) have applied these behavioral concepts to the markets. They have tested whether the stock market overreacts to information. They did so by creating portfolios of winners and losers based on past excess returns to the stock market as a whole rather than on a forecast variable, such as earnings. If the market overreacts to information, then the loser portfolios should outperform the winner portfolios in the future. As any practitioner would expect, they found this to be the case. The time period studied was January 1933 through December 1980. The "market" was defined as the capitalization weighted CRSP universe. DeBondt and Thaler found that on average the loser portfolio outperformed the market by 19.6 percent three years after portfolio formation, while the winner underperformed the market by 5.0 percent. Benjamin Graham (1959) stated that "the interval required for a substantial underevaluation to correct itself averages approximately $1\frac{1}{2}$ to $2\frac{1}{2}$ years." DeBondt and Thaler confirmed Graham's observation in that most of the relative performance occurred in the second and third years after portfolio construction. They offer this as evidence that the stock market does indeed overreact. This is an example of the representativeness heuristic in action, where more recent descriptive information is more important than prior, or base-rate data.

This tendency of the market to overreact to information, as well as to follow trends, results in much of the statistical characteristics of the markets, that is, the long-memory effects described in Chapter 7, the instability of volatility, and the fat-tails in the probability density function. Thus, it is possible that the resulting statistical structure of the markets can come from behavioral sources, at least in the short term.

16
Applying Chaos and Nonlinear Methods

There have been a number of true practitioners since the first edition of this book. Most are not entirely forthcoming with their applications. As one would expect, believers in weak form market efficiency would not like others to copy their methods and arbitrage the opportunities away. In this chapter we will briefly describe a number of practitioners who are managing real assets using some form of nonlinear analysis.

None in the group use chaos theory alone in their investment strategy. By itself, chaos theory cannot help us predict markets, only understand them. Therefore, most use chaos as a base for understanding the markets. However, the technology they apply to market prediction is a variation of standard linear methods, fuzzy logic, neural networks, or genetic algorithms. While we have discussed the first two methods, the latter two methods have not been mentioned and deserve a brief introduction.

Neural networks are mathematical models that are superficially based on the way the brain works. That is, they attempt to mimic the massively parallel methods of computing that we think underlies the functioning of the brain. Neural networks do not actually mimic the brain. Instead they are a model of how the brain works. Like all models, neural networks are a gross simplification of reality. However, neural networks have been shown to be adaptable. That is, they can learn (or readjust their parameters) as new information is received. They are also adept at pattern recognition, given enough data to learn patterns. However, in the end, neural networks are mostly another form of nonlinear, nonparametric regression. They show great promise, but care must be taken because diagnostic methods are crude and incomplete. It is very difficult to evaluate the effectiveness of neural net models. They are true black boxes. The inputs are transformed into outputs. Disentangling what is happening inside the network during transformation is very difficult. Those interested in a more complete discussion should read Refnes (1995) and Deboek (1994). Both books evaluate neural network research relative to the capital markets.

Genetic algorithms mimic evolution. Once again, we are using a model, not the actual process. Genetic algorithms can test rules and find the set of rules that optimize a particular objective function through competition. Only the best rules (i.e., the "fittest") survive into the final solution. There is more. Not only do the best rules dominate the weaker rules, they can mate to form other rules through crossover and mutation. That is, parts of a rule can change at random and be added to the mix of potential rules. Two successful rules can be combined into a new rule. If the new rules survive, they can dominate the parent rules. Crossover and mutation keep the optimization process from being stuck in a "local" maximum. When we optimize a function, we are checking whether we are at the top of a hill. For instance, the maximum of a two-dimensional parabola is the peak of the hill. Once we reach the peak, most optimization algorithms stop, saying that we have reached the maximum level. In a multidimensional problem, we can have many hills. Only one is the ultimate peak, or global maximum. However, most optimization algorithms stop once they reach a peak, even if it is only the local maximum. We cannot be sure that it's the ultimate peak. The crossover and mutation functions throw the process off the current hill in case that is not the global maximum. If it is the global maximum, the algorithm merely climbs back up. If it is not, the search continues. Therefore, the genetic algorithm becomes an efficient search method for maximizing a problem. However, it requires a substantial amount of data. Those interested in a more complete discussion are encouraged to read Deboek (1994) and Bauer (1994). Both volumes discuss genetic algorithms in relation to capital markets.

Practitioners often use these methods in combination. That is, they create *hybrid* systems. Genetic algorithms can be used to optimize fuzzy rules or the parameters for a neural net. Fuzzy rules can determine the parameters for the neural net. There are many combinations.

In the five years since the publication of the first edition of this book, a large number of people have *claimed* to apply these innovative techniques to markets. It is not clear how many have actually succeeded. Many firms have created marketing splashes, only to sink into oblivion once they are given real money to manage. In this chapter we will discuss four firms that seem to have staying power. By necessity, this chapter will be brief. As I said earlier, investment managers tend not to talk about their "technology." Therefore, there will be no secrets revealed here. I should add that I cannot endorse any firm listed here (except PanAgora). All the information is from public sources, but I cannot guarantee their accuracy. Readers interested in more information should contact the firms directly.

LBS CAPITAL MANAGEMENT (CLEARWATER, FLA)

LBS is a firm that uses neural networks, genetic algorithms, and hybrid systems. Led by Dr. Ganesh Mani as director of research, the firm offers both market timing and stock-picking strategies. They are a moderate-sized investment firm with $600 million under management. LBS is unusual in that they have a fairly long track record. Their asset allocation model goes back to 1987. Their stock selection model has real-time performance since 1992. Both strategies seem to use different technologies.

The market-timing model is an expert trading system using 260 rules and shifts between stocks and cash. According to a report in *Barrons* (Laing, 1995), the market-timing model had outperformed in the eight years ending 1994, but underperformed in the more recent five-year period. This implies that much of the return came from the crash of '87. However, in the *Barrons* article LBS admits that much of the underperformance comes from ignoring a buy signal in January 1991, during the onset of the Gulf War. This would imply that LBS is a semiquant firm. That is, they have quantitative models that they override with their own judgment as they see fit. A "true" quant firm does not override their models, except under the most extreme circumstances.

LBS also has a stock selection model that runs on neural nets. Their mid-cap stock strategy has evidently outperformed the S&P 400 Mid-Cap index by 3 percent per year from 1992 to 1994. Many may find this unimpressive, but as a professional money manager, I can tell you that 3 percent of excess return per year is great if it continues.

LBS is also testing hybrid systems. Mahfoud and Mani (1995) outlines a stock selection strategy using genetic algorithms. Dr. Mahfoud has been testing a genetic algorithm, their regular neural net, and a hybrid system in real time. The hybrid system appears to be winning.

THE PREDICTION COMPANY (SANTA FE, NM)

The Prediction Company is one of the best-known investment firms to employ nonlinear technologies. This notoriety is largely due to two of the founding members: Dr. Doyne Farmer and Dr. Norman Packard. Farmer and Packard were two members of the Santa Cruz Collective who, as graduate students, were largely responsible for formulating much of the structure of chaos theory. As scientists they were instrumental in formulating the importance of Lyapunov exponents in classifying chaos, as well as the time-delay method of reconstructing phase space. Their work was detailed in Gleick (1987). In 1991 Farmer, Packard, and James McGill formed the Prediction Company. Doctors Farmer and Packard are among the most articulate advocates of nonlinear studies. As such, they frequently speak at conferences and are often interviewed by the trade and popular press. Unfortunately, their technology is under exclusive contract with Swiss Bank Corporation, so details of their investment process and their track record are proprietary. They are also believers in "weak form market efficiency," and so are unlikely to release details in any case. Thus, the Prediction Company is one of the best-known new firms, but we know little about their investment process. However, due to the importance of Farmer and Packard's published work, they cannot be ignored.

Dr. Packard was kind enough to give some information in private correspondence. The Prediction Company has a stated goal of forecasting large, liquid markets such as currencies, commodities, equities, and interest rates. Futures are often used to implement these strategies. Modeling is done through a number of different methods. According to Dr. Packard these include genetic algorithms, decision trees, neural networks, and other nonlinear regression methods. According to published interviews, the Prediction Company believes that market returns have random periods which are followed by "pockets of predictability." That is, there are times when we can profit from the market and times when we cannot. In some ways, this seems similar to the Coherent Market Hypothesis, but there is no direct link. Dr. Packard also states that "We regard whether the predictable structure we find is related to chaos as an open question." Nonlinearity is a key factor in market behavior, but it is not necessarily chaotic according to the Prediction Company.

The Prediction Company is a true quantitative investment firm in their implementation. Dr. Packard says that "Trading is governed exclusively by our models, with no human intervention." This is, of course, in the tradition of quantitative firms (including PanAgora, the firm I work for). Discipline has always been the hallmark of a true quant.

TLB PARTNERS (NEW YORK, NY)

TLB Partners runs a hedge fund. The investment discipline was developed by Christopher May, and it is based on the concept of "nonlinear pricing." The firm is relatively new and small but has managed to create an impressive record in a short time. We will need time to judge the robustness of May's process, however. Mr. May is not a novice to the markets, bringing only academic experience to bear. Before he became an advocate of nonlinearity, he worked as an arbitrageur at Oscar Gruss & Son, and at Wyser-Pratte Company, Inc. He also worked at Baring Securities and Prudential-Bache Securities.

Mr. May is an advocate of nonlinear pricing, a term he uses frequently, and has been eloquent in his discussion of markets. His techniques use neural nets, genetic algorithms, and the Hurst exponent. While the specifics are vague (he is, after all, a practicing money manager), pattern recognition is clearly involved for both the buy and sell signals. He also says that he is not a day trader, and his investment horizon is six to nine months. Compared to many money managers, he sounds realistic in his expectations. He said in the December 18, 1995 issue of the *Wall Street Transcript,* "if you're right 53% of the time, over a long period of time, you're going to do OK. You don't have to be right on every trade." He has also said, "Chaos is legitimately new. Chaos is no Holy Grail." I could not have said it better.

In May's first year (roughly October 1994 to September 1995), TLB returned +102.63 percent net of fees. Even in the heady bull market of 1995, that is an impressive return. Of course, it's a little early to tell how his process will do in the long run. However, he is one of the few practitioners who truly use nonlinear methods to manage money.

PANAGORA ASSET MANAGEMENT (BOSTON, MA)

I am often asked how I use my own work. So, in writing this chapter, I would be remiss if I did not discuss my own place of employment. PanAgora is among the older quant firms. While we were incorporated in 1990, our actual existence goes back before that. In 1985, PanAgora was formed out of the Institutional Investment division of the Boston Company. Our original Tactical Asset Allocation and equity models date back to 1982. Parts of those models date back to the early 1970s. Our founder, Dr. Richard Crowell, won a Graham and Dodd Award from the *Financial Analysts Journal* back in 1972.

PanAgora manages about $15 billion. We are also true quants, who do not override our models with subjective judgment. It is our conviction that the subjective side of asset management is in formulating the models. Once the models are rigorously tested for robustness, they are strictly followed.

Our models, many will be surprised to learn, are based on linear regression techniques. My work in chaos theory has enhanced our ability to model using standard techniques, but we have also added some nonlinear elements. While we experiment with genetic algorithms and fuzzy logic, that work is not yet complete. We are not in a hurry. The PanAgora approach has delivered consistent results for over ten years. So any replacement technology would have to deliver overwhelmingly superior results for our client base to desire such a radical change. That is not to say that my nonlinear studies have no impact at PanAgora. In fact, the impact is quite profound.

In much of this book I have emphasized the possible fallibility of many standard statistical tests. It is possible to reject or accept bad information because we are fitting nonlinear data to a linear model. Chaos theory and fractal statistics give us a framework for evaluating our models by allowing us to see the limits of the linear approach. It is not enough to just get good t-statistics, correlations, or information ratios. The models must make intuitive sense, and be stable over many economic environments. It is possible to accept factors that have "weak" significance because they give consistent results over a long time period. It is also possible to reject a statistically significant result because its significance is tied to correctly forecasting one large nonlinear event. R/S analysis is applied to the residuals of a regression to see if persistent nonlinear structure is left unexplained by the model.

Then there is the matter of forecasting frequency. The chaotic attractor for the U.S. market has an average four-year nonperiodic cycle. This implies a long-term investment horizon. Packard, et al. (1980) have shown that it is possible to forecast a nonlinear system with linear techniques over short time intervals. At PanAgora we forecast at a monthly frequency. That is, we use monthly data to forecast one month ahead. At PanAgora, we believe that the reliable way to build wealth is to invest for the long-term. This fits in with our client base of pension funds, foundations, and endowments. Our clients are long-term tax-exempt institutions. Building wealth based on trading is not one of their goals. Indeed, we believe that consistent returns through trading activity alone is the hardest of problems.

Finally, there are nonlinear elements in our models. True to form, I am not going to go into them in great detail here. However, I can say that the antipersistent nature of volatility as seen in Chapter 9 is very important. In essence, an increase in short-term volatility is a sign of increased uncertainty in the market place, and implies negative returns in the future. Note that this is the

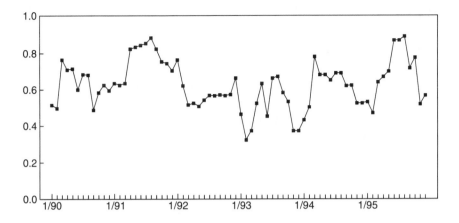

FIGURE 16.1   Hurst exponent: 1/90–12/95.

reverse of CAPM, which says that higher risk implies higher returns. At high frequencies, the reverse is true. In addition, we use the Hurst exponent as a signal. Figure 16.1 shows the Hurst exponent for the S&P 500 using monthly data over rolling twelve-month intervals. The Hurst exponent was calculated using the Hurst Empirical Law in equation (7.6). As you can see, the exponent changes over time. The natural state of the market is a persistent, trending state. However, the market can fall into a random state, or even an antipersistent state. Each state is comparable to a state in the Coherent Market Hypothesis of Vaga. Again, contrary to CAPM, a random walk state implies a loss of momentum. This again is a sign of high uncertainty in the market place. Using volatility and the Hurst exponent implies that there is both a long-term and short-term uncertainty level in the market place. When the market enters one of these uncertain states, it is susceptible to bad news. So, if unexpected bad news arrives, the market takes it badly. If, however, the market is in a persistent trending state, or has low volatility, it will tend to ignore bad news.

Future research at PanAgora centers around genetic algorithms and fuzzy logic. Both have great promise in the areas of classification. Future publications will (hopefully) deal with these applications.

Chaos theory has had a profound effect on me as a theorist and a money manager. It has given me a framework for formulating policy and creating models. My only hope is that it will have a similar impact on others.

SUMMARY

This list is, of course, incomplete. My apologies to those whom I have not included. The managers mentioned here were chosen for illustration. However, the list illustrates the growing movement toward modeling markets as nonlinear, complex systems. In the future we can expect that there will be more nonlinear technology in asset management as evidence of nonlinearity becomes more widely accepted.

17
What Lies Ahead: Toward a More General Approach

In any science, there come times when the existing paradigm raises more questions than it answers. At those times, the need for a new way of looking at the old problems becomes clear. Capital market theory and economics in general are now coming to that point. For some time, the conditions necessary to justify the use of most of our traditional analytical methods have, in general, not existed. It is time to examine alternatives. The application of these new methods is still in its infancy. There are very few "economic chaologists" in comparison with the industry's number of traditional analysts.

The sciences of complexity—of fractals and chaos—offer new tools, which may be more appropriate than traditional methods at certain times. They are, however, extensions of current techniques. When the new paradigm is examined closely, it is revealed as a generalization of existing methods.

When the Fractal Hypothesis, examined in Part Two, is compared with the Gaussian Hypothesis, its key differentiating feature is the value of alpha, or the dimensionality of the probability density function of price changes. The Gaussian Hypothesis says that alpha equals 2, and no other value. The Fractal Hypothesis differs in allowing alpha to range between 1 and 2 and to take fractional as well as integer values. This generalization of the density function has implications for the behavior of the system.

Chaos theory states that systems are generally interdependent; the relationship between the values can have exponents different from 1. Standard econometrics assumes linear relationships between independent variables. The econometric case is a restrictive form of the more general nonlinear case.

In both cases, the sciences of complexity offer more general forms of the existing paradigm. The existing paradigm becomes a special case of the new, more complex models, which can be generated using fractals, chaos, or other nonlinear methods. This increase in complexity carries with it a loss of certainty in evaluating the problem. We can no longer solve for optimal solutions, but must instead be content to examine probabilities in a world that can abruptly change when certain critical levels are passed. This new view of the world offers us less control over our environment, even as it offers us a more complete picture of how the world works.

In *The Third Wave*, Alvin Toffler observes that, in real life, there are no independent variables, but only one large, interdependent system of never-ending complexity. In the capital markets, we must begin to recognize this possibility.

SIMPLIFYING ASSUMPTIONS

When constructing models, a standard procedure has always been to assume away restrictive constraints—those that can interfere with the actual behavior of the underlying system without improving understanding. Restrictive constraints, in effect, muddy the waters so that the real phenomenon is more difficult to observe. These simplifying assumptions allow us to make simpler models, thus making a problem more manageable. The classic example of a simplifying assumption is eliminating friction from physics problems. In elementary physics, bodies are assumed to move in a vacuum. Friction is an outside influence, a complication when added to the problem, and not really a part of the interaction between bodies. A similar constraint in the capital markets is the influence of taxes. Taxes can influence the behavior of investors, but they are outside constraints that are not involved in the dynamics of buying and selling in the marketplace. When studying the basis of investor behavior, it is reasonable to assume away taxes, as though all investors were free to invest as they like.

In physics, it would be unreasonable to assume that a force acting on a body is linear, without a good deal of empirical evidence to back up that assumption, particularly when creating applications of theory. When studying the motion of a weight hanging from a spring, we cannot assume that the force of the spring is linear, in order to make the calculations easier, and then build an entire analytic framework based on a linear restoring force. It would be unjustified to proceed and speculate on other systems that are similar to the spring system, and apply the linear restoring theory to them as well.

In capital market theory, we have made such a simplifying assumption. We have long assumed that investors react to information in a linear fashion. We have built an entire analytic framework on this assumption, without sound empirical evidence that it is true. Even when searching for evidence that this assumption is true, we have used methods that have underlying Gaussian assumptions. These methods assume that certain conditions, like the independence of observations, are true when we are not sure that they are even realistic. To justify our methods, we have even built a model human called the rational investor, even though this person does not resemble anyone we know. We have ignored historical evidence that groups of people are prone to fashions and fads, saying instead that, in the aggregate, investors are rational even if they are not rational individually. Finally, we have hypothesized conditions under which all of these assumptions must hold and called them the Efficient Market Hypothesis.

I am not expressing these reservations about the past 40 years' worth of labor with an intent to destroy all of this work. I am merely pointing out that, by restricting the conditions to a very specific case, we are missing out on the wealth of methods that are available to us to extend our understanding of the markets and the economy.

THE PASSAGE OF TIME

Perhaps the most restrictive assumption in traditional analysis involves the treatment of time. In Newtonian physics, time is considered invariant. That is, time is not important to its problems. The motion of bodies in space can be undone by simply reversing the equations. Because economics and investment analysis borrow heavily from Newtonian physics, we have traditionally treated time as unimportant to our problems. An event can perturb a system, but the system will revert to equilibrium after an appropriately short time span, and the event becomes forgotten. This short memory is characteristic of most econometric methods that consider time at all.

In real life, events affect us for a long time. Certain events change our lives forever; other events change the history of the world. We have restricted the impact of events on markets to a short time span, as if the markets are different from the rest of our life experiences.

Chaos has shown us that, in natural systems, events can change the course of history, even if the total number of possible results is within a finite space. A system can lose memory of initial conditions, even if the impact continues to be felt. From a sociological point of view, we can say that certain events must have changed the course of history, even if society does not remember when those events occurred. For instance, we do not know when the wheel was invented, yet its impact remains.

In the markets, events may become forgotten over the course of time, but that does not mean their influence is no longer felt. Essentially, where we are depends on where we have been, and where we are going depends on what we are doing now. By generalizing the framework within which we view the effect of time, we enrich our analytic capabilities and our potential to understand the function of markets.

INTERDEPENDENCE VERSUS INDEPENDENCE

When using econometric models, "what if" analysis is common. In fact, one purpose behind econometric models is to isolate the influence of factors on one another. We may want to know the impact of inflation on interest rates, all other factors held constant. All of the factors are actually interdependent. Our attempts to "orthogonalize" them, or filter out dependence, is based on an underlying Gaussian assumption. We can never know the influence of *inflation alone* on interest rates, because the impact depends on other variables, and always will. Assuming independence between variables simplifies the problem, but dependence is not an outside influence, like friction, that can be assumed away to simplify the problem. It is an important part of the system itself. Assuming dependence away changes the entire nature of the problem: the model system and the actual system become no longer related.

Chaos theory generalizes the study of systems to take this interdependence into account. Generalizing the problem, rather than restricting it, will increase our understanding of the system and thus generate new applications. Quick optimal solutions may not be possible. However, the potential for substantial new applications becomes limitless as our understanding increases.

EQUILIBRIUM, AGAIN

We have discussed equilibrium in several contexts. However, the concept of economic equilibrium is so entrenched that I must address this issue one final time. Economic equilibrium is closely tied to Newtonian physics. Scientists have long known that Newtonian physics offers only optimal solutions (or, closed form solutions) for a problem involving two bodies in motion. Once we go beyond two bodies, single solutions can no longer be found, and scientists since Poincaré have given up that attempt.

In economics and investments, we continue to search for a solution to a multibody problem. We must remember that, in the multibody problem, nonlinearities between the forces can no longer be assumed away, as in a two-body problem, without drastically changing the nature of the system. This means that point attractors and limit cycles are not the only possible types of equilibrium. Strange attractors that offer infinite solutions within a finite range are a very real possibility. Only by generalizing our analytic framework can we efficiently research that possibility.

OTHER POSSIBILITIES

There are many other possible explanations for the empirical findings presented in the preceding chapters. There are also many other paradigms that may prove to be more useful than fractals and chaos. These alternative methods are still closely related to chaos. They are relatively new developments about which we are just beginning to learn. The January 1991 issue of *Scientific American* has covered two possibilities.

The first possibility is called "wavelet theory," which appears to be a generalization of spectral analysis. The creators of wavelet theory are credited as Ingrid Daubechies of Bell Labs, Gregory Belylkin of Schumberger-Doll Research, and Ronald Coifman of Yale University. Spectral analysis depends on Fourier transforms, which break a signal up into a series of sine waves that, added together, replicate the original signal. However, spectral analysis depends on the system's having a characteristic scale; that is, each smaller increment scales according to a fixed number. Spectral analysis also searches for a periodic cycle. As we have seen, fractal and chaotic time series do not have a characteristic scale, so spectral analysis on a chaotic or fractal time series results in a graph that looks like broadband noise. Nonperiodic cycles also contribute to this result.

Because wavelet theory can handle signals with multiple scales, it can be used to analyze fractal and chaotic time series. This could be a promising area of future research.

The second possibility is the concept of "self-organized criticality." The description by Bak and Chen (1991) is quite complete and has exciting possible applications to capital market analysis.

Self-organized criticality began with the study of sand piles—specifically, the stability of sand piles. Glen Held, at the IBM Thomas J. Watson Research

Center, has performed experiments using real sand piles. Bak and Chen have done such experiments mathematically. In one experiment, one grain of sand at a time is dropped onto a round, flat surface. As you would expect, the grains begin to pile up on one another and they form a cone as a large number of grains continue to be dropped. Occasionally, a grain of sand will cause a small avalanche. As the pile gets higher, the avalanches become larger, and the slope of the sides of the cone gets higher. At some point, the pile stops growing and sand begins to spill over the edge of the plate. At the point where the amount of sand being added equals the amount of sand falling off the edge, the sand pile has reached its "critical state." From that point on, the size of the avalanches can vary widely, from a few grains of sand to large slides ("catastrophes").

Strangely, even the large avalanches do not involve enormous amounts of sand. In addition, the slope of the cone does not deviate much from the slope of the critical state, even after a large slide. The actual size of the avalanches depends on the stability of the grains that the added grain hits on its way down the pile. The added grain may reach a stable position, and there will be no slide; or, it may reach an unstable section and knock loose grains that will hit other grains. They, in turn, may stabilize or may hit other unstable grains. Bak and Chen say that "the pile maintains a constant height and slope because the probability that the activity will die, is on average balanced by the probability that the activity will branch." In other words, the probability of a landslide and the probability of no landslide are essentially the same.

There are many unstable regions in the sand pile, but the critical state is robust, in that it varies little. The distribution of stable and unstable areas in the pile changes frequently, but the statistical characteristics of the slides themselves remain essentially the same.

This characteristic—local conditions in continual flux, while the statistical distribution remains the same—is closely related to fractal statistics. In this case, the amount of sand that falls off the pile varies continually. Bak and Chen say that, in a time series of such amounts, "one would see an erratic signal that has features of all durations." In other words, there is no characteristic scale or periodicity. These signals are called "flicker" noise, or 1/f noise. f is the fractal dimension, flicker noise is fractional noise, and 1/f is related to the Hurst exponent.

Self-organized criticality has been useful in modeling earthquakes and other natural phenomena, because natural systems tend to be in critical states at all times. In other words, they are far from equilibrium. In the sand pile's case, the most stable shape is not a cone, but being evenly spread out on the flat surface. Yet, the system, like other natural systems, balances itself on the edge of stability, far from equilibrium.

Self-organized criticality is promising because it offers a physical model for replicating fractal statistics. That would be a very fruitful area for future research.

In addition, unlike chaos, self-organized criticality offers the hope of prediction. Self-organized systems are "weakly chaotic," which means they reside at the edge of chaos. Their nearby trajectories diverge according to a power law, not exponentially. What this means is that weakly chaotic systems lack the time scale beyond which prediction becomes impossible, offering the possibility of long-range forecasting. This is contrary to the positive Lyapunov exponents presented in Chapter 13 for the capital markets, but it is still a promising area for research.

SUMMARY

We have seen evidence that the capital markets are nonlinear systems, and we have seen that current capital market theory does not take these effects into account. Because of this omission, their validity is seriously weakened. However, we do not have a full model of investment behavior to replace the CAPM. The Coherent Market Hypothesis of Vaga, which we discussed in Chapter 14, is more geared to equities than to bonds. What is needed is a new capital market theory that takes into account all of the nonlinear effects we have seen. Nonlinear behavior is evident in stocks, bonds, and currencies. The stock market case is not limited to domestic stocks, but extends into international stocks as well. There is ample room for more empirical research, but the next phase is to develop a capital market theory that incorporates the nonlinear structures we have seen.

Much work still remains to be done.

About the Diskette

INTRODUCTION

Appendices 1 to 5 describe the Visual BASIC (VBASIC) programs provided on the enclosed diskette. The programs replace the BASICA programs of the first edition, and run under a Windows environment. The source code is provided in files MODUTIL.BAS and MODRS.BAS for those who want to review the code or modify the code for the Macintosh platform. The diskette also provides data files. The programs can be used as a starting point for those who wish to do more advanced study.

These programs and data sets are to be used for educational purposes. They can duplicate many of the studies done in the text, although the duplication will not be exact in most cases. The data sets are generally longer and better than the ones used in the text. In addition, the programs are more efficient, reflecting the advances in technology over the last seven years.

The programs have default data files that can be used. However, you can use other files with the programs as well. In addition to the default files, the following data files are also included:

1. DJ5.TXT—Dow Jones Five day data from 1888–1990, loglinear detrended.
2. DJ20.TXT—Dow Jones 20 day data from 1888–1990, loglinear detrended.
3. NILE.TXT—Hurst's Nile River data, 622 AD–1470 AD, annual.
4. SUNSPOT.TXT—Wolfer Sunspot data, 1749–1937, monthly.

The Dow files are appropriate for the correlation integral and Lyapunov exponent programs. The Nile and Sunspot files are best for R/S analysis.

Keep in mind that these are demo programs. While they are vastly better than the ones included in the first edition of this book, they are simply learning tools. They can be adapted for serious research, but that is up to the reader. We expect to offer more powerful versions on the FMA homepage in the future.

The supporting VBASIC files necessary to run the programs are not provided due to disk-size limitations. For those who do not have access to VBASIC, those files can be downloaded from the FMA Home Page listed in Appendix 6. More advanced versions of the programs can be located there as well. You are encouraged to read the README file on the diskette as well, which may include changes made after this writing.

The programs were written by Michael Corning, who has the author's undying gratitude for his hard work and enthusiasm. Mr. Corning also supports the FMA Home Page, which he created on his own initiative with the author's complete support.

Appendix 6 lists additional Internet resources available as of the time of writing.

SYSTEM REQUIREMENTS

- IBM PC or compatible computer with 386 MHz or higher processor
- 3.5" floppy disk drive
- Windows 3.1 or higher (Windows 95 compatible)
- Visual Basic runtime files (16 bit Visual Basic 4.0)—Available from the FMA Home Page (see instructions below)

INSTALLING THE DISKETTE

The enclosed diskette contains files saved in a compressed format. Running the installation program will uncompress the files and copy them to your hard drive in the default directory C:\CHAOS.

1. Insert the diskette into the floppy drive of your computer.
2. Choose File, Run in Program Manager and type A:\INSTALL. (In Windows 95, choose Run from the Start Menu.) Click OK and the opening screen of the installation program will appear.

3. Click OK to accept the default destination drive and directory C:\CHAOS. If you wish to change the default destination, you may do so now.
4. The installation program will uncompress and copy files to your hard drive in the default (C:\CHAOS) or user designated directory.
5. A Program Group, Chaos, with two Program Items, Chaos and Read Me, will be created.

INSTALLING VISUAL BASIC RUNTIME FILES

In order to execute the Chaos program, it will be necessary to install Visual Basic runtime files onto your computer's hard drive. You can obtain these files from the Fractal Market Analysis Home Page. To install Visual Basic runtime files do the following:

1. Go to the Fractal Market Analysis Home Page at http://www.oara .org/mpc/fma and download vb4run16.exe (1.3 MB). Save the file to your C:\CHAOS\ directory.
2. In Program Manager, choose File, Run. Type C:\CHAOS\vb4run16.exe. Click OK. The Visual Basic runtime files will be copied to the appropriate directories.

RUNNING THE PROGRAM

Double click on the Chaos icon to launch the program.

From the top menu-bar, open Demonstration to access the following programs:

1. Rescaled Analysis
2. Bifurcation Graph
3. Fractional Brownian Motion
4. Correlation Dimension
5. Largest Lyapunov Exponent

Appendices 1 to 5 provide more information about each program.

USER ASSISTANCE AND INFORMATION

Please refer to Appendix 6 for author contact information.

John Wiley & Sons, Inc. is pleased to provide assistance to users of this package. Should you have any questions regarding the use of this package, please call our technical support number (212) 850-6194 weekdays between 9am–4pm EST.

To place additional orders or to request information about other Wiley products, please call (800) 879-4539.

APPENDICES

APPENDICES

Appendix 1

Creating a Bifurcation Diagram

The bifurcation diagram of the Logistic equation can be generated, as shown in Chapters 1 and 10. The program requires two inputs, the beginning and ending values of "a" for the graph. As in the text, $0 < a \leq 1$. To view the full range of values, use $0.5 < a \leq 1$, because the lower values of "a" produce a constant. This also produces a time trace of the Henon equation used in Chapters 11 and 12.

The program can draw in "draft" or "dense" format depending on the resolution desired. Higher resolution requires more drawing time, but it is worth it.

Appendix 2

Rescaled Range (R/S) Analysis

The R/S analysis provided in the diskette is not exactly the same process described in the text. Instead we use the process described in Peters (1994). R/S analysis can be biased under two major circumstances: (1) nonstationarity in the data, and (2) a short-memory process. In particular, an AR(1) process is also an infinite-memory process. Thus, it is always a good idea to take AR(1) residuals before applying R/S analysis to filter out the short-memory process. To address this problem, the program supplied here takes AR(1) residuals of the data supplied before it applies R/S analysis.

In addition, the text calculates R/S values for all values of n. If not enough data is left for a full value of n, then it leaves that data off. When n is small, this is not a significant problem. If we have a time series with 500 observations, and $n = 5$, we have 100 full R/S values to average. When $n = 6$, we have 83 R/S values with two observations left over. However, when $n = 48$, we have 10 R/S values and 20 discarded values. As n increases, more and more of the data is discarded. This results in the jaggedness of the log/log plots at high values of n. The program does not use this method. Instead it uses the process used in Peters (1994).

In Peters (1994) I used values of n that were even divisors of the total number of observations. Thus, all of the R/S values use *all* of the data. This means that the initial data set must sometimes be reduced to a number that has the most divisors. For example, 980 has more multiples than 997. What do we do with the extra data? An additional test of stability would be to do a second run with the ending values, and discard the initial values. Suppose we have 997 observations. We first perform R/S analysis on the first 980 observations, and then perform a second run on the last 980 observations. This is an example of the fact that R/S analysis should not be sensitive to starting time if there is enough data.

In addition, I must also note that this book does not have much in the way of significance tests for R/S analysis. Peters (1994) does, and I suggest that interested readers look there if they wish to continue to study R/S analysis in more depth.

The default data files are two Dow Jones Industrials price series that cover from January, 1888 to June, 1990. "DJ5DY Price" is a five day price series. "DJ20DY Price" is a 20 day price series. The program creates a file called RSOUTPUT.TXT that contains n (the number of observations) and the corresponding R/S value. The file should be imported into a spreadsheet for inspection and for regression calculation of the Hurst exponent. The only input necessary from the user is the number of observations. That is only necessary if a data file other than the defaults is used.

I also suggest plotting log(n) vs. the $(R / S_n) / \sqrt{n}$. This ratio (called the V statistic) shows a clear peak when R/S stops scaling at a faster rate than the square root of time. This is often symptomatic of the existence of a periodic or non-periodic cycle. The peak should be insensitive to the sampling interval. In Peters (1994) I found that the V statistic for the Dow Jones Industrials data file peaked at 1000 trading days, 200 intervals of 5 trading days, and 50 intervals of 20 trading days. The peak was insensitive to the sampling frequency.

All of the data files included on the diskette can be used for study. In addition, series produced by the Fractional Brownian Motion can also be checked using the R/S analysis program.

Appendix 3

Simulating a Biased Random Walk

Feder (1988) produced a formula for creating a simulated biased random walk time series, $B_H(t)$, from a sequence of Gaussian random numbers. The formula is lengthy, but not overly complicated:

$$\Delta B_H(t) = \left(\frac{n^{-H}}{\Gamma(H + .5)} \right) * \left\{ \sum_{i=1}^{n*t} (i)^{(H-.5)} * E_{(1 + n(M + t) - i)} \right.$$

$$\left. + \sum_{i=1}^{n*(M-1)} ((n + i)^{(H - .5)}) - i^{(H - .5)}) * E_{(1 + n(M - 1 + t) - i)} \right\}$$

In this equation, E_i is a time series of Gaussian random numbers, normally distributed, with a mean of 0 and a standard deviation of 1. However, we usually start with a set of pseudo-random numbers generated by an algorithm. t is an integer time step, usually one period, which is split into n intervals to approximate a continuous integral. M is the number of periods for which the long memory effect is generated. Theoretically, it should be infinite, but, for the purposes of simulation, a large M will do.

This algorithm takes a series of Gaussian random numbers and approximates the memory effect as a sliding average by weighting past values according to a power law function. By examining the equation, one can see that we need n*M Gaussian random variables to produce each biased increment. The algorithm is inefficient, because the computations needed are immense. It is effective nonetheless.

The program called Fractional Brownian Motion will accept a time series of Gaussian random numbers or will generate such a series internally. Adjustments can be made. M can be set at any value the user chooses. The longer M is, the more the result approximates the "infinite memory" concept, but there will be significant computation time. The examples used in the text use M = 200. n does not have to be a large number; it mainly affects the short-term behavior of $B_H(t)$, and we are not studying that here. In the simulations, I set n = 5 to keep the computation time down to a minimum. Therefore, in the simulations provided in Chapter 7, 1,000 Gaussian random numbers were used to produce each increment of fractional brownian motion.

This program can either generate a new random series as input, or use the file RAND.TXT which contains the numbers I used in the text. It requires inputs for the desired value of H, the value of n (the short-term memory, default of 5), the memory length M (default of 200), and the Gamma value of (H+0.50). The latter can be obtained from a statistical table. Most spreadsheets calculate the value, as well. BASIC does not, so it must be manually input. In order to examine the relationship between the original series and the subsequent transformations, it is a good idea to start with one random series. The output is a file called BROWNhh.TXT, where hh= the desired value of H. So, a run with H=0.72 will create an output file called BROWN72.TXT.

The output will be the equivalent of returns. The output file can be brought into a spreadsheet and plotted to produce graphs like those shown in Figure 7.1. By using the same input file and varying the value of H, one obtains a set of graphs like the set used in this book. They look similar, except for the value of H. A cumulative version of the output file will produce graphs like the set in Figure 7.2.

Appendix 4

Calculating the Correlation Dimension

The VBASIC program implements equation (12.2), which calculates correlation integrals for a time series. This program is not long, but it is data intensive. As a result, it can run for a long time, even on a high-speed personal computer. The calculation itself is simple. The program reconstructs a phase space for a user-defined embedding dimension and time lag, and calculates the number of points within a certain distance (R) from each other, within the reconstructed phase space. It then calculates the probability that any two points chosen at random will be within the distance (R) for the entire data set. The program does this for increasing values of R. Therefore, for each distance R, it must check the distance between each point and each other point, to see whether it falls within the required distance. It does this for increasingly higher embedding dimensions as well.

This program and the Lyapunov exponent program that follows have a similar initial step. First, a phase space must be reconstructed. The guidelines for choosing parameters is in the text. The actual program is then run on the reconstructed phase space.

1. *Reconstructing Phase Space.* The default files are Henon which generates 1000 values of the Henon attractor, or SPCPI.TXT. The latter file is similar to the inflation detrended S&P 500 file used in the text. It covers a longer period, from 1945 to 1995. The reconstruction requires

inputting the number of observations (NPT, calculated if the default files are used), the desired embedding dimension (DIMEN), and the time lag (TAU). Choose these values according to the instructions offered in the text. Press the "Reconstruct" button to start.

2. *Calculating the Correlation Dimension.* The program takes the reconstructed phase space for that embedding dimension, and calculates correlation dimensions. You must input the initial distance (R), and the increment to distance (DT) as described in the text. I recommend that R and DT be equal to 10 percent of the difference between the maximum and minimum values in the original time series. Press the "Compute" button to start calculations.

The output file CORRDIM.TXT will print the distance (R) and the correlation integral (CR) in columns for this embedding dimension. Press the "View" button to examine the output.

CORRDIM.TXT should be brought into a spreadsheet. A log/log plot of the output file will produce graphs similar to Figure 12.2 for the Henon attractor. A linear regression is then run on the linear region of this log/log plot. The slope is the correlation dimension estimate. For the Henon attractor, we knew what the underlying dimensionality was, so only one embedding dimension series was required. However, for experimental data, like our stock market time series, we do not know what the underlying dimensionality is. Therefore, we must run the program for increasing values of DIMEN until the regression converges to one value, as outlined in Chapter 13. The embedding dimension should converge before the dimensionality gets too high. Otherwise, the data will become too sparse for linear regions to be apparent in the log/log plot. If that is the case, more data will be needed to estimate dimensionality as discussed in Chapters 12 and 13.

Appendix 5

Calculating the Largest Lyapunov Exponent

The program provided is adapted into VBASIC from the FORTRAN program by Wolf et al. for calculating the largest Lyapunov exponent from a time series, or one observable. This program is the implementation of equation (12.4) used in Chapter 13. This program requires the most numerical experiments, in order to find the appropriate values. The program tracks the divergence of two points as they evolve through time. The user provides an input file of the time series, and the system first reconstructs a phase space for a user-defined embedding dimension and lag time, as was done in Appendix 4. Chapter 12 gives guidelines for choosing these parameters.

Chapters 12 and 13 provide suggestions for performing this analysis. The reader is encouraged to reread those chapters before using this program. The user also provides an evolution time (EVOLV) to measure divergence. The evolution time needs to be short enough to measure divergence, without measuring folds. However, if it is too short, there will be a high level of computation time. The maximum divergence allowed before a replacement point is found (SCALMX) can be 10 percent of the difference between the maximum and minimum value in the time series. There is no rule for the minimum divergence (SCALMN), and I have used 10 percent of SCALMX, but this depends on the level of noise that the user feels is in the data set.

The program creates a file that has the Lyapunov exponent estimate so far, the evolution time, and the current divergence between the nearby points. The program spends a good deal of time looking for replacement points when the pair diverges beyond SCALMX. The program searches through all the points in the file for a replacement point that is greater than SCALMN from the initial point, and also has a similar angle to the initial point, because we are measuring trajectories in phase space. The length of time that it takes to run this program varies, depending on the embedding dimension and the EVOLV time.

The program runs in the following manner:

1. *Phase Space Reconstruction.* This program uses the same phase space reconstruction routine and default files as in the correlation integral routine (See Appendix 4). Press the "Setup" button to initiate.

2. *Largest Lyapunov Exponent Calculation.* You must input the minimum deviation (SCALMN), the maximum deviation (SCALMX), the evolution time (EVOLV), and the minimum time between pairs (I recommend at least one full orbit). You may also input the "Time Series Interval" which is the sampling interval you wish to use. The default is 1, but if you wish to calculate over every 3 observations, input 3. Press "Compute" to start. Use "View" when the run is complete. The program generates a file called LYAPUFET.TXT.

The program also gives you the choice of using the original Wolf et al. algorithm from the first edition of this book, or a more recent algorithm from Wolf. The recent algorithm is the default. To use the old algorithm, check the box marked "original code."

Alan Wolf's Home Page contains C programs and additional insights given since Wolf et al.'s original work. The URL for that location, and other useful places on the Internet are located in Appendix 6.

Appendix 6

Internet Resources

I cannot think of a bigger advance since I wrote the original edition of this book than the growth of the Internet. It has made communication easy and commonplace. For instance, Michael Corning rewrote the original BASICA programs from the first edition into the Visual Basic programs included here, and maintains the FMA home page. Yet, Michael and I have not, as of this date, actually met. We have done all of our communicating through e-mail and the occasional phone call.

The information access is vast and overwhelming. For convenience, this appendix will list some of the many resources available that deal with nonlinearity. It is only a start. I have decided to restrict this list to sites on the World Wide Web. Most of the sites point to other sites, which are being added daily. Who knows what will be out there when this book is finally published.

The Sante Fe Institute   http://chaos.santefe.edu/
The best known center for nonlinear studies.

The Prigogine Center   http://chaos.ph.utexas.edu/
Lesser known but of high quality. Directed by Ilya Prigogine.

Alan Wolf's Home Page   http://www.users.interport.net
/~wolf/

The same Alan Wolf of the Wolf algorithm for calculating Lyapunov exponents from time series. Newer versions of the same program are offered here.

Chaos Metalink   http://industrialstreet.com/chaos//
                                       metalink.htm
    Links to many chaos-related sites.

Chaos Bibliography   http://www.uni-mainz.de/FB
                                       /Physik/Chaos/chaosbib.html
    Exactly what it says—a bibliography used as a resource by graduate students. It is mostly physical science related.

Group Fractales   http://www-syntim.inria.fr/fractales
    Many fractal-related resources.

Wavelets   http://www.mat.sbg.ac.at/~uhl
                                       /wav.html
    Dedicated to spreading the word about wavelets.

Journal of Nonlinear Science   http://www.spring-ny.com/nst/

Complexity International   http://life.anu.edu.au/ci/ci.html
    Two of the best online nonlinear journals.

Fractal Market Analysis Home Page http://oara.org/mpc/fma
    This page is maintained by Michael Corning. It is dedicated to spreading the word about the Fractal Market Hypothesis, as described in my two books. We intend to have tutorials, programs, and data. I will post changes (including errata) at this site.

Edgar Peters e-mail Address   epeters@panagora.com, or
                                       eepeters@ix.netcom.com
    Feel free to contact me to ask questions, give criticism, or just discuss things.

Bibliography

Akgiray, V. and Lamoureux, C. G. "Estimation of Stable-Law Parameters: A Comparative Study," *Journal of Business & Economic Statistics* 7, 1989.

Alexander, S. "Price Movements in Speculative Markets: Trends or Random Walks, No. 2," in P. Cootner, ed., *The Random Character of Stock Market Prices.* Cambridge, MA: MIT Press, 1964.

Anis, A. A. and Lloyd, E. H. "The Expected Value of the Adjusted Rescaled Hurst Range of Independent Normal Summands," *Biometrika* 63, 1976.

Arnold, B. C. *Pareto Distributions.* Fairland, MD: International Cooperative, 1983.

Bachelier, L. "Theory of Speculation," in P. Cootner, ed., *The Random Character of Stock Market Prices.* Cambridge, MA: MIT Press, 1964. (Originally published in 1900.)

"Back to an Age of Falling Prices," *The Economist,* July 13, 1974.

Bai-Lin, H. *Chaos.* Singapore: World Scientific, 1984.

Bak, P. and Chen, K. "Self-Organized Criticality," *Scientific American,* January 1991.

Bak, P., Tang, C., and Wiesenfeld, K. "Self-Organized Criticality," *Physical Review A* 38, 1988.

Barnesly, M. *Fractals Everywhere,* San Diego: Academic Press, 1988.

Bauer, R. *Genetic Algorithms and Investment Strategies.* New York: Wiley, 1994.

Bazerman, M. *Judgement in Managerial Decision Making,* 3rd ed. New York: Wiley, 1994.

Beltrami, E. *Mathematics for Dynamic Modeling.* Boston: AcademicPress, 1987.

Benhabib, J. and Day, R. H. "Rational Choice and Erratic Behavior," *Review of Economic Studies* 48, 1981.

Bergstrom, H. "On Some Expansions of Stable Distributions," *Arkiv for Matematik* 2, 1952.

Bezdek, J. and Pal, S., eds. *Fuzzy Models for Pattern Recognition.* New York: IEEE Press, 1992.

Black, F. "Capital Market Equilibrium with Restricted Borrowing," *Journal of Business* 45, 1972.

Black, F. and Scholes, M. "The Pricing of Options and Corporate Liabilities," *Journal of Political Economy,* May/June 1973.

Black, F., Jensen, M. C., and Scholes, M. "The Capital Asset Pricing Model: Some Empirical Tests," in M. C. Jensen, ed., *Studies in the Theory of Capital Markets.* New York: Praeger, 1972.

Bollerslev, T. "Generalized Autoregressive Conditional Heteroskedasticity," *Journal of Econometrics* 31, 1986.

Bollerslev, T., Chou, R., and Kroner, K. "ARCH Modeling in Finance: A Review of the Theory and Empirical Evidence," unpublished ms., 1990.

Briggs, J. and Peat, F. D. *Turbulent Mirror.* New York: Harper & Row, 1989.

Brock, W. A. "Distinguishing Random and Deterministic Systems," *Journal of Economic Theory* 40, 1986.

Brock, W. A. "Applications of Nonlinear Science Statistical Inference Theory to Finance and Economics," Working Paper, March 1988.

Brock, W. A. and Dechert, W. D. "Theorems on Distinguishing Deterministic from Random Systems," in Barnett, Berndt, and White, eds., *Dynamic Econometric Modeling.* Cambridge: Cambridge University Press, 1988.

Brock, W. A., Dechert, W. D., and Sheinkman, J. A. "A Test for Independence Based on Correlation Dimension," unpublished ms., 1987.

Broomhead, D. S., Huke, J. P., and Muldoon, M. R. "Linear Filters and Non-linear Systems," *Journal of the Royal Statistical Society* 54, 1992.

Callan, E. and Shapiro, D. "A Theory of Social Imitation," *Physics Today* 27, 1974.

Casdagli, M. "Chaos and Deterministic versus Stochastic Non-linear Modelling," *Journal of the Royal Statistical Society* 54, 1991.

Casti, J. *Complexification.* New York: Harper Collins, 1994.

Chen, P. "Empirical and Theoretical Evidence of Economic Chaos," *System Dynamics Review* 4, 1988.

Chen, P. "Power Spectra and Correlation Resonances," IC^2 Working Paper, 1993a.

Chen, P. "Instability, Complexity, and Time Scale in Business Cycles," IC^2 Working Paper, 1993b.

Cheng, B. and Tong, H. "On Consistent Non-parametric Order Determination and Chaos," *Journal of the Royal Statistical Society* 54, 1992.

Cheung, Y.-W. "Long Memory in Foreign Exchange Rates," *Journal of Business & Economic Statistics* 11, 1993.

Cheung, Y.-W. and Lai, K. S. "A Fractional Cointegration Analysis of Purchasing Power Parity," *Journal of Business & Economic Statistics* 11, 1993.

Cootner, P. "Comments on the Variation of Certain Speculative Prices," in P. Cootner, ed., *The Random Character of Stock Market Prices.* Cambridge: MIT Press, 1964a.

Cootner, P., ed. *The Random Character of Stock Market Prices.* Cambridge: MIT Press, 1964b.

Cox, E. *The Fuzzy Systems Handbook.* Boston: AP Professional, 1994.

Cox, J. C. and Ross, S. "The Valuation of Options for Alternative Stochastic Processes," *Journal of Financial Economics* 3, 1976.

Cox, J. C. and Rubinstein, M. *Options Markets.* Englewood Cliffs, NJ: Prentice-Hall, 1985.

Davies, R. and Harte, D. "Tests for the Hurst Effect," *Biometrika* 74, 1987.

Day, R. H. "Irregular Growth Cycles," *American Economic Review,* June 1982.

Day, R. H. "The Emergence of Chaos from Classical Economic Growth," *Quarterly Journal of Economics* 98, 1983.

Day, R. and Chen P., eds. *Nonlinear Dynamics and Evolutionary Economics.* New York: Oxford University Press, 1993.

DeBoek, G., ed. *Trading on the Edge.* New York: Wiley, 1994.

DeBondt, W. and Thaler, R. "Does the Stock Market Overreact?" *Journal of Finance* 60, 1986.

De Gooijer, J. G. "Testing Non-linearities in World Stock Market Prices," *Economics Letters* 31, 1989.

DeLong, J. B., Shleifer, A., Summers, L. H., and Waldmann, R. J. "Positive Investment Strategies and Destabilizing Rational Speculation," *Journal of Finance* 45, 1990.

Devaney, R. L. *An Introduction to Chaotic Dynamical Systems.* Menlo Park, CA: Addison-Wesley, 1989.

DuMouchel, W. H. "Stable Distributions in Statistical Inference: 1. Symmetric Stable Distributions Compared to Other Symmetric Long-Tailed Distributions," *Journal of the American Statistical Association* 68, 1973.

DuMouchel, W. H. "Stable Distributions in Statistical Inference: 2. Information from Stably Distributed Samples, " *Journal of the American Statistical Association* 70, 1975.

DuMouchel, W. H. " Estimating the Stable Index α in Order to Measure Tail Thickness: A Critique," *Annals of Statistics* 11, 1983.

Eigen, M. and Winkler, R. *Laws of the Game: How the Principals of Nature Govern Chance.* Princeton: Princeton University Press, 1993.

Einstein, A. "Über die von der molekularkinetischen Theorie der Warme geforderte Bewegung von in ruhenden Flüssigkeiten suspendierten Teilchen," *Annals of Physics* 322, 1908.

Elton, E. J. and Gruber, M. J. *Modern Portfolio Theory and Investment Analysis.* New York: Wiley, 1981.

Engle, R. "Autoregressive Conditional Heteroskedasticity with Estimates of the Variance of U.K. Inflation," *Econometrica* 50, 1982.

Engle, R. and Bollerslev, T. " Modelling the Persistence of Conditional Variances," *Econometric Reviews* 5, 1986.

Engle, R., Lilien, D., and Robins, R. "Estimating Time Varying Risk Premia in the Term Structure: The ARCH-M Model," *Econometrica* 55, 1987.

Fama, E. F. "Mandelbrot and the Stable Paretian Hypothesis," in P. Cootner, ed., *The Random Character of Stock Market Prices.* Cambridge: MIT Press, 1964.

Fama, E. F. "Portfolio Analysis in a Stable Paretian Market," *Management Science* 11, 1965a.

Fama, E. F. "The Behavior of Stock Market Prices," *Journal of Business* 38, 1965b.

Fama, E. F. "Efficient Capital Markets: A Review of Theory and Empirical Work," *Journal of Finance* 25, 1970.

Fama, E. F. and French, K. R. "The Cross-Section of Expected Stock Returns," *Journal of Finance* 47, 1992.

Fama, E. F. and Miller, M. H. *The Theory of Finance.* New York: Holt, Rinehart and Winston, 1972.

Fama, E. F. and Roll R. "Some Properties of Symmetric Stable Distributions," *Journal of the American Statistical Association* 63, 1968.

Fama, E. F. and Roll, R. "Parameter Estimates for Symmetric Stable Distributions," *Journal of the American Statistical Association* 66, 1971.

Fan, L. T., Neogi, D., and Yashima, M. *Elementary Introduction to Spatial and Temporal Fractals*. Berlin: Springer-Verlag, 1991.

Feder, J. *Fractals*. New York: Plenum Press, 1988.

Feigenbaum, M. J. "Universal Behavior in Nonlinear Systems," *Physica* 7D, 1983.

Feller, W. "The Asymptotic Distribution of the Range of Sums of Independent Variables," *Annals of Mathematics and Statistics* 22, 1951.

Flandrin, P. "On the Spectrum of Fractional Brownian Motions," *IEEE Transactions on Information Theory* 35, 1989.

Friedman, B. M. and Laibson, D. I. "Economic Implications of Extraordinary Movements in Stock Prices," *Brookings Papers on Economic Activity* 2, 1989.

Gardner, M. "White and Brown Music, Fractal Curves and 1/f Fluctuations," *Scientific American* 238, 1978.

Gell-Mann, M. *The Quark and the Jaguar*. New York: W.H. Freeman, 1994.

Glass, L. and Mackey, M. "A Simple Model for Phase Locking of Biological Oscillators," *Journal of Mathematical Biology* 7, 1979.

Glass, L. and Mackey, M. *From Clocks to Chaos*. Princeton: Princeton University Press, 1988.

Gleick, J. *Chaos: Making a New Science*. New York: Viking, 1987.

Goldberg, D. *Genetic Algorithms in Search, Optimization & Machine Learning*. Reading, MA: Addison-Wesley, 1989.

Graham, B. *The Intelligent Investor, A Book of Practical Counsel,* 3rd ed., New York: Harper & Brothers, 1959.

Grandmont, J. and Malgrange, P. "Nonlinear Economic Dynamics: Introduction," *Journal of Economic Theory* 40, 1986.

Grandmont, J. "On Endogenous Competitive Business Cycles," *Econometrica* 53, 1985.

Granger, C. W. J. *Spectral Analysis of Economic Time Series*. Princeton: Princeton University Press, 1964.

Granger, C. W. J. and Orr, D. "'Infinitite Variance' and Research Strategy in Time Series Analysis," *Journal of the American Statistical Association* 67, 1972.

Grassberger, P. and Procaccia, I. "Characterization of Strange Attractors," *Physical Review Letters* 48, 1983.

Greene, M. T. and Fielitz, B. D. "Long-term Dependence in Common Stock Returns," *Journal of Financial Economics* 4, 1977.

Greene, M. T. and Fielitz, B. D. "The Effect of Long Term Dependence on Risk-Return Models of Common Stocks," *Operations Research* 6, 1979.

Grenfell, B. T. "Chance and Chaos in Measles Dynamics," *Journal of the Royal Statistical Society* 54, 1992.

Haken, H. "Cooperative Phenomena in Systems Far from Thermal Equilibrium and in Non Physical Systems," *Reviews of Modern Physics* 47, 1975.

Haykin, S. *Neural Networks: A Comprehensive Foundation*. New York: Macmillan, 1994.

Henon, M. "A Two-dimensional Mapping with a Strange Attractor," *Communications in Mathematical Physics* 50, 1976.

Hicks, J. *Causality in Economics.* New York: Basic Books, 1979.

Hofstadter, D. R. "Mathematical Chaos and Strange Attractors," reprinted in *Metamagical Themas.* New York: Bantam, 1985.

Holden, A. V., ed. *Chaos.* Princeton: Princeton University Press, 1986.

Holland, J. *Hidden Order: How Adaptation Builds Complexity.* Reading, MA: Addison-Wesley, 1995.

Hopf, E. "A Mathematical Example Displaying Features of Turbulence," *Communication in Pure Applied Mathematics* 1, 1948.

Hosking, J. R. M. "Fractional Differencing," *Biometrika* 68, 1981.

Hseih, D. A. "Testing for Nonlinear Dependence in Daily Foreign Exchange Rates," *Journal of Business* 62, 1989.

Hsieh, D. A. "Chaos and Nonlinear Dynamics: Application to Financial Markets," *Journal of Finance* 46, 1991.

Hsu, K. and Hsu, A. "Fractal Geometry of Music," *Proceedings of the National Academy of Sciences* 87, 1990.

Hsu, K. and Hsu, A. "Self-similarity of the '1/f noise' Called Music," *Proceedings of the National Academy of Sciences* 88, 1991.

Hurst, H. E. "Long-term Storage of Reservoirs," *Transactions of the American Society of Civil Engineers* 116, 1951.

Jacobsen, B. "Long Term Dependence in Stock Returns," unpublished discussion paper, March 1993.

Jarrow, R. and Rudd, A. "Approximate Option Valuation for Arbitrary Stochastic Processes," *Journal of Financial Economics* 10, 1982.

Jensen, R. V. and Urban, R. "Chaotic Price Behavior in a Non-Linear Cobweb Model," *Economics Letters* 15, 1984.

Kahneman, D. and Tversky, A. "Subjective Probability: A Judgment of Representativeness," *Cognitive Psychology* 3, 1972.

Kahneman, D. and Tversky, A. "On the Psychology of Prediction," *Psychological Review* 80, 1973.

Kahneman, D. and Tversky, A. "Judgment Under Uncertainty: Heuristics and Biases," *Science* 185, 1974.

Kahneman, D. and Tversky, A. "Psychology of Preferences," *Scientific American* 246, 1982.

Kahneman, D., Slovic, P. and Tversky, A. *Judgment Under Uncertainty: Heuristics and Biases.* Cambridge: Cambridge University Press, 1982.

Kaiser, G. *A Friendly Guide to Wavelets.* Boston: Birkhauser, 1994.

Kandel, A. *Fuzzy Expert Systems.* Boca Raton: CRC Press, 1992.

Kauffman, S. *The Origins of Order.* New York: Oxford University Press, 1993.

Kelsey, D. "The Economics of Chaos or the Chaos of Economics," *Oxford Economic Papers* 40, 1988.

Kendall, M. G. "The Analysis of Economic Time Series," in P. Cootner, ed., *The Random Character of Stock Market Prices.* Cambridge: MIT Press, 1964.

Kida, S. "Log-Stable Distribution and Intermittency of Turbulence," *Journal of the Physical Society of Japan* 60, 1991.

Klir, G. and Folger, T. *Fuzzy Sets, Uncertainty, and Information.* Englewood Cliffs, NJ: Prentice Hall, 1988.

Kocak, H. *Differential and Difference Equations Through Computer Experiments.* New York: Springer-Verlag, 1986.

Kolmogorov, A. N. "Local Structure of Turbulence in an Incompressible Liquid for Very Large Reynolds Numbers," *Comptes Rendus (Doklady) Academie des Sciences de l'URSS (N.S.)* 30, 1941. Reprinted in S. K. Friedlander, and L. Topper, *Turbulence: Classic Papers on Statistical Theory.* New York: Wiley Interscience, 1961.

Korsan, R. J. "Fractals and Time Series Analysis," *Mathematical Journal* 3, 1993.

Kuhn, T. S. *The Structure of Scientific Revolutions.* Chicago: University of Chicago Press, 1962.

Laing, J. R. "New Brains: How 'Smart' Computers Are Beating the Stock Market," *Barrons,* Feb. 27, 1995.

Lanford, O. "A Computer-Assisted Proof of the Feigenbaum Conjectures," *Bulletin of the American Mathematical Society* 6, 1982.

Lardner, C., Nicolas, D-S, Lovejoy, S., Schertzer, D., Braun, C., and Lavallee, D. "Universal Multifractal Characterization and Simulation of Speech," *International Journal of Bifurcation and Chaos* 2, 1992.

Larrain, M. "Portfolio Stock Adjustment and the Real Exchange Rate: The Dollar-Mark and the Mark-Sterling," *Journal of Policy Modeling,* Winter 1986.

Larrain, M. "Empirical Tests of Chaotic Behavior in a Nonlinear Interest Rate Model," *Financial Analysts Journal* 47, 1991.

Lavallee, D., Lovejoy, S., Schertzer, D., and Schmitt, F. "On the Determination of Universaly Multifractal Parameters in Turbulence," forthcoming in H. K. Moffat, G. M. Zaslavsky, M. Tabor, and P. Comte, eds., *Topological Aspects of the Dynamics of Fluids and Plasmas,* Boston: Kluwer Academic Publishers, 1996.

LeBaron, B. "Some Relations Between Volatility and Serial Correlations in Stock Market Returns," Working Paper, February 1990.

Levy, P. *Theorie de l'addition des variables aleatoires.* Paris: Gauthier-Villars, 1937.

Lewin, R. *Complexity.* Phoenix: Orion, 1993.

Li, T.-Y. and Yorke, J. "Period Three Implies Chaos," *American Mathematics Monthly* 82, 1975.

Li, W. K. and McLeod, A. I. "Fractional Time Series Modelling," *Biometrika* 73, 1986.

Litner, J. "The Valuation of Risk Assets and the Selection of Risk Investments in Stock Portfolios and Capital Budgets," *Review of Economic Statistics* 47, 1965.

Lo, A. "Long Term Memory in Stock Market Prices," NBER Working Paper 2984, NBER 1989.

Lo, A. and Mackinlay, A. C. "Stock Market Prices Do Not Follow Random Walks: Evidence from a Simple Specification Test," *Review of Financial Studies* 1, 1988.

Lorenz, E. "Deterministic Nonperiodic Flow," *Journal of Atmospheric Sciences* 20, 1963.

Lorenz, H. "International Trade and the Possible Occurrence of Chaos," *Economics Letters* 23, 1987.

Lorenz, H. *Nonlinear Dynamical Economics and Chaotic Motion.* Berlin: Springer-Verlag, 1989.

Lorie, J. H. and Hamilton, M. T. *The Stock Market: Theories and Evidence.* Homewood, IL: Richard D. Irwin, 1973.

Lotka, A. J. "The Frequency Distribution of Scientific Productivity," *Journal of the Washington Academy of Science* 16, 1926.

Lovejoy, S. and Schertzer, D. "Multifractals in Geophysics," presentation to AGU-CGU-MSA, Spring Meeting, May 1992.

Mackay, L. L. D. *Extraordinary Popular Delusions and the Madness of Crowds.* New York: Farrar, Straus and Giroux, 1932. (Originally published in 1841.)

Mackey, M. and Glass, L. "Oscillation and Chaos in Physiological Control Systems," *Science* 197, 1977.

Mahfoud, S. and Mani, G. "Genetic Algorithms for Predicting Individual Stock Performance," *Proceedings of the Third International Conference on Artifical Intelligence Applications on Wall Street,* Gaithersburg, MD: Software Engineering Press, 1995.

Mandelbrot, B. "The Pareto-Levy Law and the Distribution of Income," *International Economic Review* 1, 1960.

Mandelbrot, B. "Stable Paretian Random Functions and the Multiplicative Variation of Income," *Econometrica* 29, 1961.

Mandelbrot, B. "The Stable Paretian Income Distribution When the Apparent Exponent Is Near Two," *International Economic Review* 4, 1963.

Mandelbrot, B. "The Variation of Certain Speculative Prices," in P. Cootner, ed., *The Random Character of Stock Prices.* Cambridge: MIT Press, 1964.

Mandelbrot, B. "The Variation of Some Other Speculative Prices," *Journal of Business* 39, 1966a.

Mandelbrot, B. "Forecasts of Future Prices, Unbiased Markets, and 'Martingale' Models," *Journal of Business* 39, 1966b.

Mandelbrot, B. "Some Noises with 1/f Spectrum: A Bridge Between Direct Current and White Noise," *IEEE Transactions on Information Theory,* April 1967.

Mandelbrot, B. "When Can Price Be Arbitraged Efficiently? A Limit to the Validity of the Random Walk and Martingale Models," *Review of Economic Statistics* 53, 1971.

Mandelbrot, B. "Statistical Methodology for Non-Periodic Cycles: From the Covariance to R/S Analysis," *Annals of Economic Social Measurement* 1, 1972.

Mandelbrot, B. *The Fractal Geometry of Nature.* New York: W. H. Freeman, 1982.

Mandelbrot, B. and van Ness, J. W. "Fractional Brownian Motions, Fractional Noises and Applications," *SIAM Review* 10, 1968.

Mandelbrot, B. and Wallis, J. "Computer Experiments with Fractional Gaussian Noises: Part 1, Averages and Variances," *Water Resources Research* 5, 1969a.

Mandelbrot, B. and Wallis, J. "Computer Experiments with Fractional Gaussian Noises: Part 2, Rescaled Ranges and Spectra," *Water Resources Research* 5, 1969b.

Mandelbrot, B. and Wallis, J. "Computer Experiments with Fractional Gaussian Noises: Part 3, Mathematical Appendix," *Water Resources Research* 5, 1969c.

Mandelbrot, B. and Wallis, J. "Robustness of the Rescaled Range R/S in the Measurement of Noncyclic Long Run Statistical Dependence," *Water Resources Research* 5, 1969d.

Markowitz, H. M. "Portfolio Selection," *Journal of Finance* 7, 1952.

Markowitz, H. M. *Portfolio Selection: Efficient Diversification of Investments.* New York: Wiley, 1959.

May, R. "Simple Mathematical Models with Very Complicated Dynamics," *Nature* 261, 1976.

McCulloch, J. H. "The Value of European Options with Log-Stable Uncertainty," Working Paper, 1985.

McNees, S. K. and Ries, J. "The Track Record of Macroeconomic Forecasts," *New England Economic Review,* November/December 1983.

McNees, S. K. "Which Forecast Should You Use?" *New England Economic Review,* July/August 1985.

McNees, S. K. "Consensus Forecasts: Tyranny of the Majority," *New England Economic Review,* November/December 1987.

McNees, S. K. "How Accurate are Macroeconomic Forecasts?" *New England Economic Review,* July/August 1988.

McNeill, D. and Freiberger, P. *Fuzzy Logic.* New York: Simon and Schuster, 1994.

Melese, F. and Transue, W. "Unscrambling Chaos Through Thick and Thin," *Quarterly Journal of Economics,* May 1986.

Moore, A. B. "Some Characteristics of Changes in Common Stock Prices," in P. Cootner, ed., *The Random Character of Stock Market Prices.* Cambridge: MIT Press, 1964.

Moore, A. W. *The Infinite.* London: Routledge, 1990.

Mossin, J. "Equilibrium in a Capital Asset Market," *Econometrica* 34, 1966.

Murray, J. D. *Mathematical Biology.* Berlin: Springer-Verlag, 1989.

Nychka, D., Ellner, S., Gallant, A. R., and McCaffrey, D. "Finding Chaos in Noisy Systems," *Journal of the Royal Statistical Society* 54, 1992.

Ormerod, P. *The Death of Economics.* New York: St. Martin's Press, 1995.

Osborne, M. F. M. "Brownian Motion in the Stock Market," in P. Cootner, ed., *The Random Character of Stock Market Prices.* Cambridge: MIT Press, 1964.

Osherson, D. and Smith E. "On the Adequacy of Prototype Theory as a Theory of Concepts," *Cognition* 9, 1981.

Packard, N., Crutchfield, J., Farmer, D., and Shaw, R. "Geometry from a Time Series," *Physical Review Letters* 45, 1980.

Pareto, V. *Cours d'Economie Politique.* Lausanne, Switzerland, 1897.

Peters, E. "Fractal Structure in the Capital Markets," *Financial Analysts Journal,* July/August 1989.

Peters, E. "A Chaotic Attractor for the S&P 500," *Financial Analysts Journal,* March/April 1991.

Peters, E. "R/S Analysis Using Logrithmic Returns: A Technical Note," *Financial Analysts Journal,* November/December 1992.

Peters, E. *Fractal Market Analysis.* New York: Wiley, 1994.

Piatelli-Palmarini, M. *Inevitable Illusions.* New York: Wiley, 1994.

Pickover, C. *Computers, Pattern, Chaos and Beauty.* New York: St. Martin's Press, 1990.

Pierce, J. R. *Symbols, Signals and Noise.* New York: Harper, 1961.

Ploeg, F. "Rational Expectations, Risk and Chaos in Financial Markets," *The Economic Journal,* July 1985.

Poincaré, H. *Science and Method.* New York: Dover, 1952. (Originally published in 1908.)

Prigogine, I. and Nicolis, G. *Exploring Complexity.* New York: W. H. Freeman, 1989.

Prigogine, I. and Stengers, I. *Order Out of Chaos.* New York: Bantam, 1984.

Radizicki, M. "Institutional Dynamics, Deterministic Chaos, and Self-Organizing Systems," *Journal of Economic Issues* 24, 1990.

Refnes, A., ed. *Neural Networks in the Capital Markets.* Chichester, UK: Wiley, 1995.

Roberts, H. V. "Stock Market 'Patterns' and Financial Analysis: Methodological Suggestions," in P. Cootner, ed., *The Random Character of Stock Market Prices.* Cambridge: MIT Press, 1964.

Roll, R. "Bias in Fitting the Sharpe Model to Time Series Data," *Journal of Financial and Quantitative Analysis* 4, 1969.

Roll, R. "A Critique of the Asset Pricing Theory's Tests, Part I: On Past and Potential Testability of the Theory," *Journal of Financial Economics* 4, 1977.

Roll, R. and Ross, S. A. "An Empirical Investigation of the Arbitrage Pricing Theory," *Journal of Finance* 35, 1980.

Ross, S. A. "The Arbitrage Theory of Capital Asset Pricing," *Journal of Economic Theory* 13, 1976.

Rudd, A. and Clasing, H. K. *Modern Portfolio Theory.* Homewood, IL: Dow Jones-Irwin, 1982.

Ruelle, D. "Five Turbulent Problems," *Physica* 7D, 1983.

Ruelle, D. *Chaotic Evolution and Strange Attractors.* Cambridge: Cambridge University Press, 1989.

Russo, J. and Shoemaker, P. *Decision Traps.* New York: Doubleday, 1989.

Samuelson, P. A. "Efficient Portfolio Selection for Pareto-Levy Investments," *Journal of Financial and Quantitative Analysis,* June 1967.

Satchell, S. and Timmermann, A. "Daily Returns in European Stock Markets: Predictability, Non-linearity, and Transaction Costs," Working Paper, July 1992.

Scheinkman, J. A. and LeBaron, B. "Nonlinear Dynamics and Stock Returns," *Journal of Business* 62, 1989.

Schelling, T. *Micromotives and Macrobehavior.* New York: W.W. Norton, 1978.

Schinasi, G. J. "A Nonlinear Dynamic Model of Short Run Fluctuations," *Review of Economic Studies* 48, 1981.

Schmitt, F., Schertzer, D., Lavallee, D., and Lovejoy, S. "A Universal Multifractal Comparison Between Atmospheric and Wind Tunnel Turbulence," unpublished ms., 1992.

Schmitt, F., Lavallee, D., Schertzer, D., and Lovejoy, S. "Empirical Determination of Universal Multifractal Exponents in Turbulent Velocity Fields," *Physical Review Letters* 68, 1992.

Schroeder, M. *Fractals, Chaos, Power Laws.* New York: W. H. Freeman, 1991.

Schwert, G. W. "Stock Market Volatility," *Financial Analysts Journal,* May/June 1990.

Shaklee, G. L. S. *Time in Economics.* Westport, CT: Greenwood Press, 1958.

Shannon, C. E. and Weaver, W. *The Mathematical Theory of Communication.* Urbana: University of Illinois, 1963.

Sharpe, W. F. "A Simplified Model of Portfolio Analysis," *Management Science* 9, 1963.

Sharpe, W. F. "Capital Asset Prices: A Theory of Market Equilibrium Under Conditions of Risk," *Journal of Finance* 19, 1964.

Sharpe, W. F. *Portfolio Theory and Capital Markets.* New York: McGraw-Hill, 1970.

Shaw, R. *The Dripping Faucet as a Model Chaotic System.* Santa Cruz, CA: Aerial Press, 1984.

Shiller, R. J. *Market Volatility.* Cambridge: MIT Press, 1989.

Simkowitz, M. A. and Beedles, W. L. "Asymmetric Stable Distributed Security Returns," *Journal of the American Statistical Association* 75, 1980.

Smith, R. L. "Estimating Dimension in Noisy Chaotic Time Series," *Journal of the Royal Statistical Society* 54, 1992.

Sterge, A. J. "On the Distribution of Financial Futures Price Changes," *Financial Analysts Journal,* May/June 1989.

Stetson, H. T. *Sunspots and Their Effects.* New York: McGraw-Hill, 1938.

Sutherland, S. *Irrationality: Why We Don't Think Straight!* New Brunswick, NJ: Rutgers University Press, 1994.

Thaler, R. H., ed. *Advances in Behavioral Finance.* New York: Russell Sage Foundation, 1993.

Thompson, J. M. T. and Stewart, H. B. *Nonlinear Dynamics and Chaos.* New York: Wiley, 1986.

Toffler, A. *The Third Wave.* New York: Bantum Books, 1981.

Tong, H. *Non-Linear Time Series: A Dynamical System Approach.* Oxford: Oxford University Press, 1990.

Turner, A. L. and Weigel, E. J. "An Analysis of Stock Market Volatility," *Russell Research Commentaries,* Frank Russell Company, Tacoma, WA, 1990.

Tversky, A. "The Psychology of Risk," in *Quantifying the Market Risk Premium Phenomena for Investment Decision Making.* Charlottesville, VA: Institute of Chartered Financial Analysts, 1990.

Vaga, T. "The Coherent Market Hypothesis," *Financial Analysts Journal,* December/January 1991.

Vandaele, W. *Applied Time Series and Box-Jenkins Models.* New York: Academic Press, 1983.

Vicsek, T. *Fractal Growth Phenomena.* Singapore: World Scientific, 1989.

Wallach, P. "Wavelet Theory," *Scientific American,* January 1991.

Weibel, E. R. and Gomez, D. M. "Architecture of the Human Lung," *Science* 221, 1962.

Weidlich, W. "The Statistical Description of Polarization Phenomena in Society," *British Journal of Mathematical and Statistical Psychology* 24, 1971.

Weiner, N. *Collected Works, Vol. I,* P. Masani ed. Cambridge: MIT Press, 1976.

West, B. J. *Fractal Physiology and Chaos in Medicine.* Singapore: World Scientific, 1990.

West, B. J. "The Noise in Natural Phenomena," *American Scientist* 78, 1990.

West, B. J. and Goldberger, A. L. "Physiology in Fractal Dimensions," *American Scientist,* January/February 1987.

West, B. J., Valmik, B., and Goldberger, A. L. "Beyond the Principal of Similitude: Renormalization in the Bronchial Tree," *American Physiological Society* 60, 1986.

Wilson, K. G. "Problems in Physics with Many Scales of Length," *Scientific American* 241, August 1979.

Wolf, A., Swift, J. B., Swinney, H. L., and Vastano, J. A. "Determining Lyapunov Exponents from a Time Series," *Physica* 16D, no.3, July 1985.

Wolff, R. C. L. "Local Lyapunov Exponents: Looking Closely at Chaos," *Journal of the Royal Statisical Society* 54, 1992.

Working, H. "Note on the Correlation of First Differences of Averages in a Random Chain," in P. Cootner, ed., *The Random Character of Stock Market Prices*. Cambridge: MIT Press, 1964.

Zadeh, L. "Fuzzy Sets," *Information and Control* 6, 1965.

Zadeh, L. and Kacprzyk, J., eds. *Fuzzy Logic for the Management of Uncertainty*. New York: Wiley, 1992.

Zaslavsky, G. M., Sagdeev, R., Usikov, D., and Chernikov, A. *Weak Chaos and Quasi-Regular Patterns*. Cambridge: Cambridge University Press, 1991.

Zhang, Z., Wen, K.-H., and Chen, P. "Complex Spectral Analysis of Economic Dynamics and Correlation Resonances in Market Behavior," IC^2 Working Paper, 1992.

Zimmerman, H.-J. *Fuzzy Set Theory*. Boston: Kluwer, 1991.

Zipf, G. K. *Human Behavior and the Principle of Least Effort*. Cambridge: Addison Wesley, 1949.

Zolotarev, V. M. "On Representation of Stable Laws by Integrals," in *Selected Transactions in Mathematical Statistics and Probability, Vol. 6*. Providence: American Mathematical Society, 1966. (Russian original, 1964.)

Glossary

Alpha   The measure of the peakedness of the probability density function. In the normal distribution, alpha equals 2. For Fractal distributions, alpha is between 1 and 2. The inverse of the Hurst exponent (H).

Antipersistence   In rescaled range (R/S) analysis, an antipersistent time series reverses itself more often than a random series would. If the system has been up in the previous period, it is more likely that it will be down in the next period and vice versa. Also called pink noise, or 1/f noise. See *persistence, R/S analysis, Hurst exponent, Joseph effect, Noah effect.*

Artificial Intelligence   The creation of models that mimic thought processes. See *neural networks, fuzzy logic,* and *genetic algorithms.*

Autoregressive (AR) process   A stationary stochastic process where the current value of the time series is related to the past p values, where p is any integer, is called an AR(p) process. When the current value is related to the previous two values, it is an AR(2) process. An AR(1) process has an infinite memory.

Autoregressive Conditional Heteroskedasticity (ARCH)   A nonlinear stochastic process, where the variance is time-varying and conditional on the past variance. ARCH processes have frequency distributions that have high peaks at the mean and fat-tails, much like fractal distributions. The Generalized ARCH (GARCH) Model is also widely used. See *fractal distributions.*

Attractor   In nonlinear dynamic series, an attractor defines the equilibrium level of the system. See *point attractor, limit cycle,* and *strange attractor.*

BDS statistic   A statistic based on the correlation integral, which examines the probability that a purely random system could have the same scaling properties as the system under study. See *correlation integral.*

Bifurcation   When a nonlinear dynamic system develops twice the possible solutions that it had before it passed its critical level. A bifurcation cascade is often called the period-doubling route to chaos because the transition from an orderly system to a chaotic system often occurs when the number of possible solutions begins increasing, doubling each time.

Bifurcation diagram   A graph that shows the critical points where bifurcation occurs, and the possible solutions that exist at that point.

Capital Asset Pricing Model (CAPM)   An equilibrium-based asset-pricing model developed independently by Sharpe, Lintner, and Mossin. The simplest version states that assets are priced according to their relationship to the market portfolio of all risky assets determined by the securities' beta.

Central Limit Theorem   The Law of Large Numbers states that as a sample of independent, identically distributed random numbers approaches infinity, its probability density function approaches the normal distribution. See *normal distribution*.

Chaos   A deterministic nonlinear dynamic system that can produce random-looking results. A chaotic system must have a fractal dimension and exhibit sensitive dependence on initial conditions. See *fractal dimension, Lyapunov exponent, strange attractor.*

Coherent Market Hypothesis (CMH)   A hypothesis that the probability density function of the market may be determined by a combination of group sentiment and fundamental bias. Depending on combinations of these two factors, the market can be in one of four states: random walk, unstable transition, chaos, or coherence.

Complexity theory   The theory that processes with a large number of seemingly independent agents can spontaneously organize themselves into a coherent system.

Control parameters   In a nonlinear dynamic system, the coefficient of the order parameter; the determinant of the influence of the order parameter on the total system. See *order parameter.*

Correlation   The degree to which factors influence each other.

Correlation dimension   An estimate of the fractal dimension, which measures the probability that two points chosen at random will be within a certain distance of each other and examines how this probability changes as the distance is increased. White noise will fill its space since its components are uncorrelated, and its correlation dimension is equal to whatever dimension it is placed in. A dependent system will be held together by its correlations and retain its dimension in whatever embedding dimension it is placed, as long as it is greater than its fractal dimension.

Correlation integral   The probability that two points are within a certain distance from one another. Used in the calculation of the correlation dimension.

Crisp sets   The fuzzy set term for traditional set theory. That is, an object either belongs to a set or does not. See *fuzzy sets.*

Critical levels   Values of control parameters where the nature of a nonlinear dynamic system changes. The system can bifurcate, or make the transition from stable to turbulent behavior. An example is the straw that breaks the camel's back.

Cycle   A full orbital period.

Determinism   A theory that certain results are fully ordained in advance. A deterministic chaos system is one that gives random-looking results, even though the results are generated from a system of equations.

Dynamic noise   When the output of a dynamic system becomes corrupted with noise and the noisy value is used as input during the next iteration. Also called system noise. See *observational noise.*

Dynamic system   A system of equations where the output of one equation is part of the input for another. A simple version of a dynamic system is linear simultaneous equations. Nonlinear simultaneous equations are nonlinear dynamic systems.

Econometrics   The quantitative science of predicting the economy.

Efficient frontier   In mean/variance analysis, the curve where the set of efficient portfolios lies—that is, those portfolios of risky assets that have the highest level of expected return for their level of risk.

Efficient Market Hypothesis (EMH)   The semistrong form states that current prices reflect all public information. Therefore, it is impossible for one market participant to have an advantage over another and reap excess profits.

Entropy   The level of disorder in a system.

Equilibrium   The stable state of the system. See *attractor.*

Euclidean geometry   The plane geometry we learn in high school, based on a few ideal, smooth, symmetric shapes.

Feedback systems   An equation where the output becomes the input in the next iteration, operating much like a public address (PA) system where the microphone is placed next to the speakers, which generate feedback as the signal is looped through the PA system.

Fractal   An object in which the parts are in some way related to the whole; that is, the individual components are self-similar. An example is the branching network in a tree. While each branch and each successive smaller branching is different, they are qualitatively similar to the structure of the whole tree.

Fractal dimension   A number that quantitatively describes how an object fills its space. In Euclidean (plane) geometry, objects are solid and continuous—they have no holes or gaps. As such, they have integer dimensions. Fractals are rough and often discontinuous, like a wiffle ball, and so have fractional, or fractal dimensions.

Fractal distribution   A probability density function that is statistically self-similar; that is, in different increments of time, the statistical characteristics remain the same.

Fractional brownian motion   A biased random walk. Unlike standard brownian motion, the odds are biased in one direction or the other. It is like playing with loaded dice.

Fractal Market Hypothesis (FMH)   The Fractal Market Hypothesis states that (1) a market consists of many investors with different investment horizons, and (2) the information set that is important to each investment horizon is different. As long as the market maintains this fractal structure, with no characteristic time scale, the market remains stable. When the market's investment horizon becomes uniform, the market becomes unstable because everyone is trading based on the same information set. See Peters (1994).

Fractional noise A noise that is not completely independent of previous values. See *fractional brownian motion, 1/f noise, white noise.*

Fundamental information Information relating to the economic state of a company or economy. In market analysis, fundamental information is related to the earnings prospects of the firm only.

Fuzzy logic A system that mathematically models complex relationships that are usually handled in a vague manner by language. "Fuzzy logic" refers both to formal fuzzy logic (a multivalued form of logic) and to fuzzy sets. Fuzzy sets measure the similarity between an object and a group of objects. A member of a fuzzy set can belong to both the set and its complement. Fuzzy sets can more closely approximate human reasoning than traditional crisp sets. See *crisp sets.*

Gaussian A system whose probabilities are well described by the normal distribution, or bell-shaped curve.

Genetic algorithms Models that optimize rules by mimicking the Darwinian law of survival of the fittest. A set of rules are chosen as those that work the best. The weakest are discarded. In addition, two successful rules can be combined (the equivalent to genetic crossovers) to produce offspring rules. The offspring can replace the parents, or they will be discarded if less successful than the parents. Mutation is also accomplished by randomly changing elements. Mutation and crossover occur with low probability, as in nature.

Hurst exponent (H) A measure of the bias in fractional brownian motion: $H = 0.50$ for brownian motion; $0.50 < H \leq 1.00$ for persistent, or trend-reinforcing series; $0 \leq H < 0.50$ for an antipersistent, or mean-reverting system. The inverse of the Hurst exponent is equal to alpha, the characteristic exponent for stable Paretian distributions. The fractal dimension of a time series, D, is equivalent to 2-H.

Implied volatility Using the Black–Scholes option-pricing model, implied volatility is the level of the standard deviation of price changes that equates the current option price to the other independent variables in the formula. Often used as a measure of current levels of market uncertainty.

Intermittency When a nonlinear dynamic system alternates between periodic and chaotic behavior. See *chaos, dynamic system.*

Joseph effect The tendency for persistent time series $(0.50 < H \leq 1.00)$ to have trends and cycles. The term was coined by Mandelbrot in reference to Joseph's interpretation of Pharaoh's dream of seven fat years followed by seven lean years.

Leptokurtosis The condition of a probability density curve to have fatter tails and a higher peak at the mean than the normal distribution.

Limit cycles An attractor for nonlinear dynamic systems that has periodic cycles or orbits in phase space. An example is an undamped pendulum, which will have a closed circle orbit equal to the amplitude of the pendulum's swing. See *attractor, phase space.*

Lyapunov exponents A measure of the dynamics of an attractor. Each dimension has a Lyapunov exponent. A positive exponent measures sensitive dependence on

initial conditions, or how much our forecasts can diverge based on different estimates of starting conditions. Another way to view Lyapunov exponents is the loss of
predictive ability as we look forward into time. Strange attractors are characterized
by at least one positive exponent. A negative exponent measures how points converge
toward one another. Point attractors are characterized by all negative variables. See
attractor, limit cycle, point attractor, strange attractor.

Markovian dependence   The condition where observations in a time series are dependent on previous observations in the near term. Markovian dependence dies
quickly, while long-memory effects, like Hurst dependence, decay over very long
time periods.

Measurement noise   See *observational noise.*

Modern Portfolio Theory (MPT)   The blanket name for the quantitative analysis
of portfolios of risky assets based on expected return, or the mean expected value,
and the risk, or standard deviation of a portfolio of securities. According to MPT,
investors would require a portfolio with the highest expected return for a given level
of risk.

Moving-average (MA) processes   A stationary stochastic process, where the observed time series is the result of the moving average of an unobserved random time
series. An MA(q) process is a q period moving average.

Neural nets   Models that mimic the massive parallel processing that occurs in the
brain.

Noah effect   The tendency of persistent time series ($0.50 < H \le 1.00$) to have abrupt
and discontinuous changes. The normal distribution assumes continuous changes in a
system. However, a time series that exhibits Hurst statistics may abruptly change levels, skipping values either up or down. Mandelbrot coined the term based on the biblical story of the deluge. See *Joseph effect, Hurst exponent, persistence, antipersistence.*

Noisy chaos   A chaotic dynamic system with either observational or system noise
added. See *chaos, dynamic system, observational noise, system noise.*

Normal distribution   The well-known bell-shaped curve. According to the Central
Limit Theorem, the probability density function of a large number of independent,
identically distributed random numbers will approach the normal distribution. In the
fractal family of distributions, the normal distribution exists only when alpha equals
2, or the Hurst exponent equals 0.50. Thus, the normal distribution is a special case
that, in time series analysis, is quite rare. See *alpha, Central Limit Theorem, fractal
distribution.*

Observational noise   The error between the true value in a system and its observed value, due to imprecision in measurement. Also called measurement noise.
See *dynamic noise.*

Order parameter   In a nonlinear dynamic system, a variable—acting like a macro-
variable, or combination of variables—that summarizes the individual variables
that can affect a system. In a controlled experiment, involving thermal convection,
for example, temperature can be a control parameter; in a large complex system,

temperature can be an order parameter, because it summarizes the effect of the sun, air pressure, and other atmospheric variables. See *control parameter.*

1/f noise   See *antipersistence.*

Pareto (Pareto-Levy) distributions   See *fractal distribution.*

Persistence   In R/S analysis, a persistent series is one that tends to follow trends. That is, if the system had increased in the previous period, the chances are it will continue to increase in the next period. Persistent time series have a long memory; that is, there is long-term correlation between current events and future events. Also called black noise. See *antipersistence, R/S analysis, Hurst exponent, Joseph effect, Noah effect.*

Phase space   A graph that shows all possible states of a system. In phase space we plot the value of a variable against possible values of the other variables at the same time. If a system has three descriptive variables, we plot the phase space in three dimensions, with each variable taking one dimension.

Pink noise   See *antipersistence.*

Point attractor   In nonlinear dynamics, an attractor where all orbits in phase space are drawn to one point or value. Essentially, any system that tends to a stable, single-valued equilibrium will have a point attractor. A pendulum damped by friction will always stop, so its phase space will always be drawn to the point where velocity and position are equal to zero. See *attractor, phase space.*

Random walk   Brownian motion, where the previous change in the value of a variable is unrelated to future or past changes.

Rescaled range (R/S) analysis   The analysis developed by H. E. Hurst to determine long-memory effects and fractional brownian motion. Rescaled range analysis measures how the distance covered by a particle increases as we look at longer and longer time scales. For brownian motion, the distance covered increases with the square root of time. A series that increases at a different rate is not random. See *antipersistence, fractional brownian motion, Hurst exponent, persistence, Joseph effect, Noah effect.*

Risk   In Modern Portfolio Theory, risk is measured as the standard deviation of security returns.

Scaling   How the characteristics of an object change as the size of the measuring device is changed. For a three-dimensional object, it could be the volume of an object covered as the radius of a covering sphere is increased. In a times series, it could be the change in the amplitude of the time series as the increment of time is increased.

Self-similar   When small parts of an object are qualitatively the same or similar to the whole object. In certain deterministic fractals, like the Sierpinski Triangle, small pieces look the same as the entire object. In random fractals, small increments of time will be statistically similar to larger increments of time. See *fractal.*

Single Index Model   Measures portfolio risk by measuring the sensitivity of a portfolio of securities to changes in a market index. The measure of sensitivity is called the "beta" of the security or portfolio. Related, but not identical, to the Capital Asset Pricing Model.

Stable Paretian, or fractal hypothesis   In the characteristic function of the fractal family of distributions, the characteristic exponent alpha can range between 1 and 2. See alpha, fractal distribution, Gaussian.

Strange attractor   An attractor in phase space, where the points never repeat themselves and orbits never intersect, but both stay within the same region of phase space. Unlike limit cycles or point attractors, strange attractors are nonperiodic and generally have a fractal dimension. They are a configuration of a nonlinear chaotic system. See *attractor, chaos, limit cycle, point attractor.*

System noise   See *dynamic noise.*

Technical information   Information related to the momentum of a particular variable. In market analysis, technical information is information related to market dynamics and crowd behavior only.

Term structure   The value of a variable at different time increments. The term structure of interest rates is the yield-to-maturity for different fixed-income securities at different maturity times. The volatility term structure is the standard deviation of returns of varying time horizons.

Volatility   The standard deviation of security price changes.

White noise   The audio equivalent of brownian motion; sounds that are unrelated and sound like a hiss. The video equivalent of white noise is "snow" in television reception. See *brownian motion.*

Index